REARVIEW

Raghu has been many things, from spot boy to executive producer, creative director, presenter, actor, columnist, motivational speaker, lyricist, singer and now, author.
He wishes to get paid for these things someday...

REARVIEW

My Roadies Journey

Raghu

RUPA

Published by
Rupa Publications India Pvt. Ltd 2013
7/16, Ansari Road, Daryaganj
New Delhi 110002

Sales centres:
Allahabad Bengaluru Chennai
Hyderabad Jaipur Kathmandu
Kolkata Mumbai

Edited by Janaki Viswanathan.

ISBN: 978-81-291-2911-6

First impression 2013

10 9 8 7 6 5 4 3 2 1

The moral right of the author has been asserted.

Printed at Replika Press Pvt. Ltd, India

Contents

The rudest man on television

Raghu! Raghu! Raghu!

A steady chant. I'm pacing the big, bare crew room at Laxmi Lawns, Pune. Outside, it's a lovely crisp morning. The door is shut tight but I hear them out in the halls anyway. *Raghu! Raghu! Raghu!* The chant grows louder, then wanes, but as I slip on my jacket, it's back. *Raghu! Raghu! Raghu!*

In the hall, I'm told, among the other 1,400-odd Roadie hopefuls, there is one kid, a girl, who looks like the quintessential Roadie—hair cropped close to her skull and gelled into a mohawk, Converse shoes, a black Goth T-shirt ripped just deep enough to show off the tattoo on the neck: a flock of birds flying down her back; then there is a boy who resembles a stockier version of me, complete with a shaved head, goatee, aviators and pierced ears. Another is sporting one white eye, perhaps a tribute to my get-up in the promos. Flattering? I don't know.

Raghu! Raghu! Raghu! The chanting continues.

Back in the crew room, Arjuna award-winning swimmer and special guest at the Pune auditions, Deepa Malik, all set in her military jacket, big black boots and wheelchair smiles, 'Ten years and they're still calling your name… It must be a good feeling na?' I pause for a minute and then shrug. I'm not so sure. The door opens. I automatically duck to one side as a crew member walks in. It's an instinct born out of not wanting to be seen before I'm ready for it.

Your left eye's grown smaller, he says by way of greeting. I check the mirror. Yeah, just two hours of sleep a day can do that to you. It's Season 10 of *Roadies*; the first city, the first day, the first audition and I'm already bloody tired. It'll get better, I tell myself. To be honest, I know it will. The eye, at least. The tiredness, maybe not.

Exactly twenty minutes later, I can hear Rannvijay walk up to the stage. Correction: I can hear the crowd as he walks up to the stage. In the crew room, the inimitably effervescent and absolutely crazy Bani Judge squeals in imitation of the female crowd—Oh my God, it's Rannvijay, I can't believe it—before her voice is drowned out by the chaos outside. He's got a bad throat and we've asked him to keep it soft but I know he won't. True to form, he screams anyway, and gets full-throated cries in response. He likes to feed off the crowd.

The announcements are made. This year, Roadies X—my team, made up of former Roadies—will be pitted against Rannvijay's team of new contestants. The idea is to make us compete with each other. 'Yeah right,' giggles Deepa, 'as if you two will ever fight.' I grin in reply as the door opens again and a crew member pops his head in, nodding. That's it. It's time.

I'm often asked what I feel at the exact moment I walk into an auditorium full of youngsters of all shapes and sizes calling my name. Honestly, I don't know. What I *do* know is that I'm working. I'm making my show. Everything else is a by-product. What I know is that I'm tired as hell and I'd love to be able to curl up and sleep. And sleep some more. As I walk to the stage, these thoughts in my head, I remember an earlier season, an earlier audition—it was Hyderabad, I think—and the look of wonder in my wife Sugandha's eyes as she recounted the incident in her usual animated manner: 'One minute Raghu's walking alongside us, complaining, ranting in this low, beat-up voice, "No, Kuhu, I can't handle this anymore, I'm too tired," the next minute, we hear the crowd cheering. Suddenly, out of nowhere, he starts running…all the way to the stage. The crowd is screaming and yelling and this guy, who up until a moment ago, had looked so down and out, is running.' What's that, she'd turned to ask me. What's that, I ask myself. Not me, for sure.

I walk out quickly, straight to the stage where Rannvijay is still working his audience. Looking around at them, I don't smile. Now they start screaming for me: louder, more aggressive screaming. I take the microphone and speak. They think they can impress me? Do Pune's wannabe Roadies really think they have it in them to beat the experienced ones this season? They REALLY think so? Less than a minute in and the cheers for me sort of wane, the cheers for Rannvijay turn louder. I stifle a smile. I'm pretty good at making people turn against me like this.

Jump cut to 1 p.m. We are now waiting for the group discussions to begin. Another crew member walks in holding up a bag, grinning from ear to ear—this season's spoils of war so far: 'gifts' sent or retrieved from wannabe contestants. The rest of the crew gathers around the bed as he tips it over. A T-shirt pops out, blinding white with a front that says: 'I ♥ Raghu'. Okay, that I did not expect. Flip it, flip it, says the crew member, so I do. The back reads: 'I want to spend the night with Raghu.' A loud cheer breaks out in the room and I can't help but smile. I'm SO keeping this one. What do you know…they don't all hate me! And then I see the other item retrieved: a click knife. Ah, well. Spoke too soon.

Cut to three-odd weeks later to an icy-cold night in November. It is past 11 p.m., just before the Chandigarh auditions and Rannvijay and I are at a nightclub. As we enter, two dressed-up teens clutch each other's hands looking wide-eyed. So afraid to miss a thing, they don't even blink as Rannvijay walks by, ahead of me. The next moment, they exchange a look of pure ecstasy and scream in tandem. Then I walk by. The screams die instantly. Cautious smiles now, the kind you'd give your fifth-grade teacher…or principal. Later I see them approaching my table, phone cameras held in hand, as they begged me, please…

just one photo, Raghu! I shake my head as security keeps them at bay. They continue. Please, please! We lied at home and came here just to meet you guys! Please! I relent and say cheese. I don't get it, though. What's on their mind? What do they think of me?

The next morning, however, standing in front of a 2,500-plus crowd at the Indradhanush Auditorium, Panchkula, I don't smile. I just stand there quiet, right at the edge of the stage, counting the seconds. I see the faces in the crowd, the expressions. Some screaming their throats raw, some watching me with unnerved smiles, others simply sitting quietly, wondering, contemplating... I'd give a penny to know their thoughts right now.

How about the kid who goes through the trouble of registering himself twice, so he can get into two group discussions at Pune, because that's how desperate he is to get through? What of this crazy kid in Chandigarh, who offered me ten lakh rupees as a bribe on the form, and now sits before me, grinning like crazy, trying to convince me he wrote that only so he'd come this far; I can see his hands are clammy, his left eye twitches, he's almost expecting to be thrown out. Why though? I don't ask but I don't disappoint either. I crack his goggles with perfect precision, circle him like he's prey, tip him off the chair, but he doesn't flinch... nor does he stop talking. I get mad and throw him out. The door slams after him and I can't help but laugh.

What's going on in his mind? Does he admire me, respect me, hate me? Fear me? Maybe all of the above. I don't understand it. I don't understand the *Roadies* form that has 'Fuck you, Raghu' written all over it; I don't understand the poster that was held up this year during the Chandigarh auditions that read: 'Baap toh baap hota hai. Raghu ROX'.

I see equal parts respect, equal parts loathing. Equal parts Raghu, equal parts the bully; the guy who cribs one second and runs towards a crowd the next. We're almost the same person, only that guy, the goggle-breaking, swear-word-spouting, rudest man on television—he's taller.

My mother finds out she is having a monster baby

On that sunny afternoon of 5 February 1975, more than eight weeks before her due date, Radha Vishwanath—amma to me—had worries of her own, of a different, more basic kind. As she waited in the doctor's room for her report, all amma wanted to hear was that, at six months, her pregnancy, which had made her painfully frail and her tummy unbelievably huge, was safe and her baby healthy. But it wasn't to be. Amma, poor amma. The intern at the Safdarjung Hospital touched her stomach and promptly called over a senior doctor. Tense looks were exchanged. Amma's ordeal had begun.

On her way home with her mother—my grandmother, ammamma—amma broke the news: the doctors had said they suspected twins, and they were worried because of her tiny frame. Amma was worried for other practical reasons until ammamma nodded reassuringly and said, with the unquestioning acceptance typical of women of her time, 'We were preparing for one, now we'll get ready for two.'

Amma was staying at her maternal home in Munirka for her delivery—Munirka, the urban village in New Delhi packed to the seams with Bengalis and South Indians at the time. At their DDA flat, there was just amma, her brother—an undergraduate—and ammamma. My grandfather, an engineer with the Public Works Department, had been posted in Amritsar while my dad, nanna, a bank manager, was working in Mumbai. Amma lamented the burden she was on her mother but my grandmother would have none of it. The doctor's instructions were followed completely: amma was put on forced bed rest. Not that it was of much help.

A few days later, amma was back at the hospital for another check-up. She still had more than six weeks to go until she was due. It was a typical blistering summer afternoon, and amma, painfully weak, alone in the ward, sat up slowly on the bed. On an impulse, she picked up her medical report that was clipped to the bed and opened it. She wasn't supposed to.

'TWINS???!!!' was the first word that leapt out at her. Okay, she thought, old news. They had warned her of the possibility, after all. But the three questions and exclamation marks on the report didn't inspire confidence. Amma read on. She shouldn't have. The next sentence was more detailed…and scary. The foetus, amma read, had multiple limbs. Two spines. One head. A terrified amma shut the file instantly, wishing she hadn't picked it up at all. A random thought came to mind: according to the Hindu calendar's cycle of sixty years, it was currently the year of the Rakshasa. Amma tried to make herself smile, thinking of how her little brother Narsu had joked that the twins could be named Mareech and Subahu after the two demon sons of Tathaka from the Ramayana. But she couldn't help but dwell on the three exclamation and question marks. And one head?! What did that mean? Was she going to have twins? Or just one monster baby?

Actually, let's pause here. The story of my birth doesn't begin with this medical report.

The story begins a year earlier, sometime in April 1974, in my father's hometown, Machilipatnam, sixty kilometres off Vijayawada in Andhra Pradesh. Also known as Masulipatnam or Bandara, this little city with a tropical climate plays an unwilling host to the occasional cyclone that lashes off the Bay of Bengal.

That day, though, was calm. My parents had gone to visit one of my father's sisters who had recently delivered a baby boy. My paternal grandfather and the rest of the family went to the famous Hanuman temple that he had constructed alongside his house in Edepelli Colony many years ago. What had started off as a mere photograph of the God, became, and still is, one of the most popular landmarks of the city. That evening, however, when they tried to enter the inner sanctum of the temple, Venkata Subbamma wouldn't let them. No one really knew much about Venkata Subbamma except that she was old, maybe in her eighties, and that she was skinny, didn't seem to have any living family, and spent most of her time at the temple…and yes, she was a huge devotee of Hanuman. She sprinkled water and cleaned the temple floors every day, painted the rangolis, and was just there pretty much all the time. Occasionally, she would get possessed by the Lord and make predictions that apparently came true. Lakshmi, my dad's youngest sister, had filled in amma on all these details but my city-bred mother wasn't too impressed.

That April evening, Venkata Subbamma stood at the temple, arms wide apart and evidently possessed, refusing entry to anyone. When the priest offered her an aarti to appease the God, she casually picked up a piece of burning camphor and swallowed it. Soon after, she demanded that my grandfather name his grandson after the monkey god, 'Him', which sparked off a minor confusion. Did she mean 'his' grandson; since his daughter's son wouldn't technically be 'his' grandson. It is the son's son who is one's own, thanks to the patriarchal system. My grandfather conveyed this to Venkata Subbamma, but she was in no mood for details. She merely repeated herself. As the rest of the family watched on in awe, word of this spread across the village. My grandmother, who was home with the newborn, picked him up and walked into the temple. The minute she did so, Venkata Subbamma screamed out, 'Pawan Kumaaaaaar!!!' And as my grandfather tried once again to clarify that this wasn't technically 'his' grandson, Subbamma merely said in a thundering tone, 'Hanuman (Pawan Kumar is another name for the monkey god) is here; Ram, Lakshman will come,' and promptly passed out.

There was an awestruck silence as my grandfather looked at dad and his new bride. The murmurs began: Subbamma's predictions always came true. But amma still wasn't too impressed. She hadn't even conceived then.

Now, however, as she lay back on the hospital bed, amma found herself wondering whether Subbamma's prediction was in fact, true. Did the old woman really know? Then she brushed the thought aside. Ram and Lakshman weren't even twins. And even if she was going to have twins, so what? But the one head loomed large in front of her eyes. What *was* she carrying in her womb?

The question wasn't answered immediately. Finally, one night, still some weeks before her due date, amma was wheeled into the labour room. There, the doctors consulted many other doctors, and then agreed to let nature take its course as it seemed like she was ready to deliver. So amma lay in the labour room alone all night, terrified, even though she had been reassured that it was 99.9 per cent certain it was a twin pregnancy. But it was the 0.1 per cent and the 'one head' that still haunted her. Her only company that night was the moans and sobs coming from a woman in the adjoining labour room. The woman, an ayah cryptically informed amma, was delivering her dead foetus. Talk about sugar-coating things. Amma lost whatever little composure she had left.

The woman's screams ended the next morning but amma's ordeal wasn't finished as yet. The next day, the doctors decided an X-ray would be risked for this rare situation. Much deliberation later, an X-ray machine was set up, the X-ray taken and the machine duly wheeled out. Delirious with worry, amma waited. And waited. Until the same ayah returned and when questioned, answered in a cryptic tone: sab gadbad hai! She then left as casually as she'd arrived as amma sat on, the words sinking in. At that moment my grandmother walked in, and suddenly the dam came crashing down. Poor amma was inconsolable.

Venkata Subbamma was wrong, the intern was wrong, the 99.9 per cent twin pregnancy was a lie, because 'sab gadbad hai'.

Thankfully, this time the trauma was short-lived. The doctor soon arrived, the 'gadbad' line was repeated, and she actually laughed. What the cryptic ayah had forgotten to mention was that the 'gadbad' was in the X-ray machine, not her womb. The machine hadn't worked, the X-ray hadn't happened at all, there *was* no report. Relief and worry came flooding together as amma fainted right there.

On 15 April 1975, when she woke, amma was being stitched up... and even before she could ask the question she was most scared to ask, she was informed that her 'babies' were fine. Amma couldn't believe her ears; tears of relief flooded down her face. What do you know, the small-town, mumbo-jumbo prediction had been absolutely right! Ram and Lakshman had come indeed... and were lying across the room in twin cribs. As amma turned to look at us, she tells me, my fist went up in the air, almost in slow motion. And as she watched on, not believing her eyes, a moment later, Rajiv's did too. Almost as if we were giving her a silent cheer. Venkata Subbamma was right, all was well with the world, and amma hadn't given birth to a monster baby. Well, not *one*, in any case!

Rajiv and I nearly don't make it

If amma felt heartened when her twin babies' fists went up in the air as a sign of victory moments after they were born, her relief lasted exactly three minutes. The instant the fists were down, the truth was out. And *this* is the truth. I didn't just magically turn into the tough guy you see on your television screens today—the whole process of metamorphosis was slow and painful. This was stage one, and possibly the worst for amma. I, of course, recollect nothing. But I am told that, at the time of birth, Rajiv and I were unbelievably small and underweight…and between the two of us, I was weaker. Careful consultation and approximately ten minutes later, we were wheeled into the nursery. Amma hadn't even seen us properly or held us. And as it turned out, she wouldn't for nearly ten days.

That first night after birth, amma was so weak that she couldn't even go to her own ward and had to stay back in the labour room. The next day she returned to her ward but still wasn't strong enough to come see us in the nursery, which was on another floor. Ammamma, who came to visit amma every day, would sneak a peek at us every evening from the glass window; she wasn't permitted to hold us or touch us, though, we were *that* fragile.

Aside from the fact that Rajiv and I were out of the womb a month too early, had droopy dog's ears which hadn't fully formed yet and were even having trouble breathing, amma had to make her peace with another little detail. Her babies were twins alright, but there was one tiny glitch. Identical or fraternal? It was anybody's guess.

What's the difference? Well, an identical-twin pregnancy is when there's only one sperm and one egg involved. The egg splits into two halves *after* being fertilized by the sperm. The two halves develop into two separate embryos but the babies born thus, share one umbilical cord. Basically, they were meant to be one baby but ended up becoming two. In the case of fraternal twins however, it is two eggs fertilized by two separate sperms, developing into two embryos. So, two babies, two umbilical cords. Siblings who just happen to be born at the same time. In our case, however, thanks to the whole pre-birth plot twist of two spines, multiple limbs and one head, this little nugget of information was left behind: to be determined at birth.

When we did come into this world, however, I am told there was one identifiable umbilical cord, but also one additional membrane that could either be nothing…or the other umbilical cord. Amma didn't know then. And we don't know now. Like I said, it was anybody's guess. But amma decided she wanted to *believe* we had two umbilical cords; that we were separate individuals with separate identities. As a new mother who hadn't yet seen her babies, whose husband nor father nor in-laws had been able to come by and see the babies either, the belief that her newborns were fraternal somehow comforted amma. So be it.

It did nothing to comfort ammamma, though, who had far worse things to worry about. Like the triple Rohini effect. A quick note on Hindu astrology: the zodiac consists of twenty-seven nakshatras or stars, each of which is governed by one of the nine navagrahas or planets (different from the ones in the solar system). Rohini is one of those stars and, as it turns out, it is the star under which Krishna was born. Yep, the God who, in between playing the flute, managed to save Draupadi's honour, expound the Bhagavad Gita to Arjuna before the battle of Kurukshetra, and also slay his evil uncle, Kansa. Babies born under this star, hence, are considered risky business, especially to their maternal uncles. In our case, it wasn't just one but two born under the same star. And oh, nanna (our father) as well. Hence, the triple Rohini effect, which, apparently, had all the makings of an astrological crisis.

This is why nanna was strictly advised to stay on in Bombay until further notice. He would only be permitted to see Rajiv and me after a special puja was performed for us. Ammamma drew from her ready reserve of everything-happens-for-a-reason instances, telling amma that it was perfect. In three months' time, we'd be ready to be named, and even a bit stronger. So in three months' time, after nanna had performed a puja and named us, he would be permitted to see us. Amma and nanna obeyed.

So, back to us. Day nine of being in the nursery, fed through a tube and looked at by ammamma once every day. On the tenth day of this strange routine, amma was informed that Rajiv was strong enough to go home since he'd regained his birth weight of two kilograms. I on the other hand, weighed 1.7 kilograms, clearly the weakling. Amma and ammamma were overjoyed, partly at least, and also encouraged by the fact that nanna, in all this time, had managed to get a transfer to Delhi.

The next day, late in the afternoon, amma finally came by to look at both of us. It was a heart-wrenching moment for her as Rajiv, swaddled in layers of cloth, was handed to her, while I lay back in the nursery, too weak to go. It was my first night away from Rajiv ever. It wasn't pretty. Not that things were any better at home. Rajiv was so weak and would get so tired after each feed that sometimes he wouldn't even wake up for the next one. A whole night passed by, leaving amma and ammamma sleepless, while I struggled on my own in the nursery of Safdarjung Hospital.

The next evening, when ammamma finally managed to make it to the hospital, she was given a thorough scolding by the doctors and nurses. Apparently I had suffered from a nasty bout of diarrhoea during the night, and my weight was down by twenty grams. The guilt of abandonment was added to equal portions of worry. The next morning, when amma came by with Rajiv for a check-up, she wasn't spared either, but for a slightly different reason. As it turned out, Rajiv had also dropped twenty grams. One night apart and both her twins had lost the same amount of weight. Sheer coincidence, amma told herself. Fraternal, they're fraternal, *not* identical! She would have to repeat the words to herself several more times in the coming years.

After the diarrhoea attack, I was so weak that I had to spend two nights in an incubator, and at one point, they weren't sure if I would make it. By some miracle, I did.

But after this incident, things took a turn for the better. A week later, Rajiv and I both made it to ammamma's two-bedroom flat on the first floor of Munirka's DDA colony. The highlight of this first month home was the nights. Picture this: lovely, long, sticky, summer nights of Delhi, punctuated with twin cries. As if our other complications weren't enough, Rajiv and I started to howl ourselves hoarse every night, forcing amma to take up the night-watchman duty. And it was a fine jugalbandi. If Rajiv began, I'd unfailingly join him in about a second and vice versa. Ammamma, like all doting grandparents, felt that her grandsons' sobs sounded like nothing less than the finest music. Also, despite their loss of sleep, she and amma were delighted when our cries turned louder—it indicated we were growing stronger. Not quite a theory I buy in adulthood, just so you know.

Months passed in this daze of hospital visits, crying in tandem, and amma's constant bouts of cleaning and disinfecting the house. Visitors were only allowed 'individual viewings' of me and Rajiv. In some cases, if the visitor insisted on carrying or holding us, since he was the stronger of us, ammamma would bring out Rajiv. If they asked about the 'other one', pat came ammamma's reply: he looks just like this one, anyway, so it doesn't matter.

As our third month loomed close, nanna moved to Delhi and preparations for the naamkaran and puja were in full swing. Venkata Subbamma's prediction was taken very seriously indeed by my paternal grandfather who insisted that we be named Ram and Lakshman despite the fact that the duo weren't twins. Which I guess worked well for amma's need to believe. My grandfather also came up with this explanation that I, the second to come out of the womb, was the older one, the one conceived first, and hence destined to be called Ram. So on the auspicious date, the puja was duly performed; nanna saw us, first reflected in a basin of oil, and then finally, after all ill-effects of the triple Rohini were drawn off, held us.

Soon after this, nanna's transfer was finalized and we decided to move house: two floors above in the same DDA flat. Ammamma's joy knew no bounds while amma bent over backwards cleaning and preparing the flat, hoping all would go well. But Rajiv and I didn't enjoy making anything smooth for her or the rest of the family. The day they were to move, nanna and amma, each carrying one of us in their arms, began the long strenuous journey up two floors. Three steps later, they realized we couldn't go any further. The altitude change from being three steps higher had affected us so much, I kid you not, that we had apparently developed palpitations! Amma and nanna slowly climbed down the three steps while we began to shiver. The shift was unthinkable for now. We were carried back to ammamma's, where we remained for the next month. Nanna stayed alone in our new flat on the third floor.

Then one Sunday afternoon, amma again mustered up the courage. Rajiv, the stronger of us still, was carried first. Thirty-four painstaking steps over ten minutes. He held on tight to amma, eyes shut, with amma praying all along the way. On the way, amma told Rajiv he would soon be home with nanna ... and she insists he smiled up at her. Minutes later, she repeated the procedure with me and I opened my eyes long enough to beam at her too. And so it came to be that the Ambadapudis (Vishwanath is my father's name but not our surname; my mother took it as her surname but I am Ambadapudi Raghu Ram, Rajiv is Ambadapudi Rajiv Lakshman) moved to the third floor of the DDA colony, and would live there for nearly two game-changing decades. But for now, amma was glad she'd brought her twin babies home. Oh, and did I mention they were fraternal twin babies?

◆

Amma could have screamed herself hoarse but the rest of the world didn't give a damn about the fraternal-identical detailing—to them, Rajiv and I were twins, the freaks, the odd ones out. It had, and still has, its good, bad and ugly side effects. But growing up, I guess the ugly ones outnumbered the good.

It was 5 p.m. and the place was J. D. Tytler Kindergarten, New Rajinder Nagar, New Delhi. Rajiv and I, four or five years old at most, were summoned to the principal's office. Why? To sing 'Mere paas aao mere doston' from *Mr Natwarlal*, complete with a dance routine. Why? Beats me. From then on, every evening after school when the rest of the kids would head home, Rajiv and I would be called to perform for the principal and then leave for home. Every single evening, all through kindergarten to Class One. I don't remember how or why, but clearly our performance greatly amused and entertained the principal. Bizarre, right? I think this ritual lasted about a year, and it is one of my earliest clear memories of school.

I don't understand what people mean when they say they would love to go back to school, back to their classrooms, back to that 'age' and time in life. I've been to three schools: J. D. Tytler Kindergarten up to Class One; Chinmaya Vidyalaya, from Class Two to Class Eight and the D.T.E.A. (Delhi Tamil Education Association) School where I finished my Class Twelve. Sure, my years in each of those schools made me who I am today, but if anyone, *anyone*, gave me a chance to go back to my time at either one, I'd sooner fling myself off the tallest building. I'm perfectly serious. I hated school. And for more than one reason.

Earliest School Memory No. 1

Rajiv and I were just about four years old, tiny and frail, but we held on to the gate with all our might...or it could have just been desperation. Our tiny fingers clung to the upper grills and our legs entwined on the lower ones as we shook our heads continuously, the movement almost making us dizzy. No no no no no no no! We won't go, we hate it there, we *won't*! Thatha, my maternal grandfather, heard us patiently for about a minute. The next thing we knew, his strong wiry hands plucked our hands and legs off the gate even as he made soothing sounds. It will be fine there, he said. No, I sobbed. It *won't* be fine! And boy was I right!

Earliest School Memory No. 2

Class One. Rajiv and I were inseparable. The same class, same division, same bench. The same capacity for paying attention. The same vacant look in both sets of eyes, leading to the same level of frustration in the teachers. They don't need anyone else, they're so self-sufficient, the teachers would complain to amma. And this constant need to be together all the time, every minute of the day, is unhealthy; they don't talk to anyone else! Amma knew exactly what they meant. Back at home, Rajiv and I were pretty much a single unit...so much so that our parents wouldn't even call us by our individual names but simply scream out, 'Ramaraju', and both of us would turn up.

Amma, by now, had spent the first few years of our lives trying very hard to penetrate the wall we'd so firmly erected around ourselves. She did manage to, to an extent, but the one thing she couldn't fight was how we had to do things together. Everything and I mean *everything*. Don't believe me? Picture this: My amma, with her twin monsters perched on either knee—me on the right, Rajiv on the left. A glass of milk held in each of amma's hands, held up to both our lips at the same time. If you measured the sips of milk we glugged, they'd be equal down to the last drop.

Rajiv and I would also fall sick together. Even as toddlers, if Rajiv had a temperature and the doctor stuck a thermometer in his mouth, I would automatically open my mouth too. Almost as if it were my right. In our later school years too, this continued. I once came down with jaundice and had to be taken home. Rajiv was healthier and continued to attend school. Every afternoon, though, my fever would rise just a wee bit...and there, in school, Rajiv's body temperature would go up too. But amma stuck to her guns and her fraternal twin theory. It was NOT the judwa effect—prick one and the other bleeds. Nope, she insisted, this was just a coincidence, it meant nothing. She told the teachers so too.

Our frustrated teachers, meanwhile, decided to take matters into their own hands. Rajiv and I were separated, put in different sections. Not that it made any difference. The recess bell would ring and we'd both rush out of our separate classrooms, straight to the playground, perch ourselves on the see-saw and spend all of recess swinging up and down. We really needed no one else. Actually, looking back, those days weren't so bad.

Then recesses stopped being about the see-saw or a dusty game of catch in the playground. Suddenly, for Rajiv and me, they began to mean getting beaten up. Together and separately. Why? Okay, if you are a boy and reading this, then you know what I mean when I say that there's no clear-cut answer to that question. It happens. It's disgusting and wrong but it happens.

If you're a girl and reading this, let me try and explain. Schools *are* vicious places, and some kids can be unbelievably mean. Rajiv and I were feeble and puny, our twin-ness strange. We didn't raise our voices, talk back, speak out of turn. Hence, we made easy targets. Yes, boys do pick on kids like that. It's an unfortunate, ugly truth. Remember Suchit from *Roadies* Season 8? He was bullied awfully all through his childhood and even though he grew to be a good-looking, strapping young man, even we managed to bully him. Because he let us. Rajiv and I allowed ourselves to get beaten up because it happened to us at a stage when we were too young to understand the reason behind it. We thought it was the law of the land. But when I was in Class Two and still getting punched at Chinmaya Vidyalaya, I did wonder about the whys and hows of it.

I wondered later too, in Class Four, Five, Six, Seven and Eight, when I lay flat on the playground every afternoon. I could feel the sun hitting me in the face as the big, burly boy sitting on me pounded away.

Why did the bully go through so much trouble to pick on the one weak kid who couldn't fight back? Well, *precisely* for that reason! The bully *always* picks on someone smaller than himself. But I didn't figure that out until much later. I wasn't just slow at grasping my everyday subjects; it took me a while to figure out life's lessons as well.

One of my first big life lessons came in the sixth grade. Once, when a teacher left the classroom to our devices and came back, I was scolded and my ear was twisted for 'misbehaviour'. Except that I hadn't done anything. As I stood there, nursing my red ears (Rajiv and I never ever talked back or defied an elder. Never.), I suddenly had an epiphany. I had been punished for something I hadn't done. I wasn't going to talk back or defend myself but I realized that life *wasn't* fair. But back then, I didn't stop to think of it further, I just accepted it as a fact.

When we were three years old, our mother got pregnant again. My parents made the rounds of all the temples, praying, in fact begging for, two things: 1) No twins. 2) No boys. Their prayers were answered and our little sister Supriya was born on 14 September 1978. As she grew up, Tuppi, as we called her, would crave Rajiv's and my attention. She had to know what we were up to, like any normal sibling. But she figured out her life lessons pretty early on too...that we were a unit unto ourselves and she would never be let in. Poor kid. Even today, Tuppi tells me about how we'd constantly, jointly, throw her out of our room. She'd still come back and relentlessly keep knocking on the door—anything to get a reaction. The big brotherly instincts kicked in much later. For now, she was, like all the others: an outsider.

Amma, who clawed her way into our room and our lives, had realized that, despite our tendency to lead single-dual lives, we did have different aptitudes. Rajiv was good with numbers and I had a knack for language. However, the one thing we both had an unnatural tuning for was music, a fact she had discovered long before school. When I was barely a few months old, I could tell the moods of the different ragas being sung to me. There was one lullaby which would never be sung to us, because the raga was so melancholic, amma says, that I'd get upset; not cry like babies do, but actually feel the emotions in the music. My eyes would well up, my nose would turn red and my mouth would wobble—an almost-adult reaction to a song. When we were around ten years old, Amma enrolled Rajiv and me in music class. We attended classes for about a week before our attention span—or the lack of it—caught up with us. Also, there was the little problem of it messing with our playtime. So that was it, we gave it up.

Amma tried disciplining us, oh yes she did! But as I had mentioned earlier, she could never quite gather the courage to box our ears— the memory of the once-weak drooping earlobes had stayed with her. Pitting us against each other didn't work either. Rajiv and I couldn't care less for competition, even between ourselves. *Especially* between ourselves, in fact. I am told that we would almost always take turns doing our homework. That is, one person would do the homework for both. It wasn't even a thought-out plan, it was just the way it was.

Our obsession of being together even extended to everyday things. Like pencil boxes. If Rajiv lost his, amma would have to buy a new one not just for him, but me too. And if she ever let us go buy things on our own, we were done for. Oh, did I mention that I didn't understand money? Let me explain. I got pocket money for a very brief period growing up: twenty-five paise every week. But to Rajiv and me, it wasn't 'twenty-five' paise, it was just *one* coin. Yeah, we were pretty young, but our understanding of money did not improve over the years.

Once, when we were in the fifth grade, amma, Rajiv and I went to buy geometry boxes for us. Rajiv and I both stood outside the stationery store, trying to convince her to buy a Camel Geometry Box. It cost eighteen rupees while the other brand, Bittoo Geometry Box, cost ten rupees. After a while, amma realized we didn't particularly *want* the better brand…we were arguing ourselves hoarse simply because we were convinced the Camel Geometry Box was cheaper. Our logic: amma would pay ten rupees for the other compass box and get nothing in return. On the other hand, a twenty-rupee note for the Camel Geometry Box would earn her a handsome payback of two rupees. Simple, stupid, senseless logic. It was amma's very own epiphany.

She literally dropped to her knees and, sobbing, took us in her arms. How were her twin babies going to survive in the real world without understanding money? I don't know. I still don't understand money. Ask me about my assets, accounts, finances and I'll stare right back at you blankly. Money makes no sense to me. Not then. Not now.

But the beating up slowly did. Through the years, I still hadn't figured out the bully theory, but one day in Class Seven, I suddenly realized there *was* an alternative. Fighting back. Not that I did it myself.

It was just another day, just another recess. Me, on my back on the playground, being pounded on as usual, when suddenly, out of nowhere, a boy came by. He wasn't big-built or anything but he plucked the bully off me and told him to back off. He wasn't a friend of mine but he stood up for me. As I stood there and watched him, something shifted in me and I began sobbing. It was the first time I'd ever sobbed after being beaten up. Only I wasn't sobbing because of the beating, but because it suddenly struck me that maybe the world wasn't all just bullies and weaklings and that some did care—enough to defend strangers and stand up for them. I remember the boy's face and his name to this day—Ujjwal Ramachandran.

The day I fought back and other memories

Being beaten up is kind of like being molested, I imagine. Because of the way it affects you, and the feeling you're left with—very low self-esteem. The truth is, and this is another ugly one: the bullies who beat you up, who have you scanning the hallways before walking out, who make your heart turn to lead every time you spot them…they never ever remember you years later, but you always remember them. Their faces, the smirks, the grins…and even years later, you consciously or unconsciously try to do something that you feel would impress them. Get over it I'd say. Or do something better. Like fight back.

When Rohit Batra, the BCom student suffering from thalassaemia who came to the Chandigarh auditions during *Roadies* 9, spoke of being bullied and keeping quiet, I could empathize. I've been there, I know exactly what that feels like. He had tears in his eyes when we asked him why he never fought back: he was scared of being beaten up badly, scared that he was weak. I get that too. That was me at Chinmaya Vidyalaya. Beaten, bullied, humiliated. The trauma of those beatings, I felt, made me feel even shorter than I was. The two bullies I remember most clearly were Sudhir Sachdeva and Rishabh Sood. They weren't that much older than me, they had only managed to grow taller faster. And at that age, within the span of one year, differences in physical development become stark. I lent myself to the beatings.

The beatings had, by then, become routine and I had accepted them. Except for that one day, in the eighth grade, when I wondered what it would be like to hit back. The recess bell had just gone off, and I was on my way out of the class when Sudhir Sachdeva sauntered along on one of his usual visits. It all played out according to routine. He caught me and started pounding the hell out of me for no reason, as always. Normally, I would have just borne it quietly but that day, something shifted within me. I felt the usual ringing in my ears as I got punched around... and then suddenly I raised a tentative arm, not to ward him off but to hit him back. Sachdeva was so shocked that he couldn't react to this. It felt good... for about a minute. I went all out at him but my arms flailed aimlessly, my movements those of a rookie. Most of my punches fell flat, but I didn't care about technique; I was finally fighting back!

Soon, however, Sachdeva recovered. After that, it didn't take long till I was once again on my back and he was sitting on me, punching away. By now, a crowd had gathered and begun cheering him. *Him*, not me. Why, I have no idea. Do people love bullies? Anyway, I remember feeling this cold sinking sensation at the bottom of my stomach that day. No one was cheering me on, no one cared! The thought depressed me so much, at one point I just stopped fighting. And let him pound me again. After all, who was I to dispute the law of the jungle? The bully had to win. As for the underdog... well, honestly, who gave a shit?

So, I'm sorry to say that that day didn't really end in an inspiring change of fate. The routine went on; I still got beaten up, I still loathed school. But the 'taller' guy you now see on your television screens—he was born during that ten-minute recess that day.

While I was still reeling from my routine, Rajiv had found a new way of dealing with the bullying—he had made a group for himself. The members of his group were the social outcasts, the odd ones, the kids that didn't fit in. And they had each other's backs, which made it an ideal situation. A bully only had to mess with one and the others would come rushing at his throat. Rajiv had discovered a solution to our problem: he moved around in a pack, a policy I adhere to even today.

This situation worked well for a while, but soon, the gang's activities got pretty violent and out of control, so much so that we had to change schools. So it came to be that in Class Nine, Rajiv and I were moved to the D.T.E.A. High School. Here was where, finally, I began to grow...at least where my self-esteem and a sense of assertiveness were concerned. My voice broke much later, as did my height and facial hair.

Barely a week into Class Nine, I had a déjà vu moment. Despite it being another school, another playground, I was beaten up by another bully, Umesh. But this is when things changed. The next day, smack in the middle of the playground, Umesh was called out and Kailash Arya pounded the shit out of him. For me.

A word about the Aryas: in the Munirka DDA flats where we lived, my ammamma, if you recall, stayed on the first floor, while we were on the third; the second floor was home to the Aryas. A household with five sons, theirs was a family that has had a huge impact on my life, especially Kailash, a.k.a. Kelly. He's one my closest friends to this day and even back then Rajiv, Kelly and I were known as the triplets. Anyway, that fateful day after being beaten up, when I crossed the second floor on my way home, I ran into Kelly, who was a year senior to me at D.T.E.A. and who demanded to know who had done this to me.

The next day, I watched Kelly pound my bully to pulp. Sorry bol, he roared. The bully kept quiet, the pounding continued. By now, I was really scared and kept telling Kelly to lay off; it's okay, doesn't matter, I pleaded, but Kelly wouldn't listen. His friends joined in and I have this clear memory of the bully getting thrashed and kicked, the mud flying around. And when they were done, Kelly had a short but impactful note for the bully: tell everyone *this* is what we did to you. Also tell them that the next time anyone touches these boys, they've had it.

That's the day I realized that there's only one way to react to bullying: disproportionately. Yes, it's true most bullies do have histories. They probably come from violent households but that does not give them the excuse to pick on someone weaker. So I say, when someone challenges you, the answer doesn't lie in appealing to their human side. It lies in baring your claws, in showing them what you've got. Push me and I'll punch you. Get in my way, and I won't take it lying down. Send out a message, loud and clear, so that the bully doesn't get to throw his weight around. You have made him think before he ever attempts something like that again. Sure, in the process you'll bleed some, bruise some more. But at least you will have your dignity. That's what I told Rohit Batra that day at the auditions: Fight back, you owe that much to yourself.

Now, about the auditions. Yep, some people call me a bully based on what they've watched on television. To tell you the truth, I don't give a damn about how I'm perceived, because if I did, *Roadies* wouldn't be what it has become today. I'd like to maintain that any time I've yelled at, kicked out or become physically violent with a potential contestant, I *have* been provoked. Every single time. The provocation could be anything—his manner, his writing down 'maar peet' as his answer to the simple question of occupation on his form, his belittling women, homosexuals and any other marginalized groups...*that* gets my goat. He's an obvious bully and in his face, I see them all...Rishabh Sood, Sudhir Sachdeva and the others. In my eyes then, he's asking for it. And I don't disappoint.

Also, if anyone so much as raises his voice while speaking to my crew, I do what Kelly did that day for me at the D.T.E.A. playground. Seek him out, beat him up, kick him out, and then, because I can, stick it on camera and air it, just as a warning to the others. You do not get to mess around with me or anyone associated with me, in this case, my crew. It may be violent but it is an effective message.

Coming back to the eighties, I didn't turn into a fighter overnight but I did realize something: I wasn't okay with being beaten up anymore. However, up until Class Ten, Rajiv and I remained small-built and weak, with no facial or bodily hair and with childish voices to boot. But between Class Ten and Eleven, we had a dramatic spurt of development. We grew taller, sprouted facial hair, our voices cracked— and it happened all of a sudden. But bullying, ultimately, isn't about size if you ask me. It's about the level of threat you pose to the other party. You can either keep your head bowed and go about your business without disturbing anybody *or* you can become the fucker that these fuckers are scared of. I have tried both techniques, and for me, the latter worked.

For most people, school and college are the best times ever, because maybe after that, life for them turned into one long, never-ending routine. For me, it was different. School was not great. Apart from the bullying, I think my lack of aptitude for our education system might have had something to do with it. All through school, I found very, very few classes that managed to engage me. Every time we had a maths or science class, my heart would sink with sheer fright. They were subjects that made no sense to me and I knew I'd be made to stand up, asked a question I wouldn't know the answer to, be humiliated in front of the class and eventually thrown out of the room. Remember the child from *Taare Zameen Par*? I completely identify with him. I may not have been dyslexic but I was just as lost, as out of sync with the routine of school as the kid in the movie was.

I loved history and English, though, as they were like storytelling sessions for me. Today, I know what I loathed so much about school—the uniformity and mediocrity of the system. If you measure the worth of a fish by its ability to climb a tree, it will spend its entire life thinking it's stupid. A child can be really creative but no one gives a shit—all anyone ever cares about are the marks you bring home. And you have to score well in a variety of subjects. At D.T.E.A., though, Rajiv and I both realized we had a knack for Sanskrit. We even topped but then failed in maths and chemistry.

After Class Ten, our parents made Rajiv and me take up science as opposed to arts. We did. And, as expected, the results were dismal. I remember it like yesterday: Saroj Gupta, our maths teacher, announcing the results of the first unit test. The class had performed badly, apparently. Two of the brightest kids, Naveen and Ajit, got pulled up for scoring nineteen and twenty-two respectively, out of twenty-five.

And then she called out my name. I stood up, the same ringing in my ears, and waited for the verdict to be pronounced. 'Now this,' she said, 'is not disappointing. This is exactly what I expected and it's exactly what he's scored. Zero.' Seriously. In my first unit test, I scored a zero out of twenty-five. There was scattered laughter across the class and, because I was a boy and by Class Eleven you are expected to sport thicker skin, I laughed too. Deep down, though, I wanted to be far, far away. My failure traumatized me so much that I wrote her a letter, apologizing for my performance.

Unit Test Two. Raghu! I stood up again…the moment of truth. 'There's been some improvement this time,' she said. Indeed there had been. I had scored one. While on the inside I'd have this constant sinking feeling, neither me nor Rajiv could bring ourselves to study harder. There were too many distractions, we ourselves being the biggest ones. While studying for our boards, we'd be up all night with a thermos of tea amma had painstakingly made for us. And we'd chat. All night long. Until the day amma caught us red-handed and then sat in on us every night. When she'd nod off, we'd actually have written conversations in our schoolbooks. But all through this determination to not study, there was also the feeling of not being good enough.

Despite the dislike for school and fear of academics, D.T.E.A. wasn't anything like Chinmaya Vidyalaya. And we knew this from day one. For starters, our twin status here was not only acceptable, but also 'cool'. We were no longer the freaks but objects of fascination for students and teachers alike. On our first day in school, we were paraded around the classrooms by our teachers. A couple of years into D.T.E.A., by which time the bullying had stopped and we'd become quite a formidable force ourselves, Rajiv and I discovered our talent for dance…as did the rest of the school. At our seniors' farewell, we danced—Rajiv did a very good impression of Michael Jackson—and that locked our popularity in place. By the time we got to Class Twelve and we had our own farewell, we were so sought-after that students as young as nine years old wanted us to write in their slam books. Even the teachers had come a long way—from being the 'useless twins', we were now addressed as 'my twins'.

Our popularity extended to the girls, too...though the way I handled female attention was nothing I can be proud of. I could talk to women...but only when they were in a group. One lone girl? I'd run the other way. And if she was a girl I had a crush on? I wouldn't even make eye contact, let alone tell her how I felt! As was the case with Sonika Arora, who was from our neighbourhood in Munirka and my first crush. I couldn't ever get a word out in her presence. The same happened with Kadambari, my crush in Class Eleven. Even though I suspected she liked me too (her friends had told me as much), just when I was about to be introduced to her, I backed out at the last minute and ran as fast as my legs could carry me. Bullying I could maybe handle—girls were still scary! The irony was that I was moonlighting as a writer of love letters. Because I was better at English than my friends, I was called upon to pen several love letters from my pals to their girls. But Sonika never received one from me.

Today, she's married and settled in the States and about a year ago, she told me she had caught a few episodes of *Roadies*. I can see Munirka in you, she said, at the auditions. My manner, my tone of voice, body language, the way I conduct myself...is all Munirka. It was in Munirka that I grew taller, figuratively and literally. Our bustling little urban village was right at the edge of Munirka gaon and played unwilling host to the thick population of Jats in the village. The Jat boys would come by our area, tease the girls, beat up the boys, and leave. The bullying was back, the solution to which Rajiv had figured out long ago: moving in packs. There was me, Rajiv and Kelly of course—the triplets—and several of our other friends, most of whom I'm in touch with to this day. We'd meet every evening around 4.30-5 p.m. As kids, we'd of course be playing, running around. But as we grew older and entered our teens, our attitudes and behaviour changed; we would roam the streets of Munirka and Vasant Vihar, not really looking for trouble but not hiding from it either. And we got into a lot of it. All it would take was for one of our friends to come up to us saying 'panga hua hai' and we would leave everything and follow him, ready for a fight. 'Fight first, ask questions later' was our philosophy. Life wasn't so bleak anymore: my confidence was building, I had friends, I was popular with the ladies. Studies, yes, I was still pitiably weak at—I distinctly remember daydreaming even during my Class Twelve board exams. I don't know how, but we somehow got through school. Phew!

One last random memory. In Class Twelve, before the boards, I'd wanted to study with my friend Abhijit Ghosh who was one of the brightest kids in class. But he politely declined, and he was brutally frank about the reason. Apparently his mother had advised him not to hang out with me since I could be a bad influence, weak as I was at studies. An obedient boy, Abhijit did as his mum said. I felt a stinging sense of rejection then. Three years ago, in 2010, we had a three-day reunion at D.T.E.A. For the first time, we *voluntarily* chose to stay in the principal's office, as opposed to being dragged there as punishment, because we were being mobbed by the kids. I remember bumping into Ajit, one of our school's top-scorers, at this reunion, and him telling me how life had come full circle: I, one of the school's poorer performers, had managed to turn into an achiever and our batch was now identified as 'Raghu-Rajiv's batch'.

So, yeah, a word of advice for anyone reading this book who is in school or knows someone who is. *Don't* take school too seriously. Less marks do not mean you have a lesser brain. Always remember, our education system celebrates mediocrity and schools don't have all the answers; they are *not* the real world.

That said, I'd still maintain that, despite the everyday drudgery, the heavy bags, the beatings and punishments, I do remember school with some fondness. The great thing about that age is that you are never class or religion conscious. You can be best friends with the gardener's or watchman's son, it doesn't matter to you then. The class distinctions come later in life. It is a joyful, almost idyllic existence.

But would I want to go back to it? Give another exam? Umm…there is this really, really tall tower in Tardeo…I'd rather fling myself off of it, thank you very much!

The lost years: College, whisky and a guitar

I don't think He would have approved.

It is true that at eighteen, I reeked of a good upbringing. At least on the outside. My parents didn't have to know about our wolf pack or its workings in Munirka, and how it had fast become a force to be reckoned with. They were protected from all of that and what they saw was what the world saw too—that I, Raghu Ram, was a living, breathing example of a good Brahmachari boy from a staunchly religious Brahmin family. Rajiv and I performed our Sandhyavandanam (prayers said at daybreak, noon and sundown by young boys initiated into the sacred thread ceremony) twice (yes, Brahmacharis did it only twice) every day, and underneath my shirt, I had the janayu or holy thread strung across my left shoulder at all times...

...the same left shoulder that also had a guitar strap biting into it. I had borrowed the guitar from Ravi Kapoor, a college friend, and was obsessed with it, but had no idea how to play it. I sat at the outer-inner sanctum of Malai Mandir, afternoon after breezy afternoon, not to seek the blessings of He who resided within but strumming the borrowed guitar, teaching myself to play, and perhaps, in the process, killing Him softly. Him being Murugan or Karthikeya or Swaminatha, take your pick.

Malai Mandir, a Murugan temple in R. K. Puram is South Indian in every aspect, starting from the gopuram at the top of the temple right down to the red-and-white striped walls on the outside, signalling a house of worship. But back then, I wasn't really taken in by its architecture or four-decade-old history. To me, it was just an inspiring spot to play chords whose names I didn't know. My friend, Khemraj, happened to be the younger son of the temple's chief watchman so I had unlimited access to the temple. For two aimless months, I'd tell amma and nanna that I was over at a friend's and visit the temple every single day. I practically lived there, playing, sleeping, chit-chatting with Khemraj, making friends with the flower-sellers, playing cards with Kelly, who knew Lakshman—Khemraj's older brother. Oh, and also getting initiated into drinking, courtesy the same flower-sellers.

Like I said before, I don't think He would have approved.

Before the unholy temple visits began, before we were initiated into college, Rajiv and I remained a brute force in school. The year was 1992 and Rajiv and I had passed out of Class Twelve, maybe not with flying colours but with formidable reputations. It was the same year that Tuppi, our baby sister, joined D.T.E.A. in Class Nine. Nobody knew she was our sister. One day, she came home from school and started crying. Apparently there was a boy from Class Ten who kept teasing and harassing her, mainly because he had a crush on her. Tuppi was quite traumatized because, of late, the boy had told her she had to date him, or else… Rajiv and I exchanged a look.

The next morning, Rajiv, Kailash, Bala (another of our friends) and I marched to D.T.E.A. We summoned a junior to go get this boy. But the junior refused, begged us to let him go. Apparently he was afraid he'd get beaten up because this Class Ten boy was a bully. Hmm. Even more interesting, this. I told the junior, you *don't* call him and we thrash you here. Your choice. Poor kid, he did as he was told. The bully arrived, and within minutes, the four of us managed to effectively pound into him the short message we had gone there to deliver: stay away from our sister. Mind you, we had passed out of school by then, but we still marched in there, thrashed this boy to an inch of his life and he took it because, here's the thing, and I can't say this enough: when you're a nice guy, people fuck you over. It is important to act tough sometimes so that bullies don't see you as a pushover. I realized that a long time ago. That boy, or anyone else for that matter, never bothered Tuppi again. Our reputations and egos remained intact as Rajiv and I strode forth to college.

But no, let's start from that wonderfully ego-wrecking car drive after every college in the state put up their cut-off percentages for admission. A word on cut-off percentages: it's the numbers that decide your fate after Class Twelve. With a prayer in your heart, you go to every college and hope that one of them has put up a cut-off that matches the one you have on your marksheet. Less marks mean a less reputed college and a course of 'lesser' importance and value.

Two years ago, I heard that the cut-off percentage for Delhi's Shri Ram College of Commerce was, I kid you not, 100 per cent! And it was still fucking full! Just imagine, if you've scored a 95 per cent, nobody gives a shit! You're shunted to the back of the line; fuck off, you bloody retard, didn't you study enough? You scored a 95 per cent, for God's sake, but it isn't enough. 100?! I mean, seriously!

But I digress…yeah, so back in our day, it wasn't 100 per cent but either way, Rajiv and I, yep, you guessed right, dear reader, hadn't quite made the cut.

So there we were with three of our friends, seventeen years old, fresh out of school, in the car that dad was driving, making regular stops at each college. Our friends all scored well above 60 per cent with one of them even getting a distinction (above 75 per cent) while Rajiv and I had scored only around 55 per cent. The scene almost played out like a sitcom. Dad would stop the car, all of us would get off… and inevitably, one of my friends would come back saying, uncle mera so-and-so college mein ho gaya, admission mil gayi. Oh, okay, good. We'd drive on. Next stop. Another friend would get off, come back beaming, uncle I've been selected. Great. By the end of it, everybody got admission except for Rajiv and me. And my dad was driving so you have to understand how he must have been feeling. When the second list was put up, we went on the drive again. By this time, my parents had also understood that while Rajiv and I could take on different courses, we had to, absolutely *had* to be in the same college.

And the only college that gave us both admission was Deshbandhu College; Rajiv chose economics while I took up English honours. Now, I don't know where it stands today but this was a very notorious college back in the day. Within a week, we knew our being heroes in Munirka and in school didn't matter at Deshbandhu. We were again the babes in the woods, completely lost and thoroughly bullied. Usually, each department rags its own juniors, right? Wrong. Rajiv and my twin status worked to our disadvantage again. So we were personally called to every department and ragged. Over and over. And if those were the first two weeks, what happened next didn't quite inspire confidence.

It was the day of the freshers' party for the English batch, I was in the common room where our party was being held, Rajiv was waiting for me to get done with the party and was meanwhile hanging around in a classroom within campus, with a girl. A few seniors from the English freshers' party, (my party), went sniffing for some fun and games. And walked into the same classroom. They went straight at him; three guys held a knife to his neck as they attempted to molest the girl. Thankfully, a couple of his friends had forgotten their bags inside the same classroom and came back for them. The bullies got a little intimidated that Rajiv had extra pairs of helping hands and, thankfully, things didn't turn ugly. They left, but not before one of them had grabbed Rajiv's I-card. If he breathed a word of this, he wouldn't get it back, they said. No I-card, no entry into college. In school, no one would dare to speak to us like that and get away with it. But two weeks into college and we were back to square one. Great.

The next morning, when I got to college, I met the girl from the previous day. She was telling me all about what had happened, when suddenly out of nowhere, these two guys landed up. They physically picked me up, dragged me all the way to the canteen; once inside, they took me to the kitchen and presented me in front of Bully No. 1. Now this guy was standing right there, where the food was being cooked, and shaving—shaving with a fucking knife. It was intimidating! The minute I appeared, he asked me, all cockiness and attitude, if I remembered him. I didn't and told him so. Some choice abuses later, I realized that Bully No. 1 had mistaken me for Rajiv and that he was one of the goons from the previous day. My twin story then, of course, sounded to him like a filmy ploy for getting out of a sticky spot. I somehow managed to wriggle my way out of the situation but he refused to return Rajiv's I-card.

The same evening, Rajiv and I were both summoned to meet a mystery man. It was just us again, alone against the big bad bullies. A déjà vu moment for the both of us. So, anyway, we met Bully No. 2 who asked us whether we had had a 'panga' with Bully No. 1. Yes, we conceded, he beat us, abused us, threatened us, grabbed Rajiv's I-card. Bully No. 2 listened quietly, and then told us he liked us; we were sweet, nice twin boys. And that was that. Rajiv and I were duly dismissed, and went home without a clue as to what had happened.

The next morning dawned frightful and cold. Things didn't get better when we saw Bully No. 1 waiting for us at the college gates. Deep breaths, impassive faces, we walked straight towards him. And he held out... Rajiv's I-card. Why did you say we had a panga, he asked, all sunshine and smiles this morning. Rajiv and I stayed quiet as he swore that, from that day on, he was our older brother. You see, we had unwittingly come between two warring gangs. Bully No. 2, who had strangely enough taken a shine to us, was Daagar from the Manu-Daagar gang contesting in college elections against Bully No. 1, Ajay Chauhan.

So after a false start, thanks to the bullying gangs at war, by the end of the first year, Rajiv and I had our backs covered in this college. Rajiv was even being canvassed for student body president! The same life lesson this time was taught more emphatically: logic and common sense mean nothing to bullies. Nice, meek guys do *not* inherit the world. The spoils of war are taken by the winners. I made my choice. After quite an eventful year, one that ended on a very sombre note (more on that later), Rajiv and I moved to Sri Venkateswara College for our second year.

Suddenly, none of our fighting back and standing up to the bullies mattered: we were admitted into a college that was bullied! Venky, as Venkateswara College is fondly known, situated on Benito Juarez Marg, was quite close to two rather notorious colleges: Motilal Nehru College, which was just down the road, and Atma Ram Sanatan Dharma (A.R.S.D.) in Dhaula Kuan. They were full of tough guys who would stride into Venky to tease the girls and beat up the boys... for sport. Rajiv and I, mainly owing to the reasons for our shift to Venky (again, I will explain this later) stayed away from most of these altercations. We diligently stayed away from classes, too.

This was around the time I met Ravi Kapoor and his guitar. So yeah, many temple visits later, I became quite good at playing the guitar. In fact, we formed a band—Ravi, Rajiv, Kelly who was also in Venky and technically our senior (luckily for us, Kelly lasted long, really long in college, so we caught up with him soon enough academically) and I—called Complicity. I was the frontman with Ravi while Rajiv and Kelly were backup vocals. Rajiv, Kelly and I were also the choreographers at Venky.

I should probably also mention that those were our days of very limited means. We were already hitting nineteen; Kelly was older and since he was having issues with his father, he wanted to strike out on his own while Rajiv and I had unconsciously become independent. We didn't want to take money from home, didn't want to borrow a single penny from amma or nanna. So we spent judiciously. Bad money days meant only tea and maybe one biscuit (a rupee each), coffee was a luxury (two rupees) and we would never go home from college in an auto. It cost fifteen rupees. (Of course, if our respective wallets collectively added up to fifteen ruppes, we'd hail an auto and ride home, feeling like heroes.) We would normally take the bus, with our heads bowed. To this day, I view travelling by bus as being a low point in my life. It means I can't do anything to afford better, which makes me feel like a failure. Extreme, but true. At least in my book.

The contribution system worked even when the rest of the guys had dates to go on. We'd all gather at someone's home, our meagre wardrobes on display, and the lucky devil who had a date would get to pick his favourite combination of shirt and trouser. The date: a grand ride in the bus, front row tickets to a movie, a burger and popcorn. Me, I still wasn't dating anyone, not even now that I was in college. I liked many girls, and like most boys my age (most *Delhi* boys to be specific), I pretty much had a hard-on all the time but was too shy to do something about it. Tch tch, not acceptable Brahmachari behaviour?

Which brings me back to the days at Malai Mandir. Kelly would join me on some of my visits and the evenings would see us sitting under the table where the flower-sellers sold their wares. We'd drink cheap Bonnie Scott whisky and play cards. Contemplate life. It didn't strike us even once to maybe seek answers from Him, who was just a few feet away. And for good reason. But that's another story, another chapter.

The turning point, also known as the day Rajiv slit his wrists

So even though amma and nanna were protected from our double lives all through school, we couldn't quite save them from the trauma of what happened early on in 1993.

A brief detour first.

In 2007, I produced a show with Cyrus Sahukar for MTV called *It Sucks*. It was just a fifteen-minute weekly, with every episode featuring something that irritated the aam janta: open potholes, constant calls from telemarketing executives, that sort of thing. Once we did an episode on exams and the big mad circus of their aftermath: college cut-offs and admissions. Yes, of course it was all coming from the memory of that car drive we'd had with nanna and our friends, looking for the college that would take us 'low-scorers' in.

So Cyrus pulled this imaginary gag where there was a student who had scored 95 per cent, and he didn't get admission anywhere. Not in any of the top colleges at least, because the cut-off was obviously higher. So he ended up in a mediocre college which put marks before real talent and where all the rejects from across the world were studying. Next, he did a roll call of these so-called rejects: Richard Branson, A. R. Rahman, Sachin Tendulkar, Tom Cruise, Bill Gates, etcetera. I don't think it was exaggerated at all because *these* are the people whom a system that measures capability by marks over talent rejected. They apparently did not measure up to this standard. But guess what, they *rocked* the world. So, clearly, there's something wrong with the system itself. *When* will some bloody idiot wake up to this fucking truth?!

I know I did, nearly two decades ago.

What happened that afternoon in 1993, right after year one at Deshbandhu College, was pretty much *the* turning point of my life.

Rajiv was home alone as our parents were at work. Kelly and I had just returned from college with good news and bad news. The bad news first. Rajiv had failed his first year of college. When we told him this, he nodded and then quietly asked, you? I nodded, a bit guiltily. I'd passed. Rajiv took a deep breath, looked at Kelly and me and then slowly got up, walked to the kitchen. A moment later, Kelly and I walked to the kitchen, too, though not with any kind of foreboding. And there he was, a bloodied knife in his hands, his wrists already bleeding. I remember Kelly cursing loudly, walking right up to Rajiv, making sure he wasn't hurt too badly, and then scolding him out of anger and concern. Thankfully Rajiv hadn't sustained any major injuries, he had just about scraped his skin, but it was the thought of what could have happened that terrified me.

Yes, I know amma thought of us as fraternal twins, two separate individuals, but to me, Rajiv has always been and will always be a part of me. We're one...and there isn't any thought that has gone into this, it's just something I've always known. So the idea that Rajiv wanted out so badly that he wanted to voluntarily take his life, even if his attempt wasn't successful, was what jolted my concept of the world. We were happy-go-lucky kids and we were fine, but when he failed, Rajiv felt he had brought dishonour to our family—our family of Brahmins for whom education is held in the highest regard.

I think that was the reason for my rejecting the world as a whole. You can say that I got my 'fuck you' attitude that day. It was the beginning of one of the biggest changes in me. I asked myself, what the fuck did I have to prove by giving some kind of exam? If I don't know the answers to the questions, does that make someone who has mugged them up better than me?

Quite simply put, being termed a failure is kind of when the world rejects you, right? My reaction was to reject the world. My parents are very sensible, and even while we were growing up, there was never any added pressure on us—they just wanted us to study well and pass. After a few attempts, when my mother figured there was no consistency to our scoring well in a particular subject, I wouldn't say she 'gave up', but she wasn't pushy any more. Yes, they would have been happiest if Rajiv and I had been good students, because that's a typically South-Indian attitude towards academics. I mean, I come from a family where nearly everyone from the previous generation, including my dad, spelled their degrees along with their names on their nameplates. Their educational qualifications are their identity.

MTV had conducted this survey once on the youth and their attitudes, and their findings make complete sense. All through the 1960s, success was determined by birth: which house or which last name you were born into. But over the next couple of decades, in the 1970s and 1980s, success was determined by education. Now, thankfully, talent has been given its own berth, but at that point, well, there were only so many professions. And the only way to hope to get into any was to study, study, study and get good qualifications. At that time, degrees and certificates got you jobs.

When Rajiv attempted to kill himself that day, it really shook my parents. Quite honestly, they didn't know what to do. After this incident, my parents didn't once ask Rajiv why he failed. They just kept quiet, though I'm pretty sure they discussed the matter with each other. Eventually, a week later, they sat us down, very calmly, and asked us what our future plans were. I just randomly said hotel management because I felt like it. Amma and nanna asked whether we really wanted to quit regular college. I said yes, I didn't want to graduate, I didn't want to study further. They agreed but said they'd have us get a change of scene—get us out of Deshbandhu College, get us into Venkateswara—and then figure things out.

We agreed, because well, we never really did cross our parents, but I found another way to reject the system: I didn't attend a single class at college. Not one. I spent my days with Kelly and Rajiv, hanging about campus, choreographing dances, being one of the popular guys, staying away from trouble, but also, in my own way, flipping off the system. By that time, there was a war in my head. I know it now, but back then the system just angered me, and I decided I didn't want to subscribe to it. What I do today, or what Rajiv does for a living, doesn't have any connection whatsoever with our degrees, or the lack of them.

We *are* graduates, by the way. Just not the regular way, though. One fine day, we decided we'd had enough of Venkateswara as well and duly informed amma and nanna. They agreed, but their only concern was that, at the end of the day, a degree *was* necessary. If not for job purposes, then at least officially, even for something as simple as a passport. We agreed, and dad took time off work to take us all the way to Hyderabad—to Osmania university. Back in the day, Osmania had an external students programme, wherein kids from other states could come just take an exam at the university and become graduates. That programme has been scrapped now but it's what helped me and Rajiv graduate. We were put up at the Central Institute of English and Foreign Languages (CIEFL) hostel within the Osmania University grounds. We had several relatives in Hyderabad, but nanna didn't want us to have any distractions, so we stayed at the hostel. So every morning he'd come by, wake us up, make our beds, ask us to go take a shower, sit to study. He'd drop us for the exam, go and hang out at a relative's place, then come back, pick us up, make sure we had lunch… He did this every single day for every single exam—I think there were twenty-one in all. Bless nanna!

The stay there wasn't uneventful either. Our first evening there, after nanna settled us and left to stay the night at a relative's, Rajiv and I went down to the mess for dinner, both of us wearing white kurta-pyjamas. Instantly, the pointing and staring began. By now, though, we had understood how much of an attraction our twin status was. We made friends quickly, and soon, the hostel room which was meant for one and was already being shared by two, was now being shared by three and then four of us: just guys we'd met at the mess and who'd come back to our room to group-study. I don't know about the study part but it sure was fun.

I remember nanna wanted us to hang out with the studious lot in the hostel, in the hope that we might be inspired by them. When he came by the next morning, nanna tells me, Rajiv and I were performing one of our dances on the hostel compound while the rest were cheering us on. Sure, we'd taken his advice, befriended the 'good' boys, but *they* had ended up being inspired by us!

The exams went on; Rajiv and I were almost in a stupor as we studied, ate, showered, wrote an exam, and continued the same routine. Until the final day, the final exam, last paper. I remember how, after the last exam, we sat in our little hostel room, read our books for precisely five minutes, gave each other high-fives, threw the books in the air and then looked at each other. Never again would we study for a fucking exam, EVER! Never again would I let an exam bog me down, make me feel inadequate right from the sinking feeling I would get while entering the exam hall, it intensifying when others would ask for additional sheets while I'd struggle to enlarge my handwriting to use up all the pages of the answer booklet…and the day of the results, of course, when my stomach would be made of lead. That last day of studying, we swore off all those feelings for life. And boy, that feeling of relief was indescribable.

That feeling of relief has stayed on, to this day; every year, around February and March, I feel a sense of calm as I watch the kids around the country struggling with their demons. Getting hassled about exams is pointless. I seriously believe that the only thing worth getting rattled about, losing sleep over, literally and figuratively, is and should be work…work that you love, work that involves you so deeply that it consumes you. Or is that scary? Well, then maybe you're reading the wrong book!

I'm almost a light attendant, spot boy, and obsessed with MTV

Sometime in 1993, after a press meet, then Chief Election Commissioner T. N. Seshan asked amma, a reporter from the *Deccan Chronicle*, why she always looked hassled. Amma, determined to be flippant and not indulge this gentleman she had been hugely opposed to when he was cabinet secretary, replied curtly: what do you expect from a mother of three teens? Three troubled teens, at that: one who had attempted suicide, one who was, at that very moment, probably helping himself to cheap whisky and finally, the little sister still craving her brothers' attention. Of course, amma didn't quite paint such a stark picture in front of T. N. Seshan but as the conversation went on, she finally did tell him mildly about her monster twins and how they weren't worldly-wise in any sense of the word. Seshan was intrigued. Call them to my place, he said, I'd like to meet them. And that was that.

A word about amma and her journalistic career. You see, Radha Vishwanath was trained to be a teacher but had never worked. Sometime in the mid-1980s, when she realized she had lost the ability to conduct an intelligible adult conversation, she decided to get out of the house for a few hours every day. Away from Rajiv, Tuppi and me. But she refused to take up a job in her field since the answer didn't exactly lie in being a teacher to a classroom full of brats. So she ended up becoming the telephone operator-receptionist at the newly launched Delhi bureau of the *Deccan Chronicle*. A week into the job and she had started taking dictation; a few more days and amma had written a piece on education which was received well. And just like that, she had taken her baby steps into journalism.

Soon, amma became known for her razor-sharp questions and began to cover politics. The year was 1990 and T. N. Seshan, an IAS officer, had been nominated for the post of chief election commissioner. Amma heartily disapproved, since the job demanded a legal and constitutional expert and *not* a bureaucrat. Anyway, Seshan did get the job and amma made her animosity quite evident in the many times she interacted with him. Strangely enough, Seshan developed a lot of respect for her. And hence, as the years went by, they built a cordial relationship, enough for him to demand to meet her twin boys.

Her twin boys, however, flatly refused. Who is T. N. Seshan and why should we care? Amma tried a couple of times to tell us it would be rude but we declined. It's funny, now that I think of it, how we so casually rejected the one man all politicians were afraid of: T. N. Seshan the Alsatian. At that time, though, we couldn't care less who he was. Until the day he called home and demanded to speak to me. He told me, in all seriousness, that if we did not come by to meet him soon, he would land up at our Munirka residence with his entire entourage who would set up police barricades, and no doubt set tongues wagging all over our DDA society. The choice was ours, he said.

So, finally, Rajiv and I agreed. The next Sunday dawned bright and clear as his car drove us to his Pandara Road residence. As Rajiv and I alighted, we took it all in slowly: the massive house with a lawn, a driveway, a commando standing outside the house with a gun. I remember Rajiv and I, scourge of the bullies of Munirka gaon, were rendered speechless by this scene. Who *was* this guy?

We went in and met the man along with his wife. Now, the world may say many things about him but I remember T. N. Seshan as being very cool, very chilled out. He behaved very paternally towards us. As we wolfed down some amazing dosa and chutney, and other South-Indian breakfasts over several Sundays from then on, Mr Seshan, Rajiv and I chatted. We had long, fun conversations, sometimes interrupted by calls by or to the then Prime Minister V. P. Singh. We'd hear him screaming into the phone and after he was done, he'd walk back in, pick up where he'd left off, extremely cool and calm.

Once he tried, rather unsuccessfully, to ask us what our larger plans in life were. We just shrugged and said, could he repeat the question? He did, this time phrasing it differently: what did we like doing? Dance, I said and he nodded. Classical? Rajiv shook his head. Western. Mr Seshan nodded again. So you want to get into that as a career? Shrugs again. He tried a different tactic. What else do you like doing? That was easy. Watching TV. Ah ha, he said, would you like to work for television? Would we, indeed.

◆

Up until the early 1990s, Saturdays meant piles of puris and television. In the evenings, Rajiv and I would excitedly head down to Kelly's to watch TV on their black and white set. We would rush in at precisely 6.20 p.m. and settle in front of the television for Doordarshan's three-hour telecast of different programmes. The colour bars that would appear with that God-awful 'ting' sound for at least ten minutes, but we even watched those with excitement. I think I have always loved the idiot box. So much so that even the *Saptahiki*, which was basically an anchor reading out the programme schedule, would be devoured with equal zeal.

Then in 1991, cable TV muscled its way into our lives. Star TV had arrived and our beloved idiot box was never the same again. Later that year, we also had our first ever taste of the ultimate cool: Music Television, a.k.a. MTV, which was launched as one of the channels of Star India's bouquet. Its punchline was 'Do you get it?', and boy did I get it! I knew I had fallen in love, hook, line and sinker. The rest of the country didn't, though, least of all the moral police. MTV was pronounced to be 'against Indian culture' and forcibly made to shut shop as soon as 1993. The problem was they had simply reproduced

MTV Asia for our subcontinent. It didn't work. Star India, meanwhile, very smartly brought in Channel [V]. In a way, they learnt from MTV's mistakes; they peppered international tracks with desi ones and, of course, they roped in ex-Miss India-Canada Ruby Bhatia who, I believe, gave birth to what we now know as 'Hinglish'. Her easy informal manner, 'fun' presentation and Hindi-made-cool wasn't considered so much of a Western invasion and Channel [V] stayed on. MTV understood it had to don a more desi avatar to suit India's needs and returned a couple of years later as an independent channel with more Hindi music, more relatable VJs. I was in love with it more than ever. My sole ambition in life: BE on MTV. Someday. Somehow.

So, yeah, when T. N. Seshan said he could get us to work in TV, Rajiv and I jumped at the offer. I'll speak to my friend, he said casually, he'll get you a job. The next Sunday, Mr Seshan duly informed us that he had spoken to the friend and we just had to go meet him. We nodded eagerly. The friend in question? Oh, some dude called Karan Thapar. It was a rather short interview.

Mr Thapar: What do you do?

Rajiv/Me: Dance.

Mr Thapar: No, I mean, what are your qualifications?

Rajiv/Me: (silence)

Mr Thapar: All right, the crew has decided to give you work.

And so it came to be that Raghu Ram and Rajiv Lakshman were offered their first jobs: to be lightboys at a television set. Now, the lightboy does little more than load the lights into trucks and then unload them when the trucks are driven to a location. Then the lightmen on the set would take them, set them up. At the end of the shoot, the lightboy would reload the lights, pick up the rental money and drive off. A no-brainer. Luckily for us, amma had come along and the minute she saw what the job required, she refused to let us take it on. We were capable of a lot more, she said. So that wasn't quite our first job.

Around the same time, there were these government spots

(advertisements) against child labour being produced for Doordarshan. We had a family friend, Uditanshu Mehta, a graduate from FTII, who was directing them. Rajiv and I were given jobs as spot boys on set. We'd do the oddest jobs possible, lugging chai trays, bottles of iced water, among other things. The point wasn't just to be spot boys but to observe how things functioned on a set, get a clearer picture of this world we loved so much. Uditanshu always encouraged us to be useful to the crew and not just tag along. This is a principle I follow to this day. Whenever we get new kids on *Roadies*, they have to be prepared to do anything. Learn and earn your stipend. We worked as spot boys for a few days, and this mantra has stayed with me since then.

Things had begun looking up a bit by now. Rajiv and I had successfully graduated from Osmania University. Somewhere along the way, we heard that someone called Raghav Bahl of TV18 was hiring trainees. We went and met the concerned HR person. She asked us point-blank whether we wanted to get into graphics or television production. The latter definitely sounded more exciting but she warned us that it would consist of hard work at all hours of the day and night with a huge team, and we'd be expected to do anything and everything. I instantly agreed. Hanging out with a bunch of cool people as we worked? Sounded like fun from the word go. We came back home from the interview, and then forgot about it.

A couple of evenings later, we were all home and hanging out with Kelly and the others when the phone rang. I answered it, and the same HR woman informed me we had made the cut—welcome to TV18. I was so thrilled, I let out a whoop right there on the phone and, I suspect, deeply embarrassed the HR officer.

On 4 December 1995, I officially stepped into television via TV18. Salary: ₹2,500. Post: trainee, also known as Nobody. Honestly, to quote the definition given to me by one of our seniors, we were the lowest rung of the ladder; the village bicycles that everybody got on and got a ride out of.

It was to be a one-year training programme, where we'd be working in four different sections for three months each. At that time TV18 was doing a lot of work. The channel boom had happened, and India now had Star Plus, Channel [V], EL TV (now Zee TV) and Home TV among others, playing on their TV sets every day. Game shows were huge back then. EL TV had a show called *Public Demand* hosted by Roshan Abbas and Ritu Chaudhary, who today goes by the name Mahima. That was made by TV18. Then there was the *Amul India Show*—one of the country's first magazine shows. Now, a magazine show is basically a TV programme that presents several current topics with interviews and commentaries. They're a dime a dozen on television now but, the *Amul India Show* was the definitive one at that time. That was also produced by TV18, along with something called *The Road Show*, a programme about automobiles. There was also the *India Business Report* on BBC about business and stocks.

So TV18 had their share in business shows that came under the purview of Raghav Bahl, and the entertainment shows they produced were presided over by Sanjay Ray Chaudhury a.k.a. Ray-C. Cable channels were new in India and growing, and hence needed to outsource their programming. Colleges didn't really have courses in media and communication in those days, so production houses would hire trainees and teach them all the facets of TV production. As I love saying, I was there at the very beginning. And it's hard to imagine that it all happened in Delhi, where hardly anything gets produced these days.

◆

On our first day at TV18, Rajiv and I, dropped off at the office by nanna, had unwittingly worn the same clothes. The same pair of blue jeans, black shoes and green jackets. We found ourselves in a sea of about fifty-odd trainees, and instantly there was that sense of déjà vu. You know, twins, dressed alike. Both of us sat down by the seniors, with everyone crowding around—the same thing that happened in school, college. And the first day turned out to be very, very, very confusing.

I was assigned to a show called *India Business Day* on a channel called ABNI, which is now CNN-IBN. Considering I was so well-informed about Mr Seshan's credentials, even more so about Mr Thapar's, clearly news and business were *not* my strong points. I was lost, so totally lost. Rajiv, meanwhile, wasn't doing any better: he was put on to a show called *India Talks*, which was about political developments and their repercussions. We had entered grown-up land and didn't know how to deal with it. Half the day was spent in being paraded around for the Twin Show and the rest of the day was spent in simply looking around, observing, trying to make some sense of our surroundings. I retreated into my shell of shyness and quiet. I kept quiet, kept out of people's way. You see, I have never ever initiated a conversation with strangers; I wait for someone to approach me. And that first day, no one really did.

So I sat in a conference hall, listening to people talk about SEBI and wondering whether this had been taught to me in school and if I was just plain stupid for not remembering. I didn't know what was expected of me. I sat there tight in my chair, my heart hammering... I was so sure that at any point, one of my seniors would turn to me and ask for my opinion. I'd even prepared an answer: oh I agree, fully. And then, suddenly, everybody disappeared.

One guy was nice enough to give us a tour around the office; he showed us where the various departments worked: the edit rooms, the business section, entertainment section. I was still as lost, what with my lousy sense of direction. Sometime in the evening, everyone began coming back. Today, I understand what must have happened. Clearly, they'd had a meeting about what they were to broadcast that morning, then gone out to get their stories, shoot them, and now they were back to put them together in the edit room and then finally record the news programme.

I remember walking on to the set where the news was being shot and looking around me, marvelling at how much it reminded me of *Star Trek*. Blinking lights, a flurry of activity, one guy sitting at the consoles, teleprompters, presenters. It was all analogue, the system, and everything was manual. To me, it was all space age-y and alien.

As I stepped off the set, I bumped right into Rajiv. In my enthusiasm, I told him, you won't believe maine kya kiya! What I meant to say was, you won't believe maine kya dekha. Rajiv retorted, gaand maarke aaya kya? Because that was our thing: gaand maarna. And not in a bad or offensive way, but we believed that anywhere we went, we needed to do something kickass, something that people would sit up and take notice of. Now when I think back on that interaction with Rajiv, I think it's telling of our attitude, even on Day One. Because here, nobody cared that we were bad at studies; it was a fresh start for us.

As the days went by, we sat in on the edits and during the shoots, there to help in any way possible, though our biggest contribution lay in getting tea and coffee for everyone. And we always addressed the men as sir and the women, ma'am. This would be the lone complaint against Rajiv and me during our stint as trainees at TV18. While we were judged to be the best, our seniors complained about our schoolboy syndromes.

Slowly, I started taking on more work. The first responsibility I took on was submitting tapes to VSNL. Once you recorded an episode of your show, you had to take it to the Videsh Sanchar Nigam Ltd. At the time, non-government broadcasters were not allowed to broadcast their content from India. They had to submit a tape with the episode, beam it to Singapore, and they'd beam it back. Hence, it would be telecast from Singapore. In fact, this was the case until 2008. At the end of the day, I would travel from Kalkaji to Connaught Place in an office van. The drivers of these vehicles were no less than Grand Prix racers, mainly because they had to cover this hour-long journey in twenty minutes flat in order to make the telecast time. I remember there used to be a printout every day after the meeting with the work distributed between all of us typed up on it. I'd see my name under Tape Dispatch and feel so happy, I was someone! I was a part of the team.

TV18 also had a library with tapes of stock footage used regularly for edits. It just so happened that people started asking me for tapes as I got them tea and coffee during the day. One day, I went to the library and sat and memorized all the tapes according to where they were placed: thirty minute, sixty minute and ninety minute. This way I could pick up tapes faster, knowing where each tape was, and as a result I became the 'go-to' guy for tapes.

Once, I was in the graphics room with three female trainees—they were in charge of putting in and pulling out the tapes with sound/stock shots during the recording as the editor snapped instructions. One of the girls made a mistake. There was this deathly silence as the recording suddenly stopped. The editor stood up, and right there, in the middle of the recording, he picked up the mic and hurled the choicest of abuses at the girls. They started crying, and I remember, even with my schoolboy syndrome I couldn't take his screaming. It felt wrong.

I waited it out, calmed the girls down, and then walked to the control room. The editor wasn't there but our boss, Raghav Bahl was present, along with a couple more TV18 biggies. I said I wanted to speak to him, told him that this editor whose name I didn't know had been really abusive, made the girls cry, and how I felt that was wrong, that screaming didn't help anything. My seniors nodded, promised to look into the matter. I'm sure they told the editor about the complaint, about how someone didn't like his guts. He probably asked them who this was, and they would have taken my name.

Within moments, the editor walked out in a rage from the cabin, hands poised for action, and ran straight into…Rajiv. He grabbed him by the collar, pushed him against the wall and asked him, what the *fuck* did you say? Rajiv, of course, had no clue. When he finally got away, he came looking for me saying, 'Yaar, kya kiya tune. This guy, this editor, is on a rampage.' Ladies and gentlemen, I present Rohit Vaid: friend, abrasive boss, abusive philosopher and guide, and a bloody good editor. Yes, we became the best of co-workers and friends in the coming years, but I didn't know it that day. All I knew was that I had to take off as fast as my feet could carry me; run far, far away from this college-educated bully.

Breaking the rules with MTV

Winning or respect? What would you pick? Sound familiar? It's a question I always ask wannabe Roadies during the personal interview. Not just because it's a tough one and there's no right answer, but because the question was born of my early working days.

Right from the day I joined TV18 as a trainee, I was sure about one thing: this was it. If I failed here, I had nowhere else to go. This was my *only* chance and I wasn't going to let myself fail at any cost. Because the truth, which you know as well I do, dear reader, was that I may have been a graduate but I wasn't qualified. I couldn't become an engineer or a doctor or any other staple professional. So there was also this hunger, this feeling that I just had to be the best in whatever I did, not as a competition with others, but just so I was respected. That's all I ever wanted. Respect. It meant the world to me, and it could be achieved only if I did extremely well. This much I was aware of, even if I didn't come to terms with my other complexes.

You see, despite being one of the most indomitable guys in our college and in Munirka, Rajiv and I both had several problems with ourselves. Most of these stemmed from our inability to speak English fluently, our lack of awareness of the world and our limited wardrobes. All through school and college, I possessed two shirts and one pair of bright orange trousers. You have to remember, I grew up at a time when it was uncool to look after yourself. But in the mid to late 1990s, the metrosexual man was born. And, suddenly, I was at sea. There grew in us, feelings of inadequacy and an awareness that there were people better dressed. We, however, had found our own ways of dealing with these complexes: if we came across someone who was better than us, who made us feel inferior, we just stopped feeling inferior. In fact, we made it cool—the fact that we were so different, that we had no use for such extravagances. This is something that worked for me to an extent, as it helped protect my ego and self-worth, but it also stopped me from growing because I refused to believe that anyone had one up on me. I still craved respect though.

So, yeah, what is the right answer to that question? Winning or respect? Respect comes from winning, you say? Most of the time, yes. Unless you're Avatar from *Roadies X*, who didn't have to but gave up his place in the game just so he could honour a promise he'd make to Palak. Technically he lost, technically that boy went back home, but man, he went with his head held high. Respect wins, hands down.

At the end of month three at TV18, the word was out: I was good. Real thumping good. I never said no, never looked at the time and never wondered when I'd get to go home, no, sir. I worked. And only worked.

◆

Month four began and I got on board my first ever entertainment show: *Mere Message Mere Geet* for Sony. Which lived up to its name, if nothing else. A live camera recorded a random man on the street who would pick a song from a list, dedicate it to his mother, father, neighbour in whichever city, and voice a message. We would edit it out, play it with the song and that was that. It was basically All India Radio for television. There was a director called Shankar, whom everyone referred to as Shankar Senior, because there was also a trainee called Shankar, who was obviously dubbed 'junior'. There was also an Anil Senior, whom I still call just that: Senior. And Anil Junior, the amazing editor, is to this day known as Juni, nothing else. There was also a third guy called Anil so he was called Sub-Junior, a.k.a. Sub-G. That's nomenclature on television, but I digress...

So, *Mere Message Mere Geet*, in a nutshell, was chaotic, most of all when it came to the supers: the little line that appears at the bottom of the screen that lists the name of the song, the name of the album or film, the singer and the music label. No one there could spell Hindi words in English, so *Teesri Manzil* would become Teesaani whatever. Once or twice, I sat down, browsed through some of the song tapes and created supers for them. Also, since we were living in the age of analogue editing, errors were aplenty, especially glitches and dropouts—visual errors or lines that appear on the screen because of oxidation of the tape reels. Sony was anal about any such errors and the tapes would be returned if they weren't up to the mark. One fine day, our big boss Raghav Bahl called for a crisis meeting. As far as self-affirmation goes, this was *the* meeting for me.

There we were, heads bowed as Raghav Bahl, pissed off, asked question after question. 'The tapes that were returned, that had glitches, who was responsible for them?' It was high school all over again, and like on the day the results of the maths unit test were announced, I heard my name being announced: Raghu, it was Raghu. Raghav wasn't done. 'The episodes that weren't sent back, that did *not* have glitches, who was responsible for them?' he thundered. Again, the voices echoed: Raghu. Raghav was fuming as he asked, 'Who is in charge of all the supers that go on the songs?' Guilty as charged for the third time, Raghu. Raghav lost his cool. One RAGHU is recording all the songs, recording all the messages, and is in charge of all the supers? He's doing everything?!

And despite the fact that my big boss was mad at the team and me, at that moment, I'll admit, I didn't feel remotely like how I had felt after being pulled up in school. I felt good, proud almost. I was the 'one Raghu' who was doing 'everything'. I was somebody. It was my shining moment, so to speak. I had scored the respect I always desired...in my own eyes, if no one else's. Later that day, I walked over to Shankar Senior and offered to help fix the problems. Over the next week, I tried to get those supers in place. I was working during the day anyway, because it was a daily, so I had to deliver five half-hour long episodes every week. And every night I sat and made supers for all the tapes, all the songs. There were so many that I lost count, but I also made sure that the episodes were delivered without a single glitch or dropout. There is something called a flash frame, which is an error that occurs when a frame comes between two shots (there are twenty-five frames in every second in television); which I never let happen on any of my shows, even today.

Tapes stopped coming back from Sony, and Shankar Senior really started depending on me.

◆

My four months of training at TV18 were up and I graduated top of the class again. For the third part of my training, I was sent back to the business section. A show called *Markets Today*…no, *Markets Tonight*…okay, that can't be right, because the stock market shuts in the evening…so, it probably was *Markets Today*. Anyway, whatever the name, it was a daily report about the stock market for Doordarshan. Shankar Senior was sorry to let me go from *Mere Message Mere Geet*, but the training had to go on.

Now, this new show had zero budget. Honestly. Whatever *India Business Day* did during the day, these guys would use the same content, condense it into a fifteen-minute capsule and also ship it out to VSNL. So this show had no camera setup, no edit room, no editor. It pretty much got made with a three-man team: a reporter, a director and me. There was a recorder, a player, an in-point, an out-point and that was it. Before I joined the 'team', the director/reporter would go around asking editors if they were free and whether they could cut one story of three minutes. It may have been recycled news but the footage had to be re-edited with a new voiceover.

When I came on board, I chose what I thought was the easier way out. I sat down and worked the machine, which was a simpler version of the analogue editing machine. And I got very good at it. From then on, every night I would edit all the stories. I began to develop a system for the tapes; I knew what was kept where, how things worked. This was the first time in my life where I became close to indispensible. It was kind of the same on *Mere Message Mere Geet* but that was still a bigger team; here, however, I had become the editor, the most sought-after person on the team. I stopped sleeping. If I ever had a few minutes in hand, I'd try to catch forty winks, but soon someone or the other would call to check if I was free. And I never said no. The truth is, the harder I pushed myself, the more people came to depend on me, and the more they came to depend on me, well, I just pushed harder and harder. I took pride in the fact that my presence was making them redundant. They just had to script, and I would take care of the rest. I rocked that show, ah, *Markets TONIGHT*! Of course, that's what it was called, *Markets Tonight*! In fact, I became so popular that other trainees were asked to come observe me as I worked on the edits.

◆

Time lapsed, and it was the end of another three months. Again, it was demanded that I stay back. But I refused point-blank. You see, two new shows had come to TV18 to be produced. Two new shows for, hold your breath, *MTV*. Rajiv and I almost jumped as soon as we heard about them. Decision made, we begged our seniors for a chance. When they agreed, Rajiv and I were in seventh heaven.

MTV Get a Voice was a talk show, the first one to be made for MTV. Now, talk shows were the flavour of the day and very popular. *MTV Get a Voice* basically had students sitting around, discussing issues like premarital sex, education, college politics, stuff like that. It was hosted by Uday Benegal, frontman of the band Indus Creed, earlier Rock Machine. The director was Karthik Chintamani, who became an integral part of my life later on. Karthik himself was the frontman of a band called Gravy Train.

I became—there's no other word for it—omnipotent on this show even more than I had on *Markets Tonight*. There were four episodes every month and we'd shoot them all in one go. So, from picking the topics for each episode to actually picking up these kids from the airport (MTV had decided that they wanted kids from all over the country for every episode), putting them up in hotels and so on, I was taking care of everything. Karthik was only too happy to delegate authority because, anyway, my job was to make him redundant so he could focus on other things.

I remember how, close to the end of shooting *MTV Get a Voice*, Karthik came to me and said he was giving me the designation of assistant producer in the credits roll. This was exciting because I was just a trainee and trainees never made it to the credit roll, let alone get a designation. He tried but couldn't succeed. Finally, though, when the show went on air, my name didn't ... but that didn't matter to me. What mattered was the fact that he said he wanted to. I had his respect, and someday it would work for me when I needed it most. I was right. Years later, Karthik Chintamani was the one who hired me at MTV. Here, it is important to note that the shortest cut to success is hard work. Trust me.

I clearly remember the day *MTV Get a Voice* ended, along with my training. I was pretty much top of the class once more, and in demand. I got the opportunity to pick a show that would be my first official 'job'. Obviously I chose the next show being produced for MTV: *MTV U*. *MTV U* was to be directed by ... surprise, surprise ... Rohit Vaid. Yep, the same cuss-word-spouting overgrown bully I'd had a run-in with during week one at TV18. But that's not why I remember the day I joined *MTV U*. It's because Karthik Chintamani, in my presence, told Rohit that this boy (this boy being me) was worth his weight in gold. I don't remember Rohit's reaction or even whether he was impressed; all I remember is this great surging feeling within my chest ... pride ... m, there's no other word for it, *respect*.

◆

During those days of analogue editing, VT (video-tape) editors were gods. Editing was a complicated, precise process, and only the editors knew these machines. And with knowledge came power. Rajiv and I were fascinated by the whole art of putting footage together to tell a story and couldn't wait to finish our work in the day, so that we could spend every night sitting in on the edits, watching the editors work. I'd worked on the edits at *Markets Tonight* but that had been a very basic, cut to cut setup; this was the real deal, the monitors, players, remotes, switchers and other equipment made the room look like a cockpit. They didn't mind our company, especially since it guaranteed them quick delivery of tapes and coffee. We observed and learnt the good and the bad of each editor's style and started developing a style of our own. Eventually we became good enough to be trusted by the editors to do some of the editing for them.

I was starting to become indispensible once again. This time, the proof lay in the roster at TV18, which basically listed which camera crew was going to cover which spot and when. During our time at *MTV U*, that roster alternated between two names: Raghu and Rajiv. We were there, day and night, doing several shifts every week.

MTV U was a magazine show. Now, a magazine show is divided into two parts: anchor links, in which the host of the show speaks, introduces segments and ties up loose ends to stories, and the stories themselves. Kind of like the *Amul India Show* but again, nothing like the *Amul India Show* because, let's face it, this was being produced for the channel which had built a reputation by breaking all the rules. There is a grammar to editing, there is a method to shooting. There is a line-up of shots which you don't mess with. Unless you're MTV. Okay, let me try and paint a clearer picture:

Take one—You start with the wide shot of a market. Then you zoom in to the board of one shop, point the camera inwards, go into the shop. Cut. This take looks perfect, both on paper and on screen. It's correct.

Take two—You start with an extreme close-up of a coin as it

twirls on the counter...then jump cut to the noisy marketplace, back to the man behind the counter. Cut. This take practically defies every single law in the shooting and editing book, breaks all rules of technique.

No prizes for guessing which of these takes has appealed or still appeals to me. Take one is what you would learn in every good editing class. Take two is, well, there is no better way to say this, MTV. Cutting edge, very young, very edgy.

◆

MTV U didn't just demand cutting-edge editing, it also started something of a revolution as far as television hosting was concerned. It was hosted by this guy, you may know him—Cyrus Broacha. He was wet behind the ears then, a completely new guy, barely eighteen or nineteen years old. Why was he different? Look at Cyrus and you have the answer! When MTV came to India, it was the last word in cool, not only because of its rockstars and international music but also because of the VJ trend. The VJ—video jockey—is basically a person employed by the channel to introduce a song. That's the technical definition, anyway. But VJs within themselves, within that space, became such studs, that Sophiya Haque, Danny McGill, Nonie Tao became household names. They were all so stylish, so sophisticated that VJ-ing became this glamorous, elitist profession. And then along comes this guy who is short, squat, chubby...definitely *not* a looker. But, boy, was he a trendsetter! Broacha gained a reputation for cracking poor jokes (or PJs, more colloquially), but that's not all he did. He was, and still is, fucking hilarious. He's so funny, I actually see him as India's first stand-up comic. And I can't begin to tell you the impact he has had on youth television! After Broacha happened, every kid on the street thought he could become a VJ—all he had to do was crack jokes. Cyrus made VJ-ing accessible.

◆

All that aside, what was most important to me at this point was that I was making a show for MTV, officially, as an employee of TV18. Sure, I still didn't have a designation but that was okay. Ideas were being discussed in conference rooms, people were going out to shoot stories; it hadn't gone on air yet and the production was just being indulgent. I was back to doing what I knew best: making myself indispensible.

It was on *MTV U* that I shot and edited my first story. It was for a section called *Campus Champ*, and it was with Gaurav Kapur—yes, the same Gaurav Kapur who back then was a college student, a Radio Jockey and a lot of fun. I was dead nervous, though. Sure, I'd shot for *Mere Message Mere Geet* but that was one static tripod camera, one guy looking into it, dedicating a song and cut. So I was very scared. I asked Rohit for help and he told me to think of the first five shots and then take it from there. I was pretty clueless about the first five shots themselves. It was the evening before the shoot and I had no ideas.

Which was then that the breakthrough happened at Manna, a.k.a. Manisha, a.k.a. Rohit's girlfriend and co-worker's apartment. Magazine shows also have this element called Piece to Camera or PTC, which is basically anyone giving a short report directly to the camera. That evening at Manna's house, Rohit asked me point-blank whether I could ever manage a PTC, since I was so shy and withdrawn. I said yes, I could. Manna then brought out the camera—she and Rohit had their reservations. But I remember this part clearly. The camera came on, I was standing with my back to them. The minute Rohit screamed action, I turned around and did the first thing off the top of my head: a Jim Carrey impression. It blew their minds and Manna, to this day, tells me that for a moment, she had to shut her eyes because she couldn't believe the transformation. That I, the boy who never spoke unless spoken to, was doing something as uninhibited and as out of character as this. It was freaky for both of them. They were sure now that I could do PTCs effortlessly. I felt great that night.

I was still tense about my shoot the next morning, though. Rohit finally sat me down and gave me tips. He told me to start off with a shot of the streets…then a close up of a car, the radio within the car…the voice of the RJ heard over it…the RJ was, of course, Gaurav. And the next thing you know, Gaurav is sitting in the car, and then he talks to the camera. Rohit built these few shots for me, I wrote it all down. Later that night, as Rohit worked in the editing room, I was right there, sitting behind him as usual. The clock struck 1 a.m., then 2. I gently asked Rohit whether I could go home. I had never asked to before. Rohit looked taken aback and asked me why. When I hesitated, he said, no, sit back down. And that was that. At 3 a.m., I tried once again. Rohit, can I go home? Pat came the retort: why? I reminded him that I had a shoot the next day, my very first; he apologized, said he had only wanted me to be there because he liked the company. I left and only slept for a couple of hours that night.

Early the next morning, I got up and rushed for the shoot. After spending the whole day shooting, I came back to the TV18 office and shut myself up in the editing studio with Juni. The entire night.

The next morning Rohit came in and saw the edit. It blew his mind. Apparently, I'd managed to follow his brief perfectly. I wasn't in the office then; I had finished editing at around 9 a.m. and gone home to crash. When I returned, I have this blurry image of Rohit running to me yelling, this is great, great work!

Soon after, maybe a month later or so, we had another conference, my first since officially joining TV18 as an employee. When it was Rohit's turn to speak, he got up and said, There had been four stories shot and edited that week, and three were done by Raghu. Again everyone was looking at me as I sat back, smiling inside…because by this time I had begun to enjoy this feeling, this attention. In my head, I couldn't help but think that I was good at what I did, and I would only get better. I saw Rohit looking at me with something akin to affection…and respect. I'd won it again!

As time went by, Rohit really struck a bond with Rajiv and me, mostly because the three of us were alike in that we were very different from the others. Rajiv and I started out in awe of Rohit, but eventually grew very fond of him…but more on that later.

By this time, Rajiv and I had built a reputation as the twins who never slept. And I admit, it was a reputation that was also somewhat self-propagated. I wanted this image. If people said, wow, this guy's been awake for three nights straight, it wouldn't make me think, great, now I can sleep. No, I would think, okay, now let me try and stay awake for three more nights. I enjoyed it when people had expectations of me; in fact, I strove to make these expectations grow. And to be honest, Rajiv and I *could* go without sleeping. We could stay up for one, two, three nights in a row, not eating, not sleeping.

At the time, I was a big Sherlock Holmes fan and Holmes frequently starved himself. His belief (and I should probably credit Sir Arthur Conan Doyle here) was that he didn't want to waste his energy digesting food—he wanted the blood to flow straight to his brain. It made sense to me, so I adopted this crazy ideal during those initial years. I used to starve myself, eat one meal a day. People started believing that I had near superhuman powers, that I didn't need food or sleep. It was all very well for Holmes to do this though, being a fictional character, but I was flesh and blood, and these bouts of starvation took their toll on my health. I'm still paying for them, to this day.

Normally, Rajiv and I would finish our work, then go around helping others with theirs. We had built a killer reputation by then, and the popular belief was: get these boys and you're sorted. Rohit did more than that, now that he 'had' these boys. He alienated himself from the rest of the office so that Manna, Rohit, Rajiv and I became one unit. We did everything for the show—shooting, editing, roping in the youngsters required for every episode, crowd coordinating. It was all such a blur that I don't have too many clear memories of it; but all I know is that, by this time, I had no semblance of a life beyond work—no family, no home, no friends. Work had consumed me and I loved the feeling.

What I do remember is picking up Cyrus Broacha from the airport, meeting him for the first time, and witnessing his spontaneity, his amazing talent first-hand. We shot our first anchor links with him. Now, I'd been a part of shows where the anchor would simply read off a teleprompter, but this kid! All he did was ask us what the story was, nodded a few times as he was listening, and then he was ready. He did not need a script. At all. And he would get it perfectly right every time the camera went on. He was such a revelation! *MTV U* became a huge success and, almost overnight, Cyrus Broacha became a sensation.

We worked on *MTV U* for over ninety weeks, and during this time, I not only shot stories and edited outstation stories but also did the anchor links myself (Manna and Rohit were sold on me after the Jim Carrey impression).

And eventually when *MTV U* did come on air, we watched it together, Rohit, Manna, Rajiv and I. It was the first show I'd worked on which had a detailed credit roll at the end, and as we watched the names scroll by, I stopped short for a moment...there, right there, amidst a hundred others, was *my* name. Clear, bold, spelt out for everyone to see. I had really arrived! The year was 1997; I was twenty-two and recently promoted to assistant producer.

And I had started losing hair.

The three-year itch

There was just one couch in TV18's lounge room, and it belonged to Rohit Vaid. No arguments. If anyone, *anyone* dared to sit on it, or worse still, sleep on it, he would fuck them over. Really. Rohit was not just tall and massive with a deep booming voice mostly employed to hurl abuses, he was also a twenty-five-year-old, long-haired perfectionist with bloodshot eyes (at all times) who was going through a divorce and living in a second-hand Maruti car which held his clothes. I didn't know then and I don't know now.

As an editor and vision mixer, Rohit excelled; he was a true professional. But if you didn't know your work, or if you screwed up, knowingly or unknowingly, sorry, boss, you were dead. Rohit would personally fuck you. And the funny part was, no one said anything to him. Because he was right. All the time. To me, that always seemed like a great thing—to be so sure, so *right* that no one could ever point fingers at you. A lot of what I am today, the *Roadies* Raghu and otherwise, I have imbibed from him. On screen, my abrasive quality, my attitude of taking no shit, all comes from him. That's not all that there was to him, though. Somewhere in that abrasive man lay a heart of gold.

Rohit and I had come a long way from our first run-in during my training period at TV18, so much so that over *MTV U*, Rohit became quite fond of us. Him and Manna—then girlfriend and later wife, now ex-wife—took us under their wing. They would take us out to dinner, teach us many little things (like how to use a knife and fork, for instance), help us improve our general knowledge and speaking skills. They were very well-read, and we listened to whatever they said. He loved me and Rajiv fiercely, and protected us just as much. We got so close, people started calling us Rohit's testicles.

But slowly, our friendship began taking on an unhealthy hue. You've already read about how I stayed back in the editing suite just to give him company, and you know about the evening we spent at Manna's flat where I had my breakthrough. Now, the flat was one that Rohit had just moved into after marrying Manna, in 1997. It was a 2 BHK, and one of the bedrooms was unofficially for me and Rajiv. So, every day after work, he'd tell me to come over and I would obey, because he was my boss, an elder, and I could never say no to him. I would go over and we'd sit around, chat, have coffee, eat dinner. Every single day. We already spent our working hours together, and now we would go back to the same home as well.

Soon, Rohit started resenting anyone else I spent time with. If I'd tell him I wanted to go home one day, he'd get pissed off. If I said I had plans with a friend, he'd get pissed off. As if this wasn't enough, he was the toughest on us at work, perhaps because he loved us so much. I remember when *MTV U* completed fifty episodes, we decided to film a special commemorative episode. There was a guy on the team who was responsible for delivering the finished tape. He couldn't do it for some reason, so I volunteered. I did all that I could, but at the very last minute, there was a minor fuckup and the tape did not get delivered. Despite the fact that it wasn't my job to deliver the tape, Rohit really fucked me over that day. He twisted my arm and punched me, and told me if I'd taken responsibility for something—he didn't give a shit how I did it—I had to fulfil it. There was no room for mistakes. I got it; I got what he meant and it is one lesson that has stayed with me. Even today, I tell my team that the guy who's watching the *Roadies* episode on TV does not give a fuck about what we went through to shoot it. He doesn't care how many days we've gone without sleep; all he wants is his hours' worth on MTV. And we bloody well owe it to him, so we'd better put a good episode on air! Everything else is an excuse.

There was a time when after working four days and four nights in a row, we'd say we wanted to go home and Rohit would taunt us saying, Haan aaj kal mere sheron ko neend ki zaroorat pad gayi hai. And that was it; Rajiv and I would bristle uncomfortably, and get back to work instantly. There was just one time when I contacted some kind of eye infection that Rohit freaked out and packed me off home.

Aside from my self-professed superhuman abilities of surviving with no food and no sleep, I was also very proud of the fact that I hadn't cried once since school. Until the day Rohit fired a production assistant. The assistant was at fault, he hadn't been doing his job right, but to me, it was the trauma of seeing a friend go. I may have become important in the scheme of things, turned into the boss's favourite, but I was still a twenty-two-year-old kid. I started howling and couldn't stop. Rohit quietly took me by the hand and led me out of the basement office of TV18. It was dark outside and, as I cried, Rohit said something to me that I'll never forget. He didn't ask me to stop sobbing or call me a sissy. Instead, he told me never to lose this part of myself. Being this sensitive was what would make me a great director someday.

By our second and third year of working at TV18 and of being with Rohit, Rajiv and I had come to realize that Rohit's protective instincts were growing stronger by the day and that this relationship was *not* okay. Rohit had moved a couple of houses by then and every time, there would be one room always reserved for Rajiv and me. Rajiv and I, instead of taking the bull by the horns, simply decided to quit TV18. If there's one thing I can't handle to this day, it's confrontations. I always avoid them if I can.

Every six months I would quit…rather, I'd try to quit while Rajiv would go into work. Rohit would ask him where I was and Rajiv would say, nah, he's done, he's not coming to work anymore. And that was it. Rohit would shut operations for the day, give the whole team a day off and, along with Rajiv, he and Manna would come home, meet me and convince me not to quit. This happened for a few months like clockwork. It wasn't just his affection or love; the fact that Rajiv and I had made ourselves so indispensible to Rohit professionally and personally made him incapable of letting go.

Anyway, in the interim of our attempts to quit, Rohit got it into his head that Rajiv and I would look great in front of the camera. He shot a pilot with us, a show like *MTV U* but more 'mass-y', and in Hindi, called *Campus Shampus*. The show eventually never got made, but we did it in all seriousness. Rohit and Manna took us shopping, bought us bright yellow shirts and grey trousers—I don't know what the fashion funda behind this was. But we set it up, shot the pilot, and Rajiv was really, really good. We shot it in two days, and then came back and edited it; it turned out really well. I don't know why it never got commissioned. Around the same time, TV18 produced a fiction show for Zee TV called *Vakaalat*, a courtroom drama, and one episode was written keeping Rajiv and me in mind. Yep, I acted on screen long before Abbas Tyrewala's *Jhoota Hi Sahi*…again thanks to Rohit's conviction that we'd look brilliant in front of the camera. My character was accused of a murder that he hadn't committed, and got acquitted because of reasonable doubt once my twin brother, a.k.a. Rajiv appeared on the scene. It was pretty cool and our character names were the same: Raghu and Rajiv.

Another very interesting thing that we did in front of the camera—well, Rajiv did in the same year—was on the occasion of Women's Day. Now, Maria Goretti had been newly inducted as a VJ on MTV. The story was 'become a woman for a day' which meant a guy (in this case, Rajiv) had to get under a woman's skin, literally. It started with him getting waxed and I remember him in the changing room, shrieking in pain. I was sitting outside, tears in my eyes, I could feel his pain. Eventually, Rajiv had his arms and legs shaved, got padded up, slipped into a wrap-around skirt, got his make-up done, wore extremely high heels and when he came out, man, he looked exactly like Raveena Tandon. The idea was to roam around the markets of Delhi and see how people reacted. It turned out to be a harrowing experience for Rajiv, who kept struggling with keeping his dress together and walking on high heels.

Maria walked with him, went up to people, told them this was MTV's new VJ and asked them what they thought of 'her'. The reactions were quite complimentary, which in itself was shocking; most of them found 'her' hot, one of the guys wanted to kiss 'her'. By the time they were done, it was close to 7 p.m.: that time of the day when most of us men sprout minor yet pretty visible shadows on our faces. Rajiv was close to tears at this point, accusing me of being a useless brother for going along with this charade, not supporting him, not ending his torture. Suddenly, Rohit had a brainwave: why not shoot Maria and Rajiv separately, sharing their thoughts on the day, intercut with actual shots of what had happened?

I think at that very moment, the concept of video diaries entered our lives. The little intercut shots you see of contestants talking while an episode is on, that most integral part of any *Roadies* episode, came to us way back in 1998 when we didn't even know it was called a video diary.

I had finished three years of my working career at TV18 by now. Our appraisals happened and Raghav Bahl said he could pay me twelve thousand rupees a month. I wanted fifteen. When he refused, I remember Rohit personally putting in a word, but Raghav Bahl didn't budge, said he couldn't afford me for fifteen thousand then. And I clearly remember Sanjay Ray Chaudhary—remember Ray-C, the guy who headed the entertainment shows for TV 18? He said he understood why I wanted to quit, and also told me that I would be welcomed back at TV18 if I ever changed my mind. It was a great feeling.

Of course, one of the biggest reasons for me wanting to quit TV18 was so I could get away from Rohit. I have spoken about how we grew close to Rohit, but never about why I was so desperate to get away. I guess I felt that, in a way, I had lost control over my own life. So we had our meeting with Raghav Bahl, put in our papers, came out of the conference hall...and bumped into Rohit. I told him we've quit, both of us, Rajiv and I. I remember Rohit nodding and murmuring that he'd do something about it. Now, this was barely months after Rohit had married Manna. He needed a stable job but when we quit TV 18, Rohit and Manna both, without a thought, also put in their papers. I know what you're thinking, would we *ever* get out of their hold? The truth is, at this point, I think both Rajiv and I felt very touched and guilty that, while we were leaving, literally running away from these guys, they were ready to give it all up too, just to be able to be with us. It changed the dynamics of the relationship. At least for the time being.

That's when Shashanka Ghosh came into the picture. Shashanka is the guy credited with setting up Channel [V], creating Quick Gun Murugan and directing the movie *Waisa Bhi Hota Hai Part II*. Shashanka had noticed Rohit's work, and had a meeting with him. This was still 1998, and World Space Radio was to launch in India soon. They had hired Shashanka to look after the channels, and he roped in Rohit to produce a youth-based channel.

So at age twenty-three, Rajiv, Rohit, Manna and I shifted base to Koramangala, Bangalore. Rohit took up a house on rent and in the same building, so did Rajiv and I. This time, we were literally on our own, in a new city, and in each other's hair! Rajiv and I only slept in our flat. We couldn't do anything else because we only had two mattresses. We spent eight to ten months in Bangalore and because World Space Radio had no budget to speak of, I wasn't getting paid, Rajiv was. We were two for the price of one.

Between us, we produced and recorded a pilot episode with Gaurav Kapur and Roshan Abbas, and it turned out quite, quite funny. I remember not sleeping for a whole week but still not feeling as superhuman-like as I used to in the basement office of TV18. The truth is, once you've tasted television, radio as a medium isn't as fulfilling. After making the pilot, we just waited for the green signal, and there was nothing to do but hang. So we hung around in the apartment. Eventually World Space didn't take off at that point in time, I don't know why, and we returned to Delhi.

We were now commissioned for making one-minute spots for the 1999 World Cup. There isn't much to say about this particular period in my work life, except that I came in touch with Abhinav Dhar, who was our boss. He was a very creative, very fun guy. He'd come hang with us as we ate Maggi or sipped chai in the editing room, which was where we pretty much lived. After a couple of meetings, one night, he made me take a brief break from the editing and called me outside. I was a bit apprehensive because I didn't know what this was about. Once outside, Abhinav suddenly asked me how long I'd been working. Four years, I said. He took one long look at me and said that there was a lot more I had to do. That there was a lot more I *could* do, because, he said in all seriousness, I was capable of a lot more. Now, I'd known this guy for just about a couple of days, so it was quite bizarre. It was also a first for me, being told to achieve, and also a bit strange that he said this to me and not Rohit. It is something that has stayed with me, made me surge ahead. It also affected quite a few of the decisions I was to take soon, including the moment I finally broke free from Rohit.

The 'no' man breaks free

There are three versions of me. One: Raghu Ram. The quiet, non-confrontational guy who is happy to be home, reads anything to do with Batman, Sherlock Holmes and Mohammed Ali he can lay his hands on, cuddles with his dog, indulges in continuous banter with his wife and drinks endless cups of tea and coffee. Two: *Roadies* Raghu. The only guy *you* know because you watch him on your screens. Who takes no shit from anyone, who would rather punch first and ask questions later. Three: Fun Raghu. He's the guy writing this book. To know more about No. 2, read on.

In 1999, by the time we were done producing TV spots for the World Cup, Shashanka Ghosh had also quit World Space Radio and gone back to Channel [V]. Now, [V] had always worked under the Star banner and was essentially a music channel, but that year, they started operating independently and came up with some very ambitious projects. Within the span of one week, they planned to launch twenty-five new shows, as well as twelve new VJs. They needed new guys to work on the shows, and Rohit was hired. Quite naturally, Manna, Rajiv and I followed suit. Back to square one.

Raghu No. 2, a.k.a. *Roadies* Raghu was conceived this year. You know what they say about alter egos: they take seed when the person is going through great upheaval and needs to create an alternate personality to deal with it. The great upheaval in my life in 1999 was my resentment of the increasing closeness to Rohit Vaid, and the feeling that people took me for granted because they saw me as a sweet, well-mannered guy. I decided that my joining Channel [V] was a good time to reinvent myself. We were based in the basement of Hotel Gautam Residency in Greater Kailash. And because I was getting into a new job, my new team on my shows didn't know me. They still had to form their opinions. So I decided to manipulate their perceptions. I decided to become stern. Throughout my first month at [V], I made a conscious decision to never say yes. To anything. I wouldn't initiate talks with anyone; whosoever talked to me would do so at their own risk. The thought behind this was that one fundamental aspect of my personality had to change: the need for approval. I had wanted it for as long as I could remember. From my parents, from my teachers, from classmates, my seniors at TV18 and from Rohit. But that approval came at a cost which I was no longer willing to pay. So that's it, I decided, no more Mr Nice Guy.

I'm sure it must have been difficult on the people I worked with. I even employed a body language that was downright intimidating. If anyone called out my name, I wouldn't respond instantly. Because that would mean acknowledging their power. But by not responding, by making them wait while I chose the time and manner of my response, I retained that power in my interactions. Wait a moment and then slowly look up, or turn around deliberately and fix them with a solemn gaze. I stopped using my neck so much. As a practice it may seem pretty simplistic but the thing is, it's a more deliberate, almost robotic action which can be quite disconcerting. It worked. I felt more respected, and I was largely left alone to do my work. I also employed other techniques to intimidate people. One was to just be expressionless, maintain a poker face at all times. The other was to talk softly, so that the other person had no choice but to lean in and listen, and listen very carefully indeed. I became a guy no one could question or take lightly. I still am.

◆

Personality changes aside, there was quite a bit of work to be done. We had to find new concepts for shows and we came up with [V] Dares You.

My good friend Kaustubh, a.k.a. Kausti, was the production assistant, Juni was the editor, and I was the director. Rajiv was making a show called Cool Maal about gadgets, Manna was making one called Job Shop and Rohit was the supervising producer. By this time, my equation with Rohit had really deteriorated. It wasn't exactly a power struggle but Rohit kept wanting to stamp his authority over me of which I was growing increasingly resentful.

It was time to shoot the pilot for [V] Dares You. I was looking for a camera crew in Delhi and failing miserably, because Delhi, while being the hot seat of news crews and production teams, has never scored much on the entertainment front. We needed people who were edgy, fun, who knew their stuff. After much fruitless scouting, one fine day I met this guy who claimed to be a cameraman. I remember surveying him disinterestedly. He was short, seemingly unimpressive, his jaws moved mechanically as he munched and munched paan masala all through the meeting. I found him obnoxious, uncouth, very desi, but once we got talking, I realized he knew his shit. He was Akshay Rajput. Akshay not only came on board [V] Dares You but has been the director of photography (DoP) for almost all the seasons of Roadies. He's a close work-buddy with whom I have a ritualistic fight every Roadies season without which no Roadies journey feels complete. Today if you set out to make a [V] Dares You, you'd need a team of twelve people, at the very least. But our times were different. We had no money!

Yudishtir Urs was to host the show, another first-timer in my long list of first-time VJs—Cyrus Broacha, Cyrus Sahukar, Gaurav Kapur, Maria Goretti. We were basically the generation that launched MTV India and Channel [V]. So anyway, when I was introduced to Yudi, because of my recently reinvented personality, I was my deliberate, disconcerting self. My cap and spectacles which I used as combat gear were slipped on, and Yudi couldn't even see my eyes throughout the meeting. Just to intimidate him, just to establish who was boss and who would call the shots. Poor Yudi. We went on to have a great working equation, though.

◆

So we started a work pattern—Akshay, Juni and I—and our work hours meant that between the three of us, we had roughly three to four hours of sleep every day...and for most part, my share in this was nil.

My reputation as a work machine was firmly established, so much so that I started believing my own myth. I wanted to see how much further I could go.

So I started working six days a week, day and night. I would work, work, work, without a break and on the seventh day, after dispatching the episode, I would go home and sleep for twenty hours straight. I would be dead to the world, so much so that my grandmother was convinced I was doing drugs because, apparently, I didn't even turn in my sleep. I was like a log of wood.

Once, after six days and six nights of work, I had gone to office on the seventh day with the episode ready, feeling a heady rush because we'd met an impossible deadline. I bumped into another producer called Andy and his editor, Harry. They looked like zombies, with their swollen eyes, messy hair, almost drooling—they hadn't slept for three nights, plus they were tense about something. Turns out, the show they were handling, [V] On Campus, which had a five-minute long campus profile segment, still needed editing. Now, to edit a five-minute capsule you need at least three to four shifts, and these guys had a deadline that would end in a couple of hours. I said, no problem, I'll take it on. I sat down and edited it for them. That done, I walked around, and if someone else needed a hand, I told them to pass it to me and I edited their story too. At the end of it, I wasn't tired, no way; I was thrilled that I could withstand this. And then there was a little voice in my head that said, chal na, let's see how much further you can push yourself.

So I pushed. Six days, six nights in a row as usual. Then the seventh day, seventh night. Oh, and did I mention I was unwell at this point? So I had a carefully planned-out diet of cough syrup, medicines, chai and cigarettes. Lethal mix, huh? It got me through the seventh night. The eighth day happened. Then the night. It was then that strange things started happening to me. Strobe lights went off in my head. Everything seemed to be happening in flashes—black, white, colour, FLASH! It was psychedelic. Like I said before, our office was in the basement of this hotel called Gautam Residency. All I remember is waking up in a room at the hotel the next morning. Later on, I was told I had passed out while standing and collapsed. And the team had picked me up, booked me a room and left me there to sleep. But I wasn't upset with what had happened. In fact I thought, okay, great, I know what my limits are, what I can push myself to. Seven nights and eight days without sleeping.

Push number two was to figure how long I could go without a meal. So all these days I barely ate. That didn't affect me much back then, though I am paying the price now! But I earned a reputation as the guy who didn't need to eat or sleep, and I was proud of it.

Still am. Even now, my crew members are on an average twenty-four years of age, but nobody can out-work me. In the time they've slept, woken up and slept again, I'm still up and going. Even at Channel [V], despite the crazy hours, my work was considered to be the best at the channel. There was a certain unique quality to all my shows, a certain passion, intensity, that was there for everyone to see.

Finally, it was time for Channel [V] to launch all of its twenty-five new shows and twelve new VJs, and there was this big party that happened. Ironically, I was the only guy who wasn't invited to it, mainly because by then my equation with Rohit had become extremely ugly. I felt really rejected. Even the VJs were there—Gaurav Kapur, Purab Kohli, Yudishtir…and Rajiv was there too. It wasn't an open fallout with Rohit, but I wasn't invited. I brought it up with Rohit much, much later…told him how hurt I was that I hadn't been invited. And he turned around and said, why didn't you tell me then, you should have slapped me.

◆

The new millennium dawned bright and clear for me. After the channel launch, all of us were required to shift to Mumbai and join the Channel [V] office. So I went to Mumbai, for the first time ever. I was quite scared of it, the big bad city, but at the same time I knew something good was going to happen. The office was in Khar, and Rajiv had rented a place on Yari Road, close to where I live today, and also close to, well, Rohit and Manna. Yep, that was still continuing. Such a large number of people from Delhi joining Channel [V] at the same time was in any case going to be a problem given the resentment people from Mumbai have towards Delhiites. And the management screwed it up even further by promoting Rohit as executive producer at this time. Several senior Mumbai producers quit because they didn't want to report to him which led to further negativity being directed at us, especially at Rajiv and me since we were seen as Rohit's blue-eyed boys.

While in Mumbai, I was asked to make *Oye* for Channel [V]. *Oye* was initially an MTV show—in fact, one of MTV's first Indian shows hosted by actress Anu Agarwal—but the day MTV was unceremoniously kicked out of our TV screens, Star quickly brought in Channel [V] and they retained the show. *BPL Oye* went on to become wildly popular. It was an ambitious magazine show, and we had a huge team. There was a conscious attempt on Rohit's part to include both Delhi and Mumbai people in the show. Shashant Shah (who later directed *Dasvidaniya*) and I were producers. And though the resentment against me in Channel [V] did not go away instantly, I enjoyed the love and fierce loyalty of my team. There was a sense of camaraderie, a sense of belonging, a sense of looking out for each other. That was one thing I had picked up from Rohit: he was always fiercely protective of his team, a quality I imbibed.

There was this sweet kid called Salil on the team who used to get pushed around a lot, bullied quite a bit. One day, at a meeting with the team, when I asked everyone if they had any issues, someone pushed this kid ahead, forced him to tell me what had happened. After some reluctance, Salil said, 'I don't mind being bullied, I just don't like it when they throw coffee at me.' This was really shocking stuff for me—that a kid actually had to bear someone throwing coffee at him?! It turned out it was done by some guy at the channel called Abid. So I walked up to him, introduced myself, and told him that if he ever did it again I'd kick his teeth in. Before now, I had never really threatened anyone; I'd only reacted to people when they had messed with me. But this was the first time I had openly challenged someone, when *I* had called someone out. I went back to Salil and told him he would never have a problem again. Salil did really well in my team as his confidence kept growing. This one time, I was talking to an editor when Salil came in to ask me something. The editor pushed him aside and continued talking, so I asked Salil point-blank if he was just going to take it, literally encouraging him to hit back, to not take it lying down. It was a happy moment for me, it took me back to the time I had fought Sudhir Sachdeva, and had been depressed no one cheered for me, the underdog. I cheered for Salil that day, and felt great about it.

It was all very well getting someone on my team to hit back, but when it came to me, I could never confront the Rohit issue. And it just kept getting worse. We lived in the same neighbourhood so Rohit and Manna's affections for us turned increasingly claustrophobic. Even our maids were sisters. Once, I made plans to go out with my team members while I was at Rohit's place and Manna cried! I had to actually call and cancel my plans because she wondered why I needed the company of people other than the two of them. In the office, Rohit was having problems in his position as EP, as things were getting increasingly political. There were ego clashes with other heads of department, and the atmosphere in the office was downright ugly. So somewhere around the mid-2000s, Rohit finally quit [V]. Now I was really at a crossroads. Ideally, I should have had to quit, given our history, but I'd formed bonds with my team and I was starting to like Mumbai, so I decided to stay. Decision conveyed to Rohit, I went home and slept, relieved for the first time in years.

The next morning at 7 a.m., Rohit came by, woke me up, and took me out to a coffee shop. Remember I'd told you about my time at TV18 where, whenever I'd quit, he'd come home and not leave till I agreed to come back? Well, this time he wouldn't stop convincing me till I agreed to quit with him. Beyond a point, I couldn't argue with him; I agreed, and quit. So that was the end of my stint at [V], remarkable among other things, for the fact that I was disliked for the first time in my life, and that for the first time in my life, I was okay with it. Oh, and of course, I discovered that I could be intimidating. This newfound knowledge would turn out to be of great help to me in a couple of years.

◆

The year 2001, with my move back to Delhi, this time with a job at Miditech, turned out to be one of the worst years of my life. Rohit managed to get most of our team back to Delhi; only Akshay Rajput stayed back. We started making a show called *Record Tod* for MTV, which was basically about crazy records made on college campus. It could be anything from the highest human pyramid to most number of people in a Maruti 800. I soon settled into my usual routine; I would be editing, editing, editing till I had to get out of the room to shoot at the location. I worked my butt off at this job. Once again, I had built a reputation here of being supernaturally blessed. I wouldn't sleep, I wouldn't eat, I would only work.

I managed to forge very good bonds with my team here as well… and the extent of their loyalty was obvious to me during one outdoor shoot. We had gone to Chandigarh to shoot a few more records and even though we knew examinations were on, we were confident that we would manage to get students to shoot with. But my team came back to the hotel and reported that they couldn't organize any students.

I was really frustrated because I hate excuses. It's how I'd been trained by Rohit. We'd shot in the middle of a riot, when people have been sick, when crew members haven't turned up…nothing had stopped us before. I was frustrated, telling my team off, asking them what they were good for. Could they at least press my feet? There was silence for a minute and then one guy called Abhishek actually came forward… and started pressing my feet! That shocked me so badly that I quickly made him get up, apologized and told him and the team that we would figure it out. It also made me realize that the power I was wielding had to be tempered with compassion.

◆

It didn't follow immediately but in 2001, I suddenly felt like Superman brought in contact with kryptonite. I was completely burnt out. I couldn't work any more. I had worked continuously for six years—no holidays, no time off, days that blended into nights and living on a very unhealthy diet of cola, coffee, tea and cigarettes—and, in retrospect, the burnout was inevitable. It happened at Miditech. I could not look at an edit room, I would feel nauseous if I even saw a camera, I just couldn't concentrate. So I sat with my guitar all day long at the Miditech office staircase. I played songs for my meals in the canteen, I sat not doing anything for days on end. The funny part is, both Nikhil and Niret Alva, who own Miditech, still had full faith in me. They said they'd give me time, let me get over this phase. The burnout continued but Miditech continued to pay me my salary, the super guys that they were. At the end of two months, around September 2001, I decided I was done. And this time I was really, really done. I had tried to quit the situation with Rohit around twenty times in these past six years, but this time I knew it in my head and that's probably why even Rohit knew he couldn't stop me. I remember him saying to me, 'When you go now, people are going to say I'm finished, that Rohit Vaid is done.' Now this was news to me; I had never thought of it this way. Rohit continued, 'But I'm not finished. I'll prove it, I'll crush you.' I remember feeling very hurt at this point and actually blurting out, 'Why crush me? I've given you my everything, I don't have a life or anything, you literally have it all: my blood, sweat and tears, why would *you* want to crush *me*?!' There was silence for a moment and then Rohit laughed mirthlessly as he nodded and said, 'That's right, I shouldn't have said that. Sorry.'

And that was it. Goodbye at last. I was finally free to live my life.

Meeting the wife, shaving my head and MTV at last

Nope, I didn't forget to tell you about Raghu No. 3, a.k.a. Fun Raghu, whom I mentioned in the previous chapter. I couldn't tell you then, because he was only born at the time when the events of this chapter unfolded.

The day I quit Miditech in 2001, my friends simply dragged me out and said we *had* to go out and party. I was all game; after all, I'd not only given up a job but also a deeply intense burnout and an equally intense and stifling work/personal relationship after six years. I deserved to party! My friends took me to Turquoise Cottage near Saket, where there was live music playing and two guys called Mahesh and Joe performing. I remember walking up to them, asking if I could sing a song. They said okay, I did, and it got a pretty good response. In fact, they asked if I could come back the next day. So I did. Because, for the moment, I had no job, no plans for the future, except the ever-increasing yearning to work with MTV. To become an executive producer at MTV, to be specific. Have I mentioned that? It's what I always, always wanted to become. Anyway, I returned the next day, and played for them for a few days after that. It soon grew into a business of sorts. People heard me at Turquoise Cottage and offered me other gigs, for parties and stuff. I went over, asked for measly sums, because, like I said, I don't 'get' money. But playing the guitar was a heady feeling, singing even headier, and the alcohol flowed. Oh boy, did it flow. And Fun Raghu was born. Now, this version of me is the guy who will dance on the tables while partying, he's the guy who will bring out the wild side of others at the party. He's wicked, he has *absolutely* no inhibitions, he is the jaan of the party, and if Raghu has a superhuman capacity for work, Fun Raghu has a superhuman capacity for alcohol. He can start drinking in the evening, carry on till daylight the next morning, and will talk non-stop. It's only when he wakes up with a hangover that he thinks, fuck, what happened last night? You see, personally, I *don't* like Fun Raghu; he always, always gets me into trouble. How? Why? What does he do? No chance of an answer right now, since I'm sober.

So, in the blistering summer of 2001, the general aimlessness in life had become a peer thing. Rajiv and Sumit Syal (the guy who took over *[V] Dares You* from me), had also quit their jobs at Miditech by now, and had started a production house called Shift Focus. You remember Kelly? Well, he had started his own editing studio, Icon. No one had any work. We'd sit, chat, eat and sleep at the Icon office. We'd collect money, go out, buy boiled eggs, eat a couple of plates between us. For a whole day, that's all we survived on. The parents again were kept in the dark about this; in fact, we'd hardly go home, any of us. I know it sounds rather grim and tragic but it wasn't really...it was fun in its own way. Mostly.

Or...maybe not. I remember this one day when I decided to go home from Kelly's office. It was just me, I remember (I guess Rajiv wasn't around). I got into a bus—my parents had moved to Patparganj by now—and the bus fare was two rupees. And as I reached into my wallet, I realized I was really down to my last penny. I had one rupee. I bought a ticket that would take me halfway home, and I remember getting off the bus and covering the rest of the distance, around four to five kilometres, on foot. And I howled all the way. All I kept thinking of was how I'd been top of my class right from TV18. How at Channel [V] and Miditech everyone thought I was the next big thing and here I was, without even a fucking rupee to buy myself a ticket home. Like I had mentioned earlier, I had always regarded bus travel as a sign of failure and here I was, not even able to afford that. It was a wake-up call of sorts for me. I got my act together, applied for a job at MTV, and ended up in Mumbai for the second time.

I was called to interview with Natasha Malhotra, who was the vice president of production back then. This was when MTV had their office in Tardeo. I was so excited and so sure that I would make it, that my first attempt would obviously be a success—after all I *was* the next big thing! I didn't have a showreel, which is basically a CD with your best work on it, but I did tell Natasha about my stints at TV18, Channel [V] and Miditech. She heard me out…and then said no.

I was rejected by MTV. I was stunned. I'd never even considered a possibility where I would be rejected by MTV. I was so sure that I would be hired that I hadn't even applied anywhere else. I stayed back in Mumbai for a while, trying to figure out what to do next. I had no money left but I had great friends. Nirupam Sonu, a fellow trainee from TV18 and a colleague from Channel [V] offered to put me up for a few days. He was a paying guest in a house in Nariman Point and had no money to pay his rent himself. But that didn't stop him from extending his generosity and hospitality to me. And the only way we made sure we weren't thrown out was by doing odd jobs around the house like cleaning, buying vegetables and milk every day. Another guy who really made my stay possible in Mumbai was Akshay Rajput, a.k.a. Kaandi. He was the only guy in our group who had a job and a small 1 BHK house. His wife was pregnant but once again, the doors of the small house were opened for me, and I spent many weeks there. Whenever they cooked I'd eat, whenever they went travelling, I'd go with them.

Every morning, Nirupam and I would go to the local paanwala where there was a payphone, take out our little black diary and call up the same offices, ask if anything had changed, if there was work for us. There wasn't. It was a daily, humiliating ritual. I was fed up of hearing no but I didn't know what else to do. I'd lie on the floor of Akshay's living room night after sticky hot night, watch the fan spin overhead and wonder at my life. The dead end of it, rather. There was the option of going back to Rohit but I didn't want that, never again. The situation looked pretty bleak.

That was when BBC put out an ad in the newspaper. They were making a youth travel show and were looking for young producers. The office was in Delhi, so I packed my sole pair of trousers and two shirts, and left Mumbai again. But the evening before I left, I remember watching the sunset and wondering to myself why this city kept rejecting me. When I came by for [V], I had to leave because of Rohit. This time I wanted to be here, but MTV, my dream employers, had said no. And I know it sounds filmy as hell but as I watched the setting sun, I promised myself I would come back to this city. That I'd be somebody here. I was to remember this sunset in the not-too-distant future.

But for now, BBC. When I heard they were looking, I was super thrilled and with all the exuberance of youth, having forgotten my failure at MTV, I was dead sure I'd make it here. My friends once again rallied around me, convincing me that I was sure to get this job because, after all, I was the best. I applied...and so did a thousand others. Application sent, there was nothing more to be done, so I found my way back to Mumbai. Nirupam (who had by then become a post-production director at UTV) was just about to quit and asked if I wanted to take over from him. Sure I did. It was the office where I met TV director/writer/film-maker Leena Yadav. I was really fascinated by her tattoos and told her I'd always wanted to pierce my ears. The next thing I knew, I was at a parlour in Bandra and a guy was standing, gun in hand, ready to shoot holes into my precious earlobes. He shot one ear and I remember it hurt so bad, I chased him around the shop, almost beat him up, before getting my other ear pierced as well. I remember everyone asking why I hadn't done it before as it suited me well. So if Channel [V] gets the credit for conceiving *Roadies* Raghu, Leena Yadav gets the credit for giving me my other mainstay: my piercings.

The UTV job didn't quite work out though. Barely two months

in, one day I walked in whistling, skipping as I walked (I was probably in a very good mood), when a peon came by and said I couldn't walk like that. When I asked why, he pointed to the door of a cabin marked COO, with utmost seriousness. I didn't quite see the logic, but it was conveyed that I was meant to be serious and businesslike, not hop, skip and jump. Bizarre, right? I quit the next day.

Luckily, the day that I quit, Rajiv called me saying BBC wanted to see me. Great. I went up to the office where I met the very pleasant Saul Nasse who instantly put me at ease with a 'Hi, Regu!' Now, BBC had undertaken a project for the government which was basically for AIDS awareness amongst the youth. They were doing it via three means: a fiction show, radio spots and a youth show. No prizes for guessing what I'd picked: the youth show obviously! I spoke to Saul for a while about Indian television, my work, and later he told me he'd found me to be a very passionate young man. Anyway, I was hired as producer, and they offered me a neat package of forty grand. I remember calling all my friends excitedly and saying, yaar, forty thousand... paisa hi paisa abhi! The year was 2002. It was a new beginning for me in so many ways.

Sonia Chaudhary, whom I knew from Channel [V], was my immediate boss here: my supervising producer. Owing to my Raghu No. 2 act at [V], she was initially a bit wary of me, but more on that later. What stands out about my first day at work was the fact that I walked in at 10 a.m. sharp, with the other employees. Only, everyone left at 6 p.m. like clockwork. I stayed back, of course, unused to leaving work so early. I was just sitting at my computer, trying to build a structure for our AIDS awareness show. Then I got to know this was how BBC worked. They started their days on time, maximized their work, and left office on time. It's not a work culture I can subscribe to, but in my time there, yes, I respected it.

My stint at the BBC was a career-defining experience. I learnt a lot there, which has found its way to *Roadies* as well. The safety course, for example. This was a CD with a nearly twenty-hour course on it which every new employee at the BBC had to take. Today, the fact that I always perform the tasks before the Roadies do, or the fact that no contestant or crew member (except the one time I wasn't around) has gotten seriously injured on shoot, is all because of what this course taught me. They were very thorough at the BBC. If they sent out a team to shoot something for them, the whole team had better make sure the safety norms were in place down to the T, as per the safety course. This could include basic things like temperature, humidity, possibility of snakes, whatever else. You have to actually fill up a form mentioning the presence or absence of any kind of risk for the crew members. It's very, very tedious but it also helps to a huge extent. One thing that was emphasized was that, despite all the safety norms being met, despite there being a doctor, medical help, and other things, *if* there's still a problem, the producer was responsible for it. If while shooting, you take a shot in which a safety discipline is compromised, you're not allowed to use that shot. Just like that! It came in the way of a lot of things, mostly jugaad, but it also instilled in me a great sense of responsibility for my crew. No matter who said what, I was still completely and totally responsible for anything that happened to any crew member. Still am.

The show was called *Haath Se Haath Mila* and it was to be hosted by one boy and one girl. There would be two buses that would travel all the way from Rajasthan to UP. One bus housed a male anchor, the other a female anchor. As they drove past the villages, they'd pick one boy and one girl from each village…at the next village, they'd pick up another boy, another girl. And at the third village, one girl and one boy would be dropped off and in their place, a third boy-girl pair would get on. The idea was to form a human chain. The people that came on board had little tasks to perform called 'chunautis' and at the end of the tasks there were musical gigs, all of which carried a message about AIDS. Workshops on how to talk to villagers about contraception, about sex, using Hindi words without sounding abusive or condescending were held for us.

Aside from safety courses and interactive workshops, we also had to undergo camera training. Around this time, the industry was on the verge of shifting from analogue beta to digital format and we were lucky enough to not only be among the first to use it in India, but also to be trained by the BBC itself.

The prep time for *Haath Se Haath Mila* was one of the most satisfying times ever, the training period was just amazing. And, of course, by the time the shoot started, my life had changed in more ways than one.

◆

Around this time I met three people who have had a very big role to play in my life. One: Vishal Sood, who was heading production and with whom I got along famously from the word go. He later on went to head production and operations at MTV, and is still one of my closest work associates. The second was a guy called Vivek Mathur. Now, *Haath Se Haath Mila* had two production teams who would shoot four episodes alternatively. I was heading one, the other was headed by Priyanka Dutt. Vivek Mathur worked on her team. Every day there would be at least ten stories about him floating about. Turns out, he was extremely hard-working, unorthodox, funny and eccentric (his true passion happened to be cooking). In short, my kinda guy. Vivek was addressed by his nickname 'Bumpy' but *Roadies* fans know him as Nature Baba. Yep, he's the dreadlocked guy from *Roadies*, he does have a real name! Here's where I met him. And last but not the least, *Haath Se Haath Mila* was also where I met another of our production rockstars, Ricky Saxena, now famous as Rickynaldo, also thanks to *Roadies*. What I liked about these guys was that whatever we needed on shoot, especially permissions, they would just get the job done. No questions asked, no talk of the lengths to which they had gone to get it done; it had to be done and that was it. My team on *Roadies* does just that.

Did I say I met three people who would change my life? Well I met a fourth too: Sugandha, who came on board as the anchor. But wait, maybe I ought to build that up a bit more. See, we'd been auditioning extensively for anchors, one male, one female, but hadn't found anyone. We'd finalized Daman as the male anchor but despite auditioning lots of women, we hadn't liked anyone for the female anchor. So Sonia's husband, Siddharth Bahuguna, who was with Channel [V], offered to help. [V] had recently concluded the first season of *Popstars*— incidentally shot by Akshay Rajput—and Siddharth recommended one girl who had made it to the top fifteen but then dropped out. Yep, it was Sugandha Garg, then just about nineteen years old. She came by for the audition and I thought she was great. Fun, spunky, witty, gorgeous. But above all, what I really liked about Sugandha was that she was interesting. In my experience, women in this field were not. I actually believe that Sherlock Holmes knew exactly what he was talking about when he said that the day is finite and so are mental capacities. Women who need to be in front of the camera concentrate so much on their hair, heels, nails, clothes, etcetera, that they're just cookie-cutter copies of each other: looking good is definitely a demand of their job, but unfortunately, it mostly results in self-obsession. It's easy for them to be beautiful to look at but very difficult for them to be interesting. Sugandha made it look easy. Not only was she pleasing to the eyes but I couldn't stop laughing because of her sense of humour. Sonia was very keen on another candidate called Richa, but I fought tooth and nail for Sugandha and, thankfully, won. Sugandha was hired as the female anchor of *Haath Se Haath Mila*.

◆

Cast, crew, script in place, we set off for Jaipur from where we'd be flagging off the shoot. We landed a day before, set the crew up in the hotel, set up the buses, had a pre-production meeting. It was pretty late when we turned in, and the next morning, everyone else turned up for the shoot on time except for one person—me. The producer was late. Sonia was waiting there as I hurried out from my room, feeling like shit. She took me aside and asked me why I was late. I didn't have an answer; we'd all had a late night, we were all tired. Sonia told me that I had to stop micro-managing everything. I had to learn to delegate work, then turn up on time for the shoots with just a cup of chai, and monitor everything. That's it. From that day I was never, ever late.

The other thing I learnt on *Haath Se Haath Mila* was never to ask anyone to do something I couldn't. The logic was simple. If I did something I needed, the next time I asked for it to be done, no one could really say no. Because I'd done it. For example, once we needed a sunrise shot to be taken in Agra of the Taj Mahal. I could have asked anyone to do it but I decided against it. My day as a producer/director ended much later than anyone else's. So, after a late night, I was up early the next morning, even before dawn. I got out my tripod, camera, a cup of chai and stood on the terrace, waiting, the old superhuman instincts back. As soon as it was light, I set up the tripod in the right direction, locked it in place...except that the tripod's tilt lock wasn't okay, so the camera wouldn't point up but down. Thankfully, I figured this quickly enough, but this meant that, for the next forty minutes, I had to hold the camera in my hand, waiting for the sun to rise as my tea grew cold. I remember having cursed everyone in those moments—from the crew sleeping peacefully to Shah Jahan for building the damned monument! But I ultimately got the shot, it was beautiful, and no one on the crew could ever crib about doing an early morning shoot because I had done one. It was possible. On a very basic level, this is a funda that makes perfect sense for the *Roadies* tasks too. If I do them, no one gets to say that it's too tough. Boss, I've done it!

I formed some of my basic team rules then: no one walked on my sets; during a shoot, everyone ran. And I never stayed in one place either, especially if the cameraman was planning a risky shot. Like this one time when the cameraman was convinced he could take a kickass shot: standing atop one of the buses and taking a top-angle shot of the other bus. While both buses were in motion! It would be gorgeous. Tough, but gorgeous. And also against the BBC safety course. But we did it anyway. Only that when the cameraman got on top of the bus,

I did too. I was *his* tripod, holding on to his legs while he was craning his head across to get the shot. There was another shot in which he was sitting in the middle of a rough mud patch...and I was standing behind him, again holding him as both buses whizzed past us. It was one hell of a shot; risky, but beautiful. When the shot was played in the edit, I remember Saul saying, nice shot, how did you do it? There was silence for a moment and then I lied, obviously, telling him some bull like we held the camera outside the bus window. He asked to see the shot again, paused it in between as I looked closely at the screen. There were two shadows, one of a man holding the camera, the other of this man holding him. The shot was scrapped, of course! Sometimes we'd get caught, other times we'd get away with it.

Anyway, once the episode was edited, Saul watched it, made me translate all of it and gave me twelve changes that had to be made. I returned with the corrected episode, but I'd missed out on a couple of his changes. He repeated them. Now, the third time this happened, I remember Saul said, rather coldly, that he couldn't repeat himself and that I had to pay attention to what he said. It was another lesson for me, and since that day I'd write down everything he said and even if Saul ever called me to his office, I would grab a pen and paper first and then go to him. It's a habit I've inculcated in my team as well.

◆

In between the sunrise and jugaad shots, there was another story unfolding, courtesy Sugandha. Our journey was from Jaipur to Agra, then Moradabad, then Nainital. And by the time we'd reached Nainital, Sugandha's attitude towards me had changed. I realized that when I spoke to her; the way she laughed with me, the way she spoke, looked at me, all of it was different—flirtatious, if you will.

Much later she told me she had fancied me right from the time I walked into the BBC conference hall on the day of her auditions. She had a boyfriend at the time, but she wasn't serious about him. So, anyway, we were at Nainital, right over the lake. It was a beautiful night, and there was a storm brewing, figuratively and literally. There was a blackout—the lights all over Nainital had gone out—so I brought out my guitar. We were sitting in the little gallery outside the rooms, the whole crew... and I started singing. The pitch-dark room only lit up sporadically whenever lightning struck. It hit again and again, lit up the lake, lit up our faces... and almost magically, the rest of the team went off to their rooms until only Sugandha and I remained. I kept playing, she kept listening. And I can't tell you at what moment it happened or how it happened. All I remember is, I stopped playing... and we kissed. Just like that.

By this time, I had had a couple of girlfriends and had hooked up randomly many times where I would always have this sinking feeling when I woke up the next morning, just a big 'what-the-fuck' moment. With Sugandha, that wasn't the case. Kissing her felt right. When I held her, I just couldn't let go. The next day, I felt very happy, very sunny, very pleased with myself.

BBC had a strict policy (of course) when it came to dating within the team. It was actually in the contract that you couldn't sleep with anyone from work, and if you were romantically involved, you had to officially declare it to HR. And Kuhu (as I call her) was totally besotted by me; she was almost like a fan, with a huge schoolgirl crush on me. During the next shooting schedule with Priyanka Dutt, Kuhu somehow got hold of a photograph of mine and she'd keep it with her—which was later spotted by the crew members. Even otherwise, what was between us was pretty evident. We both lived in Patparganj at the time and I remember one night, when we were both getting dropped home after work, we came pretty close to kissing but this time Kuhu backed out, saying she had a boyfriend. I retorted that that was the least of my worries, and that I was most conflicted about her age. She insisted that the official forms were all bakwaas, and that she wasn't nineteen but twenty-one. That quelled my worries for just a while, until I got to know from her mother after some random phone call, that she had lied.

When I confronted Kuhu about this, I swear (she doesn't want me saying this but, well) she looked me in the eye and coolly said that her mother was a pathological liar. I was thoroughly confused again but bought the story anyway (maybe because I wanted to believe her), and we started dating. My life then became a lot happier. I would have this stupid grin on my face the minute she'd walk into the room. We kept our relationship a secret from everyone, but obviously, everyone knew. Eventually, during a meeting in his cabin, Saul asked me about Kuhu. I instinctively denied it at first, but then came clean.

I realized everyone else knew and also that I would have to make sure there were no feelings of favouritism, even though we were dating. During the next schedule, I remember Daman being late one day, which delayed the whole shoot. I called him and Kuhu, despite the fact that Kuhu had reached the shoot on time, and blasted both, even though it wasn't Kuhu's fault. Kuhu was in tears. But I *had* to do that, because once people feel there is favouritism within the team, gossip starts to flow and they lose respect for you. I was not about to lose all that hard-earned respect, so I made it very clear that, on the sets, Kuhu was simply an anchor, that I was here first and foremost to do my job, as was she, and that she was NOT on holiday with her boyfriend. There was a Diwali party once and that's when I officially told everyone that, yes, I was dating Kuhu.

In the meantime, my work was really being appreciated. I was feeling very good about myself. Everybody from Saul to Sonia had praised...well, not just me, but my whole team, making me feel very confident. And for someone who never thought much of his looks, who had body image issues, who was losing hair at twenty-seven, being in love helped. For someone like Kuhu, who was so young, bouncy, bubbly, gorgeous, to find everything about me attractive and fascinating (she had even used the word 'hot'), it was extremely gratifying.

In fact, I felt so confident about myself that one cold December night, when I had just stepped out of the shower, I remember looking at myself in the mirror and just making a snap decision, then and there. Walking out, I strode straight into the parlour closest to home, sat in the chair and asked them to shave all my hair off. The barber was shocked; he offered to trim it for me but I simply showed him a blade and said, just shave it all off. He did. I hadn't told anybody about this, as there wasn't anybody at home to tell. I got up, still fully self-assured, opened the door of the parlour and then before the amazing confidence could hit me, fill me up, something else did.

The cold-hearted winter wind of Delhi. You see, nobody had told me that hair is not just a sign of vanity but also a protection for the head. Hair all gone, I felt so bloody cold, my teeth began chattering… hard. The other thing about shaving one's head is, you never know the shape of your skull till you actually do it. Thankfully, my skull wasn't grotesquely shaped or anything, so it wasn't that bad. That night, however, I didn't know this yet. I hadn't even looked at myself in the mirror. Nope, the first person to see me would have to be Kuhu.

She was doing voice-overs for the episode with Daman at the studio and I was to pick her up. I got into the car, drove to the studio and waited. That was the big moment for me, wondering how she would take it. And I remember it clearly even now. Kuhu came by, I rolled down the window, and she must have gotten quite a start. She looked me up and down for quite some time and then simply said, 'I like it.' And that was that. Bye, bye hair! My parents, my friends and Rajiv all reacted to it with some surprise but they all liked it soon enough.

My bald head has now become the biggest part of my identity. After *Roadies 4*, around which time the show became popular, I remember being asked by the press whether it was a style statement, and also being told that many boys across Kolkata were shaving their heads, aping me. A reporter called me and asked me if I thought being bald was sexy. Now, I don't exactly agree; a man's sexiness doesn't depend on his hairstyle, or the lack of it. But the fact remains that hair is a sign of vanity, and knocking it all off just like that implies, well, confidence. And confidence is sexy. I don't *need* the hair to feel good, I feel good anyway. I had never used any products on my hair to help the vanity.

In my growing-up years, I never had the money to buy gel and when I could afford gel, I didn't have any hair!

Bald guys are generally made fun of: they're villains, bad guys or comedians. But for me, it was the single most defining moment of my life. During the *Roadies X* auditions in Chandigarh, when we were at the pub, 10 Downing Street, I remember walking up to the DJ's console and taking off my hood. There was a stunned silence. That's when they recognized me, when they saw my bald head. And whenever I'm approached for photographs, if I'm wearing a cap, I'll be politely asked to take it off.

So back to that skull-freezing winter of 2002. Life went on, this time without hair. One fine day I heard that MTV was hiring. Again. We'd all gathered on the terrace for a chai-cigarette break—Sonia, my associate producers Tanya and Kapil Motwani, and I. And somebody, I can't remember who, said, hey, you know what, MTV's also making a travel show. It's got bikes and they're going to travel all over India. It seemed similar to *Haath Se Haath Mila* but it didn't have the element of AIDS in it. I said, okay, great, sounds interesting.

Karthik Chintamani, who had been the producer of one my first shows, *MTV Get a Voice*, was now the executive producer at MTV. He was also the guy who had told Rohit Vaid that this boy was worth his weight in gold. My one-year contract with BBC would end in another two months, but my five-year EMI for my first car (a Maruti Esteem) still needed to be paid. And this was a travel show at MTV! Did I mention I wanted to work there?

Incidentally, Manna, Rohit's (now ex) wife, was working at MTV Mumbai, and she suggested my name to Karthik who instantly went, fuck, of course, *that's* the guy! He called me immediately. I told him I was with the BBC, and he asked whether I'd like to work for MTV. Pause. Not for effect, but for it to sink in. Would I like to work for MTV? Hell, yeah. I agreed to fly to Mumbai the coming Monday. Then I promptly went to Saul, told him what had happened. Because, you see, Saul was not just my boss, he was my mentor. In one year, he taught me stuff that some people go through their entire careers without learning. And he did it without being obnoxious or authoritative. He empowered and supported, firmly and politely guided. I didn't want to go behind his back; it's a policy I've followed all my life, to let people involved know what I'm about to do. And then live with their reaction.

Saul was quiet for a bit, and then said, 'Well, go, meet them, and come back and tell me what happens.'

I left that Saturday. Later that night, I remember partying with Sonu and Akshay. Sunday night, I partied till very late once again, as a result of which I woke up with a horrible hangover on Monday morning…but it didn't matter. MTV had called me and I was *not* going to be rejected this time, no sir! Not by MTV, not by this city.

I walked into the MTV offices wearing my best (and only) bright orange half-shirt, track pants, running shoes, earrings and bald head, met Karthik who was happy to see me and said great, now come meet Cyrus Oshidar. You may remember Cyrus Oshidar from a very interesting credit title he was given on most MTV shows: 'Guiding Light: Cyrus O'. He's just that. That man has been credited with creating Brand MTV, which is crazy, irreverent, against the rules…and it was an embodiment of all those who worked there. And boy, they were a mad, mad bunch. There was Vasant Valsan, a very genial, highly entertaining guy, and the brain behind *MTV Bakra*. Then there was David Polycarp, an eccentric guy like you won't believe, who created *Fully Faltoo*. David is a paradox of sorts. He's very good-looking and soft-spoken—in fact, he hardly talks—but makes sure he gets his point across. Oh, and he's mental. Vasant and David are best friends and today run their own company called The Company. And the baap of all the mental patients was Cyrus Oshidar. If you talk to him for fifteen minutes, he'll come up with five different ideas, each madder than the next; his brain is just wired differently.

The year was still 2002 and there was a huge power tussle going on within MTV between shows and promos. Shows were handled by Natasha Malhotra, the lady who had rejected me, and Cyrus Oshidar handled promos. Only, by this time, Natasha had been promoted and had moved to Singapore. And Cyrus Oshidar was put in charge of shows and promos. More madness. The minute I sat down, Cyrus quoted from *Jerry Maguire*. Now, the movie is about this guy who works in a sports management company. When the film starts, the company is at the top of the business But Jerry feels they've lost their spirit somewhere down the line. So the movie opens with him writing (well, technically screenplay writer Cameron Crowe wrote it) a mission statement titled 'The Things We Think But Do Not Say'. It is a brilliantly idealistic piece of writing and I remember getting excited when Cyrus asked if I remembered it. I knew it by heart, and he said it's what they tried to do at MTV. Less is more. Do less work but do it better; do it really, really well. So, Cyrus didn't quite interview me—he chatted with me, and in such a way that I felt I was already a part of the company.

Next up, I had to meet Alex Kuruvilla, General Manager, MTV. I had a very short chat with Alex of which I only remember one thing very clearly: Alex asked me why I wanted to work for MTV. Now, it wasn't a question I'd prepared for, but the answer came out instantly: because I know I'll do my best work here. Alex seemed to like my answer a lot, and the meeting was done.

I came back to Delhi on Tuesday. When Saul asked to meet me, I told him everything had gone off well, and that I was pretty much taking up the job. Now, Saul is your classic British guy, which means he's all stiff upper lip, and he will never ever betray his emotions. But I remember that day, the first words that escaped him when I said this were, 'Don't go.' He checked himself as soon as he said them but the words were out, I'd heard them, and to me, it was one of the biggest compliments I have received. EVER. The next minute, he was back to his businesslike manner, saying they were planning a second season of *Haath Se Haath Mila*, but this stayed with me. I swear that at that moment, I would have agreed to his terms and conditions, taken up his offer…but the truth was, I could taste MTV.

Saul understood. All this happened in December 2002 and I joined MTV in February 2003.

I went back to *Haath Se Haath Mila*, shot it, edited the rest of the episodes, and soon it was the night of my departure. I had worked non-stop without sleep for three days and nights, and was dog-tired. Rajiv and Kuhu drove me to Hazrat Nizamuddin Railway Station so I could take my train to Mumbai. The train was about to come. I was sitting on my suitcase, chatting, when, suddenly, I felt something fall on my head. When I lifted my hand to see what it was, rose petals fell into my lap. I was sure there was a wedding or something going on, but when I looked up, I was shocked. Standing in front of me was Saul, Sonia and the entire BBC team with garlands, flowers, a bagful of condoms, I kid you not! Saul had this stereo in hand and he played this song, a song we played at the end of every *Haath Se Haath Mila* episode, a song about parting, about the journey continuing—it seemed symbolic—and they showered me with flowers. Kuhu, Rajiv and I were stunned. The train arrived, I started saying my goodbyes... and Sonia broke down. This was another big compliment for me. I was emotional myself but couldn't express it, so I completely shut down—I didn't cry, not because I didn't want to but because I'd gone without crying for so long.

I sat in the train, numb. The minute the train began to move, a flashback began in my head. It had been such a big year for me, one of the best of my life. I'd found love, I'd worked under an amazing, amazing boss and with a wonderful team.

During the eighteen hours of my journey, all I did was look out the window and think about my life, and how it was about to change. The memories that came to me were all intense, but one memory stood out, shining above all the others—the memory of myself standing in a pigeonhole of a flat in South Mumbai, looking out at the sun setting over the sea, with no job, no money to speak of, and promising myself that someday I'd be someone in this city that kept rejecting me.

I was getting there. At the other end of my train journey lay

Mumbai, in Mumbai lay Tardeo and in Tardeo—gleaming, bursting at the seams with energy and a whole new bunch of ideas, madness and creativity, and my apparent BEST work—lay my dream office: MTV.

My first day at MTV... and hitting the road, finally

Random Trivia No. 1: I don't think I would have been hired by MTV to produce *Roadies* if David Polycarp didn't have a bad back.

Random Trivia No. 2: The word 'Roadies' is not synonymous with the contestants of my show and/or me. In the dictionary, it refers to members of a crew in a travelling group of musicians or other entertainers, whose work usually includes the setting up of equipment.

Random Trivia No. 3: Roadies was just a working title and was never meant to be the real thing. The titles considered were 'Saat Saath' and 'Road Raj'. But 'Roadies' stuck and we let it stick.

But I'm getting ahead of myself. It's still February 2003, there were still a couple of months to go before *Roadies* took shape. Meanwhile...

I took a cab from Mumbai Central to Andheri, landed up at Manish's, whose place I was to share. He had a flat just down the street from where I live today on Yari Road. I reached on a Saturday, and on Sunday night, Melly (Manish) and I hosted a little housewarming party. It was a cosy get-together—the two of us, Akshay, Nirupam and their better halves, plenty of alcohol and my guitar. After drinking, chatting, singing the night through, the others had left but I wasn't done yet. I dragged Melly down for a walk just before dawn. We walked and walked and walked... and I talked and talked and talked. For an hour or two. And all I kept saying was, dude, I am going to rock it, I am going to kill it this time. The MTV guys, they have *no* clue *who* is coming to work for them. I don't get tired, I don't need to eat, I don't need to sleep, I have the best ideas, I'm creative, I've been called the best at my work... Melly they have no clue, they have never seen anyone like me Melly...and they will never see anyone like me. And poor Melly just kept walking with me saying yeah, yeah... And I would shake my head and say, no man, you don't understand. This is it, I have a job, at MTV, and I am going to KILL it. I am the king! They have never seen anyone like me. And Melly kept nodding dutifully.

The next morning, I hadn't seen anyone like me either—I had such a *mother* of a hangover. It was 10 February 2003, my first day at work, at long last, for MTV.

First days at work are weird. When I walked into the MTV office that day, I couldn't help but remember my first day at work at TV18. Rajiv and I had spent a clueless hour at the big conference hall, entered the *Star Trek*-ish world of the editing room, and then been given tapes to transcribe. Transcribing is basically playing a tape and writing down every single thing that people say on it. It's a mind-numbing job, the original donkey work that is done by those at the bottom-most rung of the ladder. But at least it kept us busy. At MTV, however, I was too senior to spend my first day doing that. So I looked around, spoke to Karthik, who told me *Roadies* still had about a couple of months to go (we're getting there, we are, honest) but meanwhile I could look at tapes of *MTV Loveline* and figure out ways of making it better. Yes, the same show in which anchor/agony aunt Malaika Arora Khan solved love problems and granted grateful viewers a glimpse of her legs as she sat on a candy-coloured couch. By the time I joined MTV, however, Malaika had left and it was Sophie Chaudhary and Cyrus Broacha hosting the show. I walked on to the set as senior producer and met the two producers of *Loveline*: Vrushali Samant and Ranjit Phatak. Vrushali is someone who later became an integral part of *Roadies*, as did Ranjit Phatak.

A word about Ranjit: this guy is 6'3" and I remember looking him up and down once or twice thinking, fuck man, he's *really* tall. So, naturally, when I needed to call him over for something, I turned around and called out, 'Eh, Chhotu, idhar aana!' I remember he had looked around himself the first time, not believing what I'd called him. The crew was dumbfounded, too, as I pointed to him and repeated, 'You, Chhotu, come here.' And Ranjit is so sweet, he laughed, as did the rest of the crew, and he came over. That's Chhotu, by the way, the really tall dude you've seen on *Roadies* and that's the day he got named. On my first day at MTV. For me, it was just a fun way to establish my alpha male status. I didn't know whether he'd laugh or get offended. He laughed. The name stuck.

◆

The other memorable thing that happened at *Loveline* was on April Fool's Day. By 2003, *Bakra* was MTV's biggest property and they had advertised 1 April as 'Bakra Din', promising a day full of pranks on everyone—from the VJs to the man on the street. A prank—or a 'bakra' as it was popularly known—had to be pulled off on Sophie and I was appointed as the 'bakra-maker'. I'd heard that Sophie was, like most girls, touchy about comments regarding her body, and her worst fear was being called fat. Aha! So on D-Day, I landed on the set, Sophie came out to shoot and right before action, I shook my head, said I didn't like what she was wearing, that it made her look...pause for effect... *big*. Sophie was a little taken aback, but agreed to change. Moments later, she came back, got into position and again I frowned. 'What's the matter, Sophie?' I asked in all seriousness. You're looking...*fat*. Silence. And then Sophie blurted, 'Excuse me?' Unperturbed, I went at it again: 'You're making *Cyrus* look skinny.' Now Cyrus is really round, and Sophie gaped at me for a moment...as did the rest of the crew around us. She got up, went into her room, and called me in a moment later. I got a mic fixed on me and went in. She was crying but she composed herself, told me she didn't appreciate how I spoke to her, and that my tone lacked in common courtesy and respect. I nodded most seriously, agreed with her, apologized, and requested her to come back to the set. The poor girl took a moment to collect herself, then walked back in. The camera started rolling and then again, I maaroed the same line, with the words 'big' and 'fat' thrown in for effect. This time she lost it, argued with me and I shrugged. 'Why should I pussyfoot?' I said. 'I'll say it like I see it.' Now she started really crying, right outside there, in front of the crew. I felt terrible and told her, please don't cry because it was time. The bakra cap was duly brought in, pinned to her head and I feebly screamed out, 'Bakra!' Sophie was unimpressed, found nothing funny about it and flatly refused to shoot for the rest of the day. I heard she cried for three days about it. Sophie went on to become a really close friend, but to this day, I regret how I spoke to her during that shoot. I was rude and I think it was stupid. But I also realized that I have the potential to perform a certain way, to suppress my natural polite instincts, and be another guy if I needed to be. The taller guy, remember him?

Meanwhile, *Roadies* continued to be discussed among the top brass at MTV—Karthik, who was then the executive producer, Anil Nair, who was heading MTV online, and supervising producers David Polycarp and Vasant Valsan. They told me there were going to be these kids who would ride bikes from Chennai to Chail. The kids were to ride bikes all the way to the cricket ground, (incidentally the highest in the world), because, well, 2003 was also when the World Cup was to happen. What MTV thought was that we would get the *Roadies* here, get a prominent cricketer of the time like Rahul Dravid or Saurav Ganguly, and the finale would be a friendly cricket match.

Now, technically speaking, Chail isn't an end point to a journey. In every subsequent season of *Roadies*, I have always made sure that the end point *is* a fitting end point, either you touch a border, or there's sea beyond—a natural end to the journey. This was the first (and last) time it so happened that the end point wasn't a natural 'the end'. But we went with it. Like we went with the name of the show. The name 'Roadies', as you've read earlier, was a working title. I was told that Miditech was the company making the show, and I was glad because I was on excellent terms with them.

◆

The first question I asked and kept asking was, why are they travelling on bikes? From Chennai to Chail, why? The question hadn't been asked earlier. People were confused; they shrugged and said, because Hero Honda is the sponsor. I said I got that, but that was no justification for a viewer. Karthik smiled and said, you figure it out. Someone suggested we take up a social issue. Start a signature campaign, get the kids to collect signatures from all the states they ride through and ultimately, end the journey not in Chail but in Delhi, then hand the signatures to the president of India. That didn't mean anything to me. Because such a move doesn't change anything. Moreover, I'd just come from BBC and they're very particular about issues; this campaign seemed rather casual to me. I shot down the idea.

I had a couple of meetings with Miditech who had already made a rough structure for a few episodes. The episodes went along this line: the kids would ride up to a village, park their bikes there, and the task would be to build a cricket pitch and then play a cricket match with the villagers. Again, I was confused. What did that mean? How were we to assume that the village would even want a fucking cricket pitch? And how would it help the village?

There were several other ideas about *Roadies* that came from Miditech and MTV, ideas that I loved, that I inherited. One was the idea that these guys had to survive on a budget of five hundred rupees per day. I liked the idea of a fixed budget, and the fact that seven of them had to spend it between them over one day. I looked at it as survival within limited means, which appealed to me.

But the one question that kept coming back to me was, why are these guys travelling by bikes? Why not by train, why couldn't they fly, or if they had to take the road, why couldn't they just drive in a car? It was definitely more comfortable! The answer came to me in bits and pieces. A train journey isn't exactly a journey: it's time consuming, yes, but it's full of only destinations. You get on at one station, you stop by at many others, but you don't actually get to explore your surroundings. Not beyond the railway platform anyway. Planes are even worse: there's just a starting point and an ending point, but there's no journey.

Driving on the road is definitely better, even if it's in a car, because you're looking out at the places that pass by, you can halt anywhere you want. But the car as such is an insulated means of travel. The windows are up, the AC is on, you've got music blaring. You're isolated from your environment. Irrespective of whether it's hot, cold or wet outside, you're comfortable inside. But a guy who rides a bike is really interacting with his environment. If it's hot, he's sweating; if it's cold, he's freezing; if it's raining, he's drenched. He's really *feeling* the journey, experiencing it. That to me signified a mind that seeks new experiences, a mind that *wants* to experience. Such a person would be open to finding new things and learning from them. Hence, the bikes. Drum roll, please.

This led to the idea of challenges where they explored the culture of the places they visited and also tested their own personal limits.

The next logical step was to go on the reconnaissance, a.k.a. recce. This is basically a trip that a crew makes to the place they have to shoot at to figure out its feasibility as a pre-production procedure. In this case, we had to make a trip from Chennai all the way to Chail. The recce was going to take twenty-five days. I started on it with very little idea of what to do. We needed to make twenty-six episodes of half an hour each and we had to plan twenty-six stops in between Chennai to Chail. I made this trip with Nivedith Alva, the youngest of the Alva brothers and the designated director of the series, and with another guy, Vikrant Bhardwaj, who was a friend of mine from Delhi and was in the production team. Vikrant and I both shared a passion for North Indian food. Our first stop was Chennai and I remember both of us had a simultaneous craving for rajma chawal. Well, it was Chennai and the rajma chawal, to put it mildly, was PATHETIC! As we picked at the stringy grains of the rice, we made an unofficial pact that through this recce trip, we would find out which state makes the best rajma chawal. Now we travelled to many, many states: Tamil Nadu, Karnataka, Goa, Maharashtra, Gujarat, Rajasthan, Uttar Pradesh, Delhi, Haryana, Punjab, Himachal Pradesh. We tried rajma chawal in every single state and I happen to know which place in India serves the best rajma chawal, or at least did, ten years ago. But that's my little secret.

◆

This was around the time I developed darker aspects to my personality. I had been dealing with my many issues with religion, morality, life and death, and God. The day the Babri Masjid tragedy happened, I gave up my holy thread, I gave up being a Brahmin. The day the Godhra riots happened, I gave up religion entirely. I wanted no part in any system that needed people to kill one another, or even claim to have all the answers. No one fucking does. End of story. Civilized society as such is an oxymoron. Because everything happens within our society: elderly people get murdered, younger people get molested, abused, raped. It takes very little need or greed for that wall of society to crumble and for the animal instinct—actually no, scratch that, not even animals are like this. Animals hunt when they're hungry, eat their fill, and that's that. Animals don't have the concept of killing something for the sake of killing, humans do. This whole thing is civility. If you go to a dinner party, everyone is clinking glasses, talking politely, all very well-mannered. I would wonder, what would happen if I were to lock them up in this room. How long would it take for this politeness, for this fucking façade to crumble and for people to start snapping at each other…and how much would it take for them to start killing each other? This is kind of like *Big Brother* but back then I didn't know what that meant. I just kept thinking these things while travelling.

I've easily spent a decade of my life looking at the world through the window pane of a car. And the car journeys on this recce are particularly significant. I found that I loved them, absolutely loved them. I have David Polycarp to thank, I guess. It's his bad back that landed me here, after all. No, seriously, David and Vasant Valsan were supervising producers, and Vasant was involved in *Bakra*. So technically—logically—the responsibility of *Roadies* should have landed on David Polycarp but he had a bad back: he couldn't sit in a car for too many hours. Nobody has explicitly told me this, but I'm pretty sure this is why MTV hired me. Because they wanted someone to go on the journey. And I'm glad they did. I adored the car drives. I could read, I could think, I could have a conversation if I felt like it. On the recce, I also started thinking of the whole five-hundred-rupees-a-day-to-survive idea. I thought, let me take the word 'survive' and make that an integral part of the show.

Roadies was a travel show when it was conceived. No bike manufacturer would say, hey man I've made a bike, let's make a reality show. Nope, they'd say: if it's a travel show I'll be a part of it. In the end, a road trip was decided upon. In fact, the name that Hero Honda had suggested was 'Saat Saath', which basically translated to 'Seven Together', since there were to be seven contestants. I hated the title— it sounded like a fucking Karan Johar film. It's all about loving your friends?! What the fuck! It just didn't sit with my new world view. I wanted reality. I wanted to put to practice my dinner-party-civility theory. And as we travelled on, I found a few ways to do it.

Today, *Roadies* is *all* about that. Neither Hero Honda, nor MTV, nor Miditech wanted it to be like this. But anything else would not sit well with me. When I came to MTV, I realized what kind of mad fuckers work there: Cyrus Oshidar, Cyrus Broacha, Vasant Valsan, David Polycarp. If you see their work, you can get a very good idea of who they are, which means that they're able to express themselves through their work. And I knew that at this place I could finally express myself. I really wanted to put my thought process into the entire thing, and what *Roadies* became was the expression of my thoughts at the time.

Done with the recce, we came back with the thought that somewhere, in different parts of the country, there were seven idiots whose lives were about to change. It was time for auditions. It's a common misconception that I was a judge in the first season but I wasn't. Being a trained cameraman and audio recorder, I was the guy *shooting* the auditions. The judges were Karthik, Anil, David and Vaibhav Vishal (V2), a guy from marketing who would have a significant role to play in the *Roadies* story.

◆

These guys decided to just sit and chat with the people who had come in to audition. A bench with four people and a guy in front of them. A form was filled, a group discussion carried out, and there was a short chat. There was a camera on a tripod recording every audition, not for any other purpose but only so we'd have the chats and the wannabe contestants on record; so if we wanted to go back and see if any had the potential, we just needed to turn on the tape. That's how recording the 'audition chats' came in to being. I also had the idea to film them outside the room. So the kids who came for the first ever *Roadies* auditions will all remember a bald guy with a camera, shooting them, talking to them. The guy would speak to them just as they were going in, ask them how they were feeling, and then the minute they were out, the same question would be repeated. That guy was me, and this exercise has now caught on as a reality show trend. Usually people are very fussy about framing, everyone likes to think that they're an artist. The frames looked good but I felt the process then lacked spontaneity. But I'd learnt at my stint in the BBC that if what a guy or a girl was saying was interesting, the fucking background didn't matter. All you needed to do was point the camera into his or her face and *let* them talk. Forget backgrounds, forget directing them to speak a certain way…just get them to say what they want to.

So, there we were in Pune, which is where I think the first set of auditions happened. It was the first day of the shoot, and I had a fucking temperature. Mine was a very lonely job; the MTV guys were together, the event guys were together, I was all alone, feeling like shit…

and eventually, I just kind of fainted. I was standing, shooting, and then I was on the floor. Two guys came by, one had a bike, the other claimed to be a doctor. The doctor said I had to go to the hospital and the kid with the bike offered to drop me. I didn't and eventually they got me meds, sorted me out, and I thanked them. You may remember them as Tony Cordolia and Dr Iknoor Bains, contestants on *Roadies 1*.

The next auditions happened in Delhi and Kuhu came by to surprise me. I was delighted. We made plans for that night and I went to the auditions. On the first day, auditions were held at Modern School, Barakhamba Road. As I was shooting the hopefuls, I came across this one girl, sporting jeans and a vest, a bandana on her forehead, bag slung over her shoulder—she really stood out. I remember shooting her to see how she'd look on camera. She looked good. I conveyed her registration number to the MTV guys and told them that this girl seemed like she had potential. They thought so, too, and the girl was Natasha Gulati, who was also cast on the show.

The first day of the auditions was done. Day two came by. I would shoot them just before they'd go in, and then wait to shoot them when they came out. We broke for lunch and I remember sitting by myself, eating. There was also this guy who was around, waiting for his interview, who asked me how the food was, did I like it? I said, yeah, thanks. I noticed he was rather sweaty and flushed, waiting for his interview. He didn't look nervous though, he looked kind of bored. I didn't know then that I'd just met my second brother.

How I met Rannvijay, bikes, fights and television gold

Rannvijay never wanted to audition for *Roadies*. Really. He comes from an army background, he had cleared the Services Selection Board and was to report to Chennai within two or three months as an officer. He was into sports, and he had earned the reputation of being a stud. And he was really good at riding bikes. The ad for *Roadies* that ran in the newspapers asked readers whether they could ride bikes and were ready for the adventure of a lifetime, and the prize was a Hero Honda Karizma, the brand new one that had launched then. Rannvijay's friends had told him about the ad and he had said, great, I want the bike, I'll win the bike. He wanted it, sure, but he wasn't very driven.

The night before the auditions, he had partied and then stayed over at a friend's place. The next morning, another friend, Kabir, came by to pick him up for the auditions. Rannvijay still says that if Kabir hadn't come, he would have backed out, not turned up. But since Kabir was waiting downstairs, Rannvijay got the better of his hangover, changed his clothes, and left with him. When they got to Modern School and Rannvijay saw the long queue, he backed out again, saying, forget it. But on his way out, one of his classmates who was manning the gates as a volunteer, saw him, called him back, and let him go in a little ahead. So that's why Rannvijay came back, because he didn't have to stand in the long queue. Else he would have just left. He had to wait for his turn, though, and a while later he got quite bored.

There were some kids playing basketball in the court, he started playing with them. Soon he was drenched in sweat, but he kept playing. Now, the MTV guys had noticed Rannvijay, noticed him playing continuously. He took a break in between, and someone from the event management company went to him and asked if he had a registration number. He did. It was stuck to his chest but drenched in sweat, so this guy told him, no issues, and got him a new number. He led him to the front of the line. Rannvijay then got through the group discussion and that's how I came to meet him, waiting to go into the interview room as I ate lunch. The interesting thing about Rannvijay is how he didn't want it, he didn't even want to come and audition, but people kept noticing him and pushing him ahead. And that's how he got on to it.

The format of the auditions has always been the way it is today. It hasn't been tweaked or changed. I don't know who came up with it but having a group discussion and then a personal interview, made logical sense then—as much as it does now. And like the working title, it stuck. A funny thing would happen when I would shoot the GDs: I'd get involved in the fights. I'd point the camera at someone who was making a point, ask them a question, push my point across! The MTV guys would ask me what the fuck I was doing, but I couldn't help it…how can you not react?! And I'd be politely told that all they wanted to do was to observe what the contestants' point of view was. This mentality of mine came out fully when I later landed on the judges' table, but I have always been very vocal about my opinions.

As we watched the footage once we got back, I realized that the auditions were all in English and this rattled me no end, mainly because I'd just come from the BBC setup, had made a Hindi show and to me, that was the language of communication. The MTV guys said this was how they spoke. Now, MTV's shows were all in English except, of course, for *MTV Bakra*, which was candid camera and featured regular people. But I was very sure I wanted to make my show in Hindi. *Roadies* is pretty much the first Hindi show in youth television in India. Maybe people didn't think Hindi was cool, but I didn't care about that. The panel of judges weren't working for me.

But we had managed to get an interesting cast and were ready to shoot. We landed in Chennai with the entire crew; this was 14 August 2003. I remember clearly because we kick-started *Roadies* for the first time on 15 August. Independence Day! Even though the recce was done, we didn't have a clear idea of what we were shooting, I just had a clear idea of how I wanted to shoot it. We made it up as we went along.

◆

There's this place called Golden Beach Resort near Chennai. It's significant because the first episode for *Roadies* was shot there and the first time we went abroad, we took off from there again. We had no plan, just kept shooting. In the middle, we suddenly wondered where one of the contestants, Divya, had gone. We had lost a contestant on the first day! We finally tracked her down…talking on her phone to her boyfriend, then her mother, relaying everything that was going on. Nope, she wasn't breaking any rules, not yet. You see, this was the first day of shooting, and like I said before, we were making it up as we went along. Nivedith said, dude, we must take their phones away and I instantly agreed it made sense. We sat and brainstormed about it. Phones would be taken away, but what if someone used a payphone? Okay, let's take away their money and the five-hundred rupees per day if that happens, and monitor their activities carefully. No phones in the hotel rooms, no TV either.

If you remember the episode, the contestants are told to get ready for a party and then a faceless voice—the 'producer'—asks them to deposit their cell phones in a bag. That's me and that was how one of the basic, most integral rules to the show came to be. Just like that, in the spur of the moment. The first night we had a party…and later that night, we put up cameras outside the contestants' rooms. But of course they could see the fucking camera light from the window, so it didn't quite serve its purpose. We brainstormed again and figured that this candid camera shit wasn't going to work and we'd just have to shoot them with our crews.

◆

The *Roadies* party wrapped but the MTV party continued. I got drunk and, of course, Fun Raghu came out. There was music, a guitar. And then a mother of a hangover. It was the day of the first task and I woke up late. A couple of hours late, and this became an issue. Nikhil shot a mail to MTV saying, your senior producer was late for the second day of the shoot. I felt terrible, terrible. It was the first time it had happened since BBC.

Anyhow, we got down to the shoot...day two, day three...and now we were faced with a strange problem. We didn't have a host. Sure, we had Cyrus Sahukar, but he was only shooting anchor links with us, which meant he wasn't technically on the journey. We couldn't interact with the crew, so how would we convey messages to them, on camera, to the viewers? And then Nivedith came up with this great idea to start a scroll. It's one of the integral parts of any *Roadies* journey. Also Nivedith, perhaps owing to his convent education, used the word 'scroll' instead of 'note'. It's not a commonly used word, but it stuck.

Another internally used technical term that stuck was 'task'. Now, the first ever task on *Roadies* involved making the statue man at the resort move, collecting a clue from a boat and then finding the bikes. It was basically to flag off the journey. Mini was the captain for day one but Rannvijay and Tony, being the rebellious boys they are, refused to accept her captaincy. So after they swam in the water, they decided to go take a shower. And Mini and the crew and the rest of the Roadies waited. Eventually, our two boys made a freshly showered appearance and an exasperated Mini went: 'Vijayyyy, *where* were you?!'

Rannvijay, who had pinned the Indian flag to his T-shirt, just unpinned it, gave it to her, and asked her to chill with it. A little friction, I realized, a little interpersonal drama had begun. I liked it.

Nivedith was great fun to work with. He came up with a lot of cool ideas, but the one place we both had a huge gap in communication was the video diaries. I had heard this term for the first time at BBC and had figured it was similar to how we had shot Rajiv's narrative during his 'woman-for-a-day' story on MTV. I had tried it out during my stint at *Haath Se Haath Mila* during the end of the schedule. I had affixed a camera at the back of the bus and told the contestants to each go there and speak their hearts out. It was an abject failure. Later when I saw what had been recorded, none of the content was exciting or usable in any way. They were just talking about what I'd already seen. This time around, however, I had a fair idea of what mistake I had made and I had formulated a new way of getting content. I wasn't the first in the world to do it but in our space, yes, it was a first. I also learnt the hard way that you had to sit down the contestants, ask them questions and then use the answers as a narrative. If the answers weren't interesting enough, then you asked them another question, this time in such a way that the answer could be interesting. That's your narrative. The story is told by the contestants themselves as it unfolds, through these video diaries. I told Nivedith the concept, but he didn't get it. We shot the video diaries, him and me, with all the contestants every day. And then he said, this will look great at the end of the episode. I hit my forehead with the palm of my hand. I tried to explain to him again that I planned on using it all through the episode, making it the means of telling every episode's story. I was also worried about what kind of content he may have shot if he thought it was to be aired at the end of the episode. We got past that, though.

◆

Another little issue I had on the show with this crew was with the Director of Photography (DoP)—this guy called Alok, a very senior guy, white hair, white moustache and beard, referred to as 'the old warhorse' by Miditech. He had the most amazing ideas when it came to making a shot look lovely but had absolutely no clue when it came to sound. Framing was all he cared about. So what he'd do was, if the kids were walking around, he'd make them stop, change the background, make it look picture perfect, and then ask them to walk back. As a result, mics were abandoned. The visual was all he cared about, not the audio, not the capturing of thoughts, feelings...and I could not agree less.

We once threw the Roadies a party on a barge in Goa, and I wanted to get their reactions when they saw the party setup, but I didn't get any of that. Because I knew they weren't wearing mics, and I knew Alok would only set up the cameras for a pretty shot. I remember asking Nivedith what the hell was happening, and how I wanted to see their reactions, hear what they were saying when they saw the barge all lit up and decorated. Just put the camera in their faces and let's get their reactions, I roared, but it didn't quite happen. The problem was that both Nivedith and I were bacchas, and this guy was senior, so it wasn't really our place to tell him how to do things.

But my frustration was growing. If it's a fiction show, I can tell the actor to look surprised, look sad, look scared. But if it's a reality show, I can't do that. I have to fucking wait for the reaction and when it comes, I should be able to capture it! If we miss it, we have to live without it.

Anyway, that apart, Season 1 did have a lot of parties. The one in Bangalore was the most interesting, because somehow Divya managed to get through to her boyfriend, tell him where we were and then he landed up at the pub! Now the strange part was, when her boyfriend did land up, they refused to be seen together and when we pointed the camera at him, this kid ran to the bathroom and shut himself there for an hour and a half. Weird, right? Well, yes, but it also made for good content. We made the other Roadies force him to open the door but he wouldn't budge. Nikhil Alva finally managed to talk him into coming out. He cursed us, threatened to sue us but finally came out, jacket over his head. He ran, the cameras ran after him; he got on a bike, the camera guys got into an auto and gave chase for quite some time. It was so crazy, so much fun. And I was glad we managed to make good airtime of such a bizarre situation.

Another funny thing I remember was a strict instruction from David Polycarp that I shouldn't talk to any of the contestants. I didn't understand why that had to be so, but I obeyed. So this one time when there was a rappelling task at Tipu's Drop in Karnataka, I was below the cliff with the cameraman shooting the Roadies as they came down... Natasha Gulati was the last to come down, the cameraman had to go ahead to put the stuff in the car and then we had to follow him. Which resulted in me being left alone with Natasha. She started talking to me. And I kept quiet. You've been doing this for long? Silence. What's going to happen to us today? Are we going to get any rest? Quiet. Are you not supposed to talk? You could have heard a pin drop. And just like that, at the silliness of the situation, at the fact that I wasn't even telling her that I wasn't supposed to speak to her, Natasha burst out laughing and I joined in.

◆

A week passed by. The shoot was going great guns but not my relationship with Miditech. I'd come into this thinking we shared a great rapport because we had worked together earlier, but they treated me as a client, an outsider. Every morning, they'd have these team huddles and I wouldn't be a part of it; I'd just look at them from my room and feel left out. And things got a bit strained with Nivedith as well. He had a different view of the shoot, and I don't blame him, because the show was very different from anything that had been done before. But the one thing I had a *very* clear idea about was *how* I wanted to shoot it, and on that, we couldn't see eye to eye. Then there was the DoP who was treating it like a music video, directing the fuck out of the contestants. Soon, I started feeling isolated and I started thinking, it's a fucking forty-day journey... seven days in and I'm all alone. And then the Roadies came to my rescue.

Eventually, I did break David's rule. I started talking to them, and soon become a part of their group. I'd only spend time with them, and got very interested in each of their personalities. Tony and Rannvijay were pretty close to each other, they almost became one unit. And Rannvijay had this easy charm, so much so that, no matter who the captain of the day was, people would look up to him for instructions. By the end of the journey, the Roadies were the only people I spoke to. It was wrong, but I was just twenty-eight, feeling lonely on the shoot, and the Roadies were the only people I could gel with.

◆

So, the Goa party. The MTV VJs came once again, and this time I was desperate for some interesting things to happen. Rannvijay and Natasha, much to my disappointment, hadn't gotten together or even come close...and Iknoor and Tony, much to my surprise, were just not on good terms. It was unpredictable, but soon I'd learn that that's the best way to be on reality TV. Anyway, I got Sophie to flirt with Rannvijay, I got Nikhil to get Natasha to speak, Anusha chatted up Divya and so on. The party was a blast and, finally, all the VJs left... except Cyrus Sahukar. Yes, by now you may have guessed what was in store, but this was the first time it ever happened, so it came as a shock when he said, 'I'm here not for the party actually, but for a vote-out.' And bam! It was the first ever vote-out and the expressions were... well, stunned, to put it mildly. It was chaotic; people went to different corners to chat...and we got it all on tape. And this first vote-out of *Roadies* was the most shocking and unexpected of all: there were seven votes, all against Iknoor. Even Iknoor voted against himself.

We found out that Iknoor had asked to be voted out because his family had been waiting to emigrate to Canada for a while, and their visas had just come through. I don't know how he got to know—I'm convinced these kids were up to something with the five-hundred bucks we'd give them every day. Anyway, he got voted out because he wanted to leave. Only, the minute he got off the boat after saying his goodbyes, Iknoor instantly regretted it. And I'm so glad there was a camera by the car as he left, because we got that reaction. It was ugly framing, terrible background but the most precious fucking content. The minute he left the barge and got on land, Iknoor was retching, almost puking as he sat in the car, looking out, sobbing his heart out. The camera was right there with him. And that was awesome footage. It might have been chaotic and badly shot, but it was television gold.

Meanwhile, in Goa, the *Roadies* song took seed. It was set as a task for the Roadies: they met ace musician Vishal Dadlani, who spoke to them about their journey and asked them to come up with lines for a *Roadies* theme song and to write them down. I remember Mini came up with the line, 'Chennai se Chail tak, apni apni bike par…', and then someone else added lines to it. The idea was that Vishal would then start work on it. The song started in Goa and ended in Delhi.

Now in Goa, on one of our holidays, I got a panicked call from the crew saying the Roadies have left, they've taken the bikes and fucked off! Like I've been saying over and over, we didn't have firm rules in place. The crew got a holiday every seventh day, so they weren't around. The kids had access to their bike keys. They got up one morning and Rannvijay had a brainwave—he decided he didn't want to rot in the hotel, especially since he had never been to Goa, so he led the rebellion. And they just vanished! They didn't have cell phones, so there was no way we could contact them. Miditech was shitting bricks. It's funny now, but back then it was really scary. Nivedith said, I'm gonna punish them, and I told him to chill, they'll come back. They're not idiots. They did come back eventually.

This had happened before. Once at a dhaba, I remember, the crew and cast ate separately. And these kids knew that five hundred bucks wasn't enough. So they ate their fill, went and washed their hands, hung around for a few moments, and then before we knew it, they had zoomed off on their bikes, gone off without paying the bill! They had one meal for free. It was against the rules but, of course, there were no rules then! It was also funny. Now. Actually then, too…a bit. I kind of admired them for it. They were thinking on their feet.

From Goa we climbed up to Maharashtra: Ratnagiri, then Satara and then a Sainik School. It had a swimming pool and an obstacle course, and we'd decided to do a task there. We joined the morning physical training and the Roadies had to compete with the Sainik School students. Rannvijay performed the obstacle course. He didn't win it, but he performed really well.

◆

Later, when the show began to air, around the time we came to the Satara episodes, Rannvijay's mother had started telling him, I think Raghu is fond of you. It was true. Because every time Rannvijay appeared on screen, he had this hero kind of vibe which made for beautiful cuts—which I'm famous for, because my edits were and *are* (screw modesty) the best; they were like nothing anyone had seen before, just as I'd claimed to Melly that drunken night before I joined MTV. Anyway, every time Rannvijay was in the frame, I'd get the kind of shot I wanted and I'd use it to my advantage.

In Hindi poetry, there's the concept of 'ras', which means 'flavour'. There are many that are used to describe a form of art, including haasya-ras, which is comedy, and veer-ras, which is not bravery, not courage, but the portrayal of a hero. With Rannvijay, it became that. There was a feeling of him being more of a leader than the others. And by the time the show came on air, he almost seemed like the lead, the hero of the show. Also probably because I was really fond of him and also, well, because I'd edited it. Those edits went a long way in giving him a career in television.

Anyway, back to the Sainik School tasks. The next one after the obstacle course was a swimming competition. The Sainik cadet, an eleven year old, came by, splashed into the pool...and within no time had swum eleven lengths like he had a motor up his ass! And Tony had to compete with this kid. He dove in. The first lap he swam very well, very fast...the second lap, he started getting tired...by the third lap, he was fucked. But here's the thing...he felt like giving up but he went *at* it. He kept going. There was too much chlorine in the water and he couldn't see after a while. He changed his stroke; he knew he would lose but he didn't give up. I was, of course, with the cameraman, and I went back and forth with Tony for every lap that he took while everyone cheered him on. I found myself joining them because *this* was *my* kind of shit. This sort of attitude really inspires me and what Tony did that sweltering day at the pool has somewhere become the brand image of *Roadies*: that you *don't* give up, you show so much heart that you are the victor in people's eyes no matter what the outcome of the task might be. Tony did that. I was so proud of him! I actually had tears in my eyes. Now, they had lost two rounds out of three... but they still took on the third challenge. It was a boxing match in which Ranjeet took part, got beaten but again, he didn't back down.

And later when the Roadies came back, having lost all three rounds, came one of my favourite parts of the show and the season—the scroll which said, 'Proud of you. You lost all three competitions but you showed so much heart, you're winners not losers. These watches are for you... and say goodbye to Divya, she's leaving.'

Now, Divya was the only contestant who has ever been thrown out of the show in the history of *Roadies*. I threw her out. Because after what happened in Bangalore with her mad boyfriend, she came to the crew and demanded that we not show the footage of her boyfriend having come over. I told her that was out of the question. The contract said that anything can happen and anything that happens will be shown. A couple of days later, she came with a stamped paper saying, you guys will not show it. I shook my head. No, not happening. Then she made a phone call to her father and told him: 'I'm not comfortable here, not being fed properly and being made to wear clothes that I'm not comfortable in.' (Now, contestants' clothing is something I have been very particular about. For me, what they choose to wear indicates their personality. And I have never entertained any interference in that. In fact, before the shoot, I had had a fight with Hero Honda when they insisted that we make the contestants wear Hero Honda T-shirts. So there has never been a question of dictating what the contestants wear.)

The next thing I know, her dad called the crew! This was the first time my face came on *Roadies*. During this phone call, I got a mic fixed on me, a camera in my face. We had a less-than-calm conversation at the end of which I threw her out. Despite what her lawyer dad told me, I'd used the situation for great content.

We moved on to Pune, and Kriti Malhotra came in as a replacement for Divya.

We went on to Rajasthan, then Delhi, which is where we recorded the final *Roadies* song at the same studio where I'd shot the *Haath Se Haath Mila* song with Silk Route.

The journey went on. I still remember two or three of the final days of our shoot, though. The Roadies had to set up camp, and I couldn't camp with them. I remember feeling really bad and sulky at having to spend the night in a lonely hotel room, because these guys had all become my friends, and I, theirs.

The journey went on and we finally reached Chail. The Roadies reached Chail Palace after an excruciating trek and Luv Barunia, who had been a replacement for Iknoor, a hefty, overweight, unfit guy whom no one liked from day one, trekked the whole way, puffing and panting. He delayed the rest of the Roadies but he gave the trek his all...and finally, as he plonked himself right outside the Chail Palace, I remember him panting and asking the others, now do you consider me a Roadie? The sight of this kid seeking acceptance was both sweet and sad. But it was a thing of wonder, too, that he wanted to 'be' a Roadie. Even before the first season had aired. That meant something—for him, as for countless others after him, for whom it had become a code word for respect.

Now I'd like to clarify another misconception—that Rannvijay won *Roadies 1*. He didn't. There was no winner. Season 1 was not a competition, it was just a road trip. It was never meant to have a winner. We did have vote-outs though, because elimination is an integral part of any reality show. As an exercise, it is one that polarizes gangs, causes friction, promotes games...not to mention, it's up my alley: the dinner-party-civility theory? But Rannvijay didn't win the season. No one did. Everyone did.

On the last night, after pack-up, Miditech's Nikhil Alva came and addressed the crew. They had these miniature bikes that were given to every member of the cast and crew. I wasn't called, I wasn't given one. I felt really bad about it but I thought, fuck it. Maybe they were sending me a message or maybe it was their revenge.

But the fun part was, I'd invited Silk Route to Chail for the finale to just chill and party with us. Mohit Chauhan was singing folk songs sitting there at the bonfire. Open air, starry skies, guitar, folk songs. That was the end of the first season. Everyone partied. I hung out with Tony, Rannvijay and Ranjeet. We drank, then set out to find a beautiful picturesque place to pee. We were determined to hold it in until we'd found said beautiful place! Finally, we did—I think it was a cliff with a nice view or something.

I came back and went to Miditech's office in Delhi to supervise the editing of the first episode. I remember finding the edit quite weird, and learnt that Nivedith had gone to Milan to shoot a fashion show. Because that's what production houses do: the direction and editing teams are different. But that's not how I have worked. I have always wanted to sit in on my own edits, not edit someone else's work, because I have always shot something keeping a certain story or idea in mind, and with reality TV, you don't have a script to explain it. Anyway, I decided to sit in on the edits. The tapes with footage had been logged by the trainees at Miditech. Now, as I've mentioned before, logging tapes is basically noting down what's happening between counter time XYZ to counter time ABC on the tape. The logs of our shoot were, to put it mildly, *fucked*. So, I sat down, started logging the tapes myself, got an assistant to help. I'd gone back exactly where I had been many years ago, at TV18.

Today, *MTV Roadies* has eight or nine edit suites which are networked together, five or six producers, more editors, different ones for the day and the night. There I had only one room, one editor, one me, and twenty-six weeks. I'd spend eighteen to twenty hours every day at the edit table, where I believe that the show is made. What you finally see on TV is an edit. And with reality, there's no rigid structure to the storytelling. Also, since this show was the first of its kind, we could twist it any way we liked. I remember Nikhil had come up with tag lines and labels for each of the contestants in the first episode, so Tony was Biker Boy, Rannvijay was Superstud and so on. I came up with the idea of giving each of the Roadies a signature tune, which we'd use during crucial moments on the show. It added layers to the characters and their story.

We decided to shoot one last episode in Mumbai in ITC Grand Maratha. We brought everyone back except Divya. A lot of people had issues with each other, a lot of angst, because they had watched the show and seen the video diaries. Which made it very interesting! The surprise was that Hrithik Roshan would be there, because he was the brand ambassador for Hero Honda Karizma.

I met Hrithik at his hotel room, briefed him about the Roadies and the fact that seven of them would get bikes. And he turned around and said, I thought there were ten guys. I said, yeah but only the seven who had finished the journey would get bikes. Hrithik felt it was unfair. He had a word with the Hero Honda guys and they agreed. So, in the end, all ten Roadies received ten bikes, thanks to Hrithik Roshan.

It was a season I was very proud of. I had made friends, I had made up a show along with my crew with some help from the cast, too. But more than pride or anything else, I remember the absolute, undiluted joy I felt during this one particular journey.

After a night they had spent camping out in interior Karnataka, the Roadies had received a scroll which told them that they would be given no money today, but if they wanted it, they'd have to reach XYZ place by this time. They had no bikes, no money...they'd have to hitch-hike. The scroll ended at 'whatever you're thinking about the crew, same to you'. Yes, the scroll was my handiwork!

At this point, I still wasn't talking to the Roadies, but I was shooting them. They hitch-hiked a ride on a tempo and I got on, too, cameraman and all. It rained, the wind blew, these kids listened to 'Must Be the Money' on their iPods and later, while editing, we even set that part of the episode to the same track. It was just the nine of us, travelling, feeling the journey, the road spread out ahead. That journey, that drive, encapsulates Season 1 for me. I was not talking to them but I was with them, *one* of them.

A new VJ I'm proud of, and a season that still makes me cringe

So I walked into the MTV office after the final edit had wrapped up for *Roadies*, expecting a hero's welcome... and I was asked for my identity. They didn't recognize me. It felt awful but come to think of it, I couldn't blame the security at MTV. They hadn't seen me enough. I'd joined in February, by April I had left for the recce, then the auditions, then the forty-day journey. In my time of ten months at MTV, I'd been missing from office for eight months.

They may not have recognized me, but they knew my work. There was a sense at MTV that something really good had happened. At that point, MTV had three new properties: *Style Awards*, *Roadies*, and their first fiction show, *Kitni Mast Hai Zindagi*, an Ekta Kapoor production. The awards and the fiction show had both bombed. And *Roadies*, which had been the cheapest to produce, had done well. They felt good about it and they decided to do it once more. That whole journey again, with new people, new places and new experiences, I was really thrilled!

Actually, let's backtrack a bit to Delhi, and the final days of the *Roadies 1* edit. Rajiv had edited the song, and quite a few of the Roadies were in Delhi, since they were based there. This one night, we were all partying together and Rajiv met Rannvijay for the first time. Rajiv was generally chatting with Rannvijay when he got to know he was to join the army in about a month, and told him he ought to hold on, he had a chance at something—he could stay on at MTV. He asked me, and I agreed that he should try. Rannvijay went back and spoke to his parents about it. They couldn't understand it at all. Because Rannvijay belongs to the fifth generation of a family full of army officers, it's what they do. And for them—and it's amazing they feel this way—the army is a safe option! They don't understand life outside it. So they were quite distraught with his sudden change of heart. His mother called me in tears, saying the army is all we know, but tell me, what does it mean to be a VJ? What is the career like, what is the shelf life? I tried to reassure her that, while it was a chance-based career, he seemed to have a personality that could work. Her main concern was that he was letting go of a pensionable job for a profession that had no guarantees. I assured her that, while I could not promise a job or success here, if he were to succeed, he would earn more than his pension in less than five years. And if it didn't work out, he could always go back to the army after one year. His parents couldn't find fault with the plan, and gave him permission.

Anyway, back to Mumbai. I was excited about the second season and had started thinking about the route. I dismissed the idea of Kanyakumari to Kashmir as soon as I thought of it because we'd be crossing many of the states that we had been to already. My next thought—something I still want to do, but haven't been able to—was to travel to Pakistan. Start the journey in India, end it in Pakistan. Since it didn't happen, for Season 2, I had to settle for the Grand Trunk Road from Kolkata all the way to the Wagah border in Amritsar. All through, we kept trying to get visas and permissions, and if it had happened, we could have gone to Lahore. It was the first of my two dreams for *Roadies*, and the only one that still remains unfulfilled. The other was for the show to go international. It did. But Pakistan never happened. *Roadies* now regularly airs in Pakistan, so I suppose I'll have to be happy with that!

I was at the water fountain at MTV one day and General Manager, MTV, Alex Kuruvilla, walked up to me and said, 'Good work, Raghu. And good to know you're working on a second season. You ought to double your average ratings this time.' I replied with a: 'Yes, I will.' And I did. Season 2's ratings were exactly double of Season 1's. It's another matter, of course, that I wasn't proud of this season. Not one bit.

But let's start with the good stuff. I was still brainstorming, picking my own head about the season, when Cyrus Oshidar asked me a question that stunned me to silence: What *was* the funda of the tasks? What was the incentive? I didn't have an answer. The fact was that if these guys didn't feel like it, they could just refuse to do a task. There was no penalty, there was no incentive. I felt like I was back to square one. In Season 1, I'd had a fundamental question: why are they travelling on bikes? I'd found the answer myself. This time around, I had to find another answer. I did. I decided to make it a competition.

Now this is 2004, still very early on in the show. The idea was this: we would conduct online voting, let audiences vote for their favourite contestant and he or she would be given prize money of five lakh rupees. So if the contestant refuses to do a task, he may lose out on votes. And the votes would have to happen only once the show went on air, because it was a delayed telecast.

◆

We all sat in for a meeting, both MTV and Miditech, and I told them this time I needed a full-time presenter. There was a lot more I could do with a full-time VJ when it came to tasks and vote-outs. Since all the MTV VJs were in the music/comedy space, I decided they wouldn't work for *Roadies*. I needed somebody with the personality that would reflect the show. I had someone in mind. Rannvijay. I thought he'd have credibility since he's been a Roadie. I remember Karthik Chintamani got very excited and liked the story Rannvijay would bring with him— army kid joins a bike reality show, goes all the way, does all the tasks, then leaves the army, comes back to become a presenter. I was asked to give him an audition. Rannvijay, by this time, had come to Mumbai and plonked himself in my house; he was pretty much living at my place. I'd grown very fond of him over the past few months. He had come close to being a younger brother. And I knew he was just as fond of me, though you know boys, they never say anything.

But one incident stands out in my memory, a sort of cementing of our equation. Soon after *Roadies 1*, I remember we'd all gone partying to this place called Pluto in Vasant Kunj: Tony, Rajiv, Rannvijay, Ranjit, Kriti Malhotra, Natasha Gulati, Natasha Rodrigues and me. The three girls were the only women in the club. They got recognized by some people, and were having a good time. But this is Delhi, so something was bound to happen. A couple of guys took me for the leader of the group, maybe because I looked older, and called me out. There were six guys outside, drunk and talking shit. I was the only guy representing the group that had the only girls in the club. They kept asking me if I knew who they were and who they knew. Typical Delhi stuff. I sensed trouble. Asking them to wait for two minutes, I somehow scampered back in, grabbed Tony, Rannvijay and Ranjeet, told them to take the girls, take the car, and get the hell out. Tony and Ranjeet took the girls and left instantly. Rajiv stayed back with me. Now, the girls leaving annoyed the hell out of the guys. The shit hit the fan, and what may have been a little scuffle now became a free-for-all fist fight. Soon, there were easily thirty people surrounding Rajiv and me. It wasn't an equal fight; I was getting grabbed, punched, kicked…my kurta got ripped, Rajiv's shirt was torn. Then I saw Rannvijay; he had stayed back and dove in, blocking people from us, taking hits for me, for Rajiv. I remember being scared for him, because even though he is a solid guy, he was a kid and I felt responsible for him. I yelled at him to leave but he wouldn't move out. Not without the two of us. And this I respect. The three of us kept getting thrashed, and eventually managed to get out. This incident brought me and Rannvijay closer still.

So, back to Rannvijay's audition. I sat with him, told him my fundas about presenting, anchoring. I've worked with so many VJs and presenters; I've seen the good ones, the not-so-good ones. For two days, we had long sessions at home after work. Finally, I auditioned him. Actually, before that, I appointed myself as his stylist, went out, bought him a lovely flowery shirt. And I shot him reading links off a teleprompter, and I shot him interviewing Tony without a script—oh yeah, Tony was also around—and I shot him interviewing me. I then made sure the MTV top brass watched the edit of the audition, not the actual footage, so that it gave me the freedom to knock off shots which weren't up to the mark. Anyway, the audience does not see the out-takes, and for me, the MTV guys were my audience for this and I put Rannvijay's best foot forward.

They liked him, and agreed to try him for one season.

◆

There was another discussion happening at this time between Karthik and Nikhil about how the show would rate better if it aired twice a week instead of once. It made no sense to me. I felt that not only were we taking a risk in assuming that viewers would tune in twice but I also has serious concerns about how we'd manage to double our output from one episode to two per week.

And then they revealed their masterplan: I'd have a separate edit team. So I would keep sending the tapes back, and the edit teams— groups of seven to eight people—would work in shifts to deliver two episodes a week. I had a problem with this, my usual problem: how would the editor know what I had in mind when I was taking a particular shot? It's a question that never got answered.

They went ahead with this masterplan and I must say, it was the worst decision that could have been taken. *Roadies 2*, in my opinion, is a shit season, and I'm actually ashamed to be associated with it. By the time I came back from the shoot, I couldn't bear to watch the episodes, they were such crap! With weird, inappropriate Bollywood numbers in the background put in just for the fuck of it. Boring edits because no one had the time to fine-tune them, because we had to go on air twice a week *and* go on air *as* the journey was being shot. Bad, bad end product!

The only good thing about the season was Rannvijay becoming

an anchor. Having being instrumental in convincing his parents as well as MTV about his talent as an anchor, I was heavily invested in his career as a VJ. And sitting behind the camera, watching him, I couldn't help but remember his journey in the first season, and how here he was, representing the show with a mic on the same channel. It was a proud moment for me.

◆

By this season, I'd made it clear that Hindi was to be the only language of communication, because I wanted to make my show fully Hindi. Now these guys tried to hold the conversation in Hindi in Pune, but it would inevitably go like this: when a contestant would walk in, they'd ask him for his name, he'd most likely say, 'Myself XYZ.' And they'd ask in halting Hindi, 'Hindi bolni aati?' And he would reply in broken English, 'Yes I English talk.' Anyway, the point is, I wasn't happy. It still meant the contestant wouldn't speak in the tongue he was most comfortable in, so I told them that and they said, 'Well, then *you* come on board.' So that's why I'm on the panel of judges at the personal interview. Because I can speak Hindi.

I sat in with David and Karthik; this was the time when auditions weren't aired. They weren't even considered content, it was a necessity for the show, so nothing was done because it had to 'look' good. I remember David, eccentric as he was, had an unusually soft voice. He wouldn't talk much but when he did, he made the other person quite nervous. I picked up my cues somewhat from David. Talking softly, saying things bluntly with a deadpan face, helped in intimidating the contestant and in turn, getting to know what we needed to about their personality.

An interesting thing happened during the Kolkata auditions: I lost my temper with a contestant for the first time. A guy called Varun came in to audition and David asked him, 'Why are you here?' And Varun turned around and asked him, 'Why are *you* here?' David stayed calm, but I lost it. I remember that being among the first few times

I really lost my temper because we had been sitting there for quite a while by then. And all I wanted to do was to get to know this guy who was giving attitude to my senior. I screamed my head off at him and shut him up. Who do you think you are, it's obvious why we're here, looking for a cast, not for idiots like you! But interestingly, because he got a reaction like that from me, Varun was selected.

This tendency of mine to lose my temper has really helped us pick the people for the show over the years. This was something I discovered about myself. I can say stuff which can rattle people, and also make intelligent guesses about what kind of people they are... and I have been right most of the time. To top this, when I lost my temper, the interactions came alive. They were anything but boring. I remember one contestant from Chandigarh who, after he came out of the personal interview and was asked what he thought of each of the judges, mentioned me and said, 'Life mein kissi se bhi pangaa lena par iss aadmi ke saath bilkul mat lena!' I was starting to make a reputation for myself.

Auditions done, we came back to Mumbai and I had another meeting with Cyrus O. True to form, he gave me a brilliant idea within three seconds. If I liked many guys at the auditions, I ought to call them for a second round of auditions, where I would actually make them do stuff. If they claimed they were bindass, if they claimed they were fun, or had an easy way with people, I ought to test them on that basis. Shoot it, and air it. The idea blew my mind, and it was also the first time we aired an audition.

One audition I remember clearly is Ayushmaan Khurana's. He'd been recommended to us by MTV; he had auditioned for *Kitni Mast Hai Zindagi*, and though he hadn't made it, they had liked him. Ayushmaan had also made it to the final level of *Popstars 2* at Channel [V]. His personal interview was rather interesting. I wasn't angry, I wasn't rude...I was just a little bitchy with him. There was Cyrus O, Karthik, Anil Nair and me on the panel. He was refreshingly frank and forthcoming, disarmingly honest. Saying what he had in mind but not offensively so. It was endearing. I remember telling him that as an actor, with his put-on charm and his put-on smile, he may be interesting but that wasn't the real him, he said no, this is me! And I muttered, 'Really? Then God help us all.' Everyone guffawed, and poor kid, he didn't know what hit him. I gave him the feeling that I didn't like him at all. Every answer he gave me, I turned it around in such a way that he felt he had given a wrong answer.

The auditions were rather eventful. I sat in on the panel, and my 'rude' image sealed. We aired a bit of the auditions with Rannvijay as presenter. By then, Rannvijay had met VJ Anusha Dandekar. Several VJs would make appearances during the auditions, and Rannvijay and Anusha had a pretty obvious chemistry. I was happy for them, of course, but initially, I wasn't sure about her, because I felt they came from very different backgrounds. All the girls in MTV were good at their jobs but they were all about style, looks and being celebrities… they just inhabited a very different world. But they were happy, so I was happy for Rannvijay.

◆

We got to Kolkata, the first point of the journey. Rannvijay and I entered the room that we were sharing. We were staying at a small place, nothing fancy. He was so excited; he had hosted the auditions but this was the real deal. It was his second *Roadies* journey but his first as a presenter. I remember he threw his bag on the floor and then launched himself in the air to jump on to the bed… BAM! There was barely any mattress, just a thick bed sheet over a hard wooden bed. It hit him so hard, it knocked the breath out of his body. I was laughing so hard as he kept gasping and laughing. It was like, 'Hey, I am a VJ…BAM!' I remember that being his entry into the world of VJ-ing. The other thing I remember is going shopping with him, I hate shopping but he loves it. We went to the market in the evening; no one recognized us then, so we spent hours there…and came back with a plastic airgun and pellets. We then spent all night trying to shoot at different targets in the room from the door.

The night before the *Roadies* journey was to be officially flagged off, we had a crazy MTV party at Tantra. I wanted to turn in early, but Rannvijay wanted to spend time with Anusha. I told him he had to sleep early to make the early morning flag-off, but it so happened that he managed to convince me. So we partied all night, stayed up all night. And the next morning, it was a very tired, very sleep-deprived Rannvijay who flagged the journey off.

Though it wasn't a season I particularly enjoyed and the Grand Trunk Road didn't really give us much scope to experiment, I clearly recall one place we visited during this journey: Bodh Gaya. This was the time in my life when I was coming out of my spiritual crisis; I was now following Nichiren Daishonin's Buddhism, and I'd started chanting. I liked the fact that, more than a religion, it was a philosophy. Coincidentally, the *Roadies* journey went through Bodh Gaya where Siddhartha became Gautam Buddha. What appealed to me about Buddhism was that it's based on logic; it's not a theology but a philosophy, and there's no practise of praying to a vindictive God, unlike some other religions. Everything was fine till the time at a prayer meeting, some of the followers started discussing how anyone who opposes Buddhism is pure evil. That broke it for me. It doesn't matter what the fucking philosophy is, but when people get together, they start thinking, 'I am better than everybody else, only I know the truth.' I'm not that guy, so I stopped following it. I don't chant anymore but if I have a religious philosophy, it's Nichiren Daishonin's Buddhism.

One of the bizarre tasks on this journey, my idea (naturally), was that our contestants donate sperm...and we had on board with us, our very own Vicky Donor, only we didn't know then! So Ayushmaan Khurana made his glittering TV debut donating sperm in 2004. Who knew he would win all the awards in 2012 while doing the same thing in a movie! What are the odds, huh?

◆

Anyway, back to Season 2. I had decided that since this was Rannvijay's first time as presenter in front of the camera, my boy needed make-up. After all, every VJ got it and I didn't want him to be at a disadvantage! Miditech didn't have a make-up person, so, just like I'd appointed myself stylist, I thought I'd do the make-up too. We asked one of the girls on our team, Tanushree, to help. She drew up a list with alien words like foundation, moisturizer, etcetera, on it. I remember walking into a store in Kolkata and being laughed at by the female shop attendants. We didn't even know the names of the products, forget brands! Rannvijay finally called up Anusha who instantly took charge, spoke to the manager and soon we were walking back with our loot. The next day we shot something in the night—Rannvijay had to blindfold the Roadies, lead them to an open area with mashaals all around and a bed of fire which they had to walk on. He looks ghost-white in that episode, because I had done his make-up. Later, while watching the episode on air, I could only think of my relatives in Andhra Pradesh who would apply generous amounts of talcum powder before heading out. Eventually, the powder, along with rivulets of sweat, would form a strange mixture. But even they didn't look as comical as Rannvijay did that night! And I felt terrible. All other VJs had make-up artists and air-conditioned studios and my poor boy had to make do with me.

Rannvijay didn't start off being the VJ he is today. What I noticed in his stint as presenter for the first time was that he was trying to be me. He probably wanted to emulate me because he looked up to me; he felt I *was* the show somewhere, and that's why he became me on camera. But this just resulted in him looking morose, morbid even, on camera, while off it he was his usual bouncy, fun self. He got better, though, as the days went by. He was able to take the brief and stick to it. We usually don't cut in-between a shot and with him, despite my expecting that I would have to do a retake, I didn't have to. The one thing I really liked about him, and still do, is that when he's on camera, I can convey any change I want in the middle of a shot, and he can deliver it right then and there, while the camera is still rolling.

✦

I told Rajiv about this when I spoke to him, so he could pass it on to the bigwigs at MTV. Hold on a minute, I haven't told you the story behind Rajiv working with MTV as well, right? Okay, let's backtrack a bit to our birthdays earlier that year, in 2004. 15 April dawned, I had a nice big cake waiting for me at the MTV office, and in keeping with our tradition every single year, Rajiv had come down from Delhi to spend our birthday with me. It was great fun. I introduced him to everyone, and when Karthik and Cyrus met him, they exchanged looks, called him to their office…and offered him a job. At this time, Rajiv was running a production house, Shift Focus, in Delhi. But he moved bag and baggage to Mumbai. Now, I did take it as a huge compliment that MTV had such regard for me as a professional that they hired Rajiv without so much as an interview. But in no time, Rajiv proved to be even better than their expectations. So, anyway, I'd call him from time to time, share titbits of Rannvijay's foray into presenting: how he was good, how he didn't need too many cuts to get it right, etcetera.

The journey had moved to Lucknow when Rajiv called me. I was still travelling with Rannvijay. Rajiv said he had some news, but to try and not react in front of Rannvijay. Rannvijay had been confirmed as a presenter with MTV, and they were making a contract. He suggested I didn't tell him right away, to have some fun with it instead. I was thrilled and suppressed a smile.

That day went by, we went to our hotel room, this time a big one with a double bed, a cupboard and a terrace. I remember sitting Rannvijay down and asking him, now that you've missed out on your chance of going into the army, what if you don't make it on TV? What then? Rannvijay was quiet for a while and said his next option was to do an MBA. I asked him which university, he said maybe correspondence, named the course, and when I started asking him about, it kind of gave him the idea that I was trying to break bad news to him. Finally, I turned around and told him, quite simply, that he didn't have to consider the options because he had been made a VJ, congratulations. Silence. I have this image in my head of Rannvijay standing in front of me with a big smile, then clamping his hand to his mouth, tears in his eyes, tears in my eyes. It wasn't just him becoming a VJ, it was two friends, two comrades, achieving something. It was my achievement as much as it was his. I was laughing, and he didn't say anything. He just spun around the room…then went into the cupboard and shut it. Then he came out, hugged me; we did cartwheels and Michael Jackson steps. It was awesome. We had nothing to celebrate it with then, but I just remember it as being this really, really happy moment.

◆

The last thing that happened at the end of the Season 2 journey was nothing happy, though. It was a huge fucking screaming match. Who screamed? That's easy. Me. Why? Well, Rannvijay had gone on a whole *Roadies* journey for the second time, this time presenting it, but he still nursed a craving to ride the Karizma. Miditech had extra bikes and he asked me, then asked them whether he could ride one, and every time they'd tell him 'later, later'. Finally, he was told he could ride one but after the journey was wrapped up. It didn't make sense, but I told him to go with it, respect them. Done. Season 2 ended with aplomb at the Wagah border; I'd just run all the way to the border, flag in hand, and Poro yelled: 'Pack up!' And now Rannvijay sprung up from nowhere, super excited. 'Raghu, *now* can I ride a bike?' I said, of course he could. Tanushree from production was around and I told her to organize it, and walked off to congratulate the team. Minutes passed and when I looked back, Rannvijay was standing there, looking crestfallen. I asked him about the bike and Rannvijay said, his voice shaking, that they'd said no. As he said it, he suddenly started crying. And watching him cry, my blood started boiling—this was my kid brother crying because he felt shitty, rejected, humiliated.

I told him to hold on a minute and I started running towards the crew. I let them have it. The volume at which I screamed, the language

I used, I was in full Munirka form. Who the FUCK do you guys think you are, what the FUCK is your problem, when you've told me, told him, he can ride a bike at the end of the season, which makes no logical sense in the first place, but which we fucking respected. Now the season's over, pack-up has been announced, *now* what the fuck are you doing! And I took all their names individually, fuck you XYZ, fuck you ABC, don't show me your faces. I grabbed Rannvijay with me, took him to the crew bus—we refused to sit in our car—and we sat there, with me fuming.

A while later, Poro and Tanushree came in with the crew, saying, yaar Raghu come on… I refused to let them in, threatene to punch them. They said they'd made a mistake, and agreed to let him ride the bike, begged me to let it go. I wondered why they couldn't have just agreed to it earlier without creating a scene. Rannvijay got the keys, he took off. But I *still* don't know why they refused him initially. I guess, on some level, it was them being vindictive. I was from Miditech, and now I was at MTV, and they probably felt I was lording over them. They had this one chance to get their own back by bullying Rannvijay. Bad idea.

Well, the season ended, Rannvijay got to ride his bike. I attended the wrap party at Amritsar, then took a train to Delhi the next morning, I was really missing Kuhu. She was in Delhi, having been hired by Miditech to be casting director for *Indian Idol* which was just launching that year. Casting directors are the ones who do the preliminary auditions. Their job is to pick the best guys and the worst guys before the actual official judges get to see them. This is just a screening process, it doesn't make it to the telecast. Anyway, I got to Nehru Stadium where the auditions were being held; I meant to surprise Kuhu, so I called Nivedith, who was the director, and told him that I had come but not to tell Kuhu. It was all hush-hush. Nivedith called Kuhu out, I was there to surprise her, it all went off perfectly well and then out of nowhere Nivedith said, why don't you go in, audition, and pick a fight with the judges. I asked why? Nivedith said, dude, it'll be kickass!

Nivedith had been a part of the auditions for Season 2 and my temper had made an impression on him. He thought it would be good content for someone to give it back to the judges. I didn't see the point to it, but Kuhu said why not. Now, the judges were Farah Khan, Anu Malik and Sonu Nigam, who, through the show, were also going to publicize their film, Farah Khan's directorial debut *Main Hoon Naa*. They said, no need to get in line, just go into the room. Everyone knew it was a set-up except for the judges.

I went in, they said I had two minutes. I started stretching. Farah Khan asked me what the hell I was doing, I told her I needed to warm up. I warmed up, then I sang 'Aaj Jaane ki Zidd Na Karo'. Anu Malik stopped me midway. He started saying something in a roundabout way but now I stopped him midway, asked him yes or no. He said no, and I asked, 'Yeh baat tameez se nahi bol sakte the?!' Basically, I just picked a fight out of nothing, like I was asked to. I left the room, there was a camera pointed in my face. Now, of course I knew the crew, so I kept up the act; I made a gun sign and made a shooting sound on my way out. Later, I was told, the judges had felt threatened. It was quite funny really. I came out, and Mini Mathur—the show's host—was there. She didn't know me, but knew of me, and I kept up the act with her as well, telling her that the judges were being rude.

Interestingly, this video went viral on YouTube recently and turned into a controversy. I completely get it. Because, right now, *I* am the rudest man on television, so for *me* to have called *them* rude... Well, what can I say, the fans just lapped it up.

Anyway, Season 2: shot by me, not edited by me. By the time I returned to Mumbai, MTV had moved office from Tardeo to Parel. Same shit, new day. With the new office, new security, the who-are-you ritual played out all over again! To cut a long story short, we had a meeting. Sure it was a fuck-all, shameful season (in my opinion), but the ratings had doubled. Rajiv and I sat at a meeting with MTV's top brass, and Karthik asked whether I'd like to produce Season 3 in-house. I said I'd rather nail myself to the wall of a burning building.

Four new producers, a healthy dose of madness, and *Roadies* comes into its own

It was a lovely evening, my parents were visiting, and Rajiv and I had our first fight. Actually it was just me raving and ranting and him listening. All because he'd said yes. When I'd said no.

Back to the MTV office, back to the conference hall, where I'd been asked to produce *Roadies 3* in-house. I had refused because I had no respect or patience for the so-called calibre of the so-called producers employed by the channel. What did they have to do anyway? A VJ stood against a chroma (green) screen, a scriptwriter would write the lines, an editor would edit, they would dispatch the tape and be called producers! Really? I hated their Mumbai attitude, these kids who dressed well, talked with an accent, but looking at their work, I wouldn't even hire them as assistant producers!

To make a show like *Roadies*, you needed an army who had that kind of mentality: a mad bloodlust. Because on *Roadies*, you did go to war. I thought I'd made my point at the conference, and I actually had. But then the only person who could disagree with me, disagreed with me. Rajiv said, no Raghu, I think we can do it in-house. And now everyone started chanting with Rajiv, yeah, yeah Rajiv thinks we can, we can do it in-house. It was decided. Sealed.

And so I went at Rajiv, and my parents were scared because I was so livid. What the FUCK were you thinking?! I asked Rajiv. Do you even know the kind of situation you've put me in? These fuckers are useless and you know it! I'm going to have to put together a show with *these* people! Rajiv heard me out calmly and then when I paused to breathe, he calmly said, 'I will give you four people who can do it. They have potential.'

◆

And that's how the team came together, the team that made the show what it is today.

Team Member No. 1: The inimitable Bumpy/Nature Baba, whom I had hired from BBC after Season 1 just to produce the single Season 2 audition episode. He did a great job, MTV offered him a permanent job, and he stayed on. Now, a word about Bumpy. He's mad, a total whack job, with a real passion for food. He would spend hours at the MTV office, surfing the net, looking up recipes, taking printouts, putting them in a folder, just so he could go home and cook. As for his dedication, he took the term hard-working to another level altogether. Right after Season 2, MTV had a new show called *Scam TV*. It was a rubbish show based on a stupid concept, but anyway, that's not the point. Bumpy was handling it all alone and once Rajiv, who had also joined MTV by now, had gone to check out the edits. Bumpy was editing at some godforsaken studio, where in the room next to his, a Tamil porn film was being edited. Anyway, when Rajiv walked in, he saw a pair of boxers dangling from one corner. Bumpy claimed it as his. What was it doing there? Apparently, Bumpy the Great had worn the underwear on day one. On day two, he had turned it around and worn it again. When day three dawned, Bumpy realized the underwear had only two sides…and it was promptly discarded. Conclusion 1: Hard-working man doesn't go home despite underwear emergencies. Conclusion 2: Hard-working man is mad man.

Team Member No. 2: Chhotu. Yes, Ranjeet Phatak. I was really sure of Chhotu from day one because he's the ultimate yes man. I have never heard him say no. If you ask him to come up with ten ideas, Chhotu wouldn't even be able to come up with one. In fact, if I told the team, let's brainstorm tomorrow, come up with five ideas, the rest of the team would actually come up with surplus ideas and coach him: here are five ideas, this is what you should say. He's not the creatives guy, but he *is* the execution guy. If I tell him I want XYZ and I have a specific visual in mind, Chhotu can, I kid you not, execute it *exactly* as I had envisioned it. He's a fantastic member to have on a team. If you tell him that, for the next two days, he will be shooting day and night for sunrise and sunset shots, he'll nod and say, okay, chalega. I love that quality.

Team Member No. 3: Debbie, a.k.a. Danger Debbie, David Polycarp's sister, who was just as soft-spoken, and just as eccentric and weird. Now if David is soft-spoken, Debbie mostly doesn't even talk. All her communication is non-verbal. One flick of an eyebrow, or one turn of the body, and she's made her point. She never ever loses her temper. Rumour: Debbie counts the number of times she chews her food, a rumour still believed to be true. Rumour created by: yours truly.

Team Member No. 4: Zulfiya. What do I say about Zulfiya? Remember how I always took notes when Saul spoke to me? Well, Zulfiya took enough notes for everybody; she would even make copies and distribute it to the rest of the team. Zulfiya is such a happy soul, I didn't even have the heart to give her a nickname. She's a sweetheart, always smiling, always laughing, a plump bubble of positive energy floating around.

And, with her, the perfect team was created. My producers, Nature Baba, Chhotu, Danger Debbie and Zulfiya, went on to become very popular amongst *Roadies* fans, and Season 3 was, in many ways, the beginning of *Roadies* as we know it today. These guys coming in made all the fucking difference. They were ambitious, they wanted to do something interesting and they knew they'd have to unlearn a lot of shit. It changed the show. Another person I hired around this time was Ricky, also known now as Rickinaldo. Another hard-working, irreverent, completely mental guy.

A word about madness: it's a crucial job requirement, at least for me, because nothing interesting ever came out of someone normal. My producers weren't normal and the team was a perfect nightmare. And I'm very convinced that if *these* guys hadn't come on board *Roadies*, I wouldn't be writing this book today. Really.

I got them to watch Season 1 and Season 2—Season 1 so they knew what the show was, Season 2 so they realized what we shouldn't do ever again.

Hang on, though. There was another element to the mad mix as well. Rajiv had shot an international travel show called *D-Tour*, which was basically about five beauty queens from five continents travelling together. It was a project for MTV International and MTV had hired an executive producer called Janet Price from it. Janet hadn't worked with an Indian crew before, but Bumpy and Rajiv were the only Indians on the crew and she fell in love with both of them. She hadn't seen this kind of hard work or whackiness, ever. So Rajiv decided that Janet ought to come on board *Roadies* as well. He wanted me to direct it, to invest in the show creatively, and for these guys to handle the rest of it. If Janet hadn't come on board, I don't know if *Roadies* would have turned out like this. I learnt so much from her; she made me look at even basic things differently and contributed a lot to finding a method in the madness. She'd sit with legal, production, and every department, do all it took to make our work easier, better.

The team was put together—a team that met my required levels of madness—and now the brainstorming began.

◆

I had decided that I didn't want to do viewer votes with Season 3 as we had done with Season 2. I have a basic problem with this format of viewer voting on reality shows, but let's start with their panel of experts. *How* does a Bollywood actress qualify as an expert on singing?! But I get the logic behind it: it's a formula. You need one hot girl, one young star and one veteran to add some credibility to the mix. All right, fine,

I give you that, but then why are the viewers deciding who wins? Are they the experts? If they are, why do you have the panel in the first place? This is a fucking loophole in the whole talent show business. I understand the concept. It's a revenue generator and it promotes a feeling of ownership and participation from the viewers. But I hate it. I don't think the viewer has any business deciding the winner because viewer votes can never be fair. They will vote for someone from their own region, or someone who looks good. This system leaves room for this sort of bullshit. So, for Season 3, I was very sure I didn't want viewer votes. How, then, would I pick a winner?

I also wasn't satisfied with voting being the incentive for a Roadie to do the tasks. The incentive needed to be much more tangible. Therefore, money tasks. Not only would they promote competition but I loved the dynamic of people working together as a team for money but only one of them walking away with it in the end. To help your chances of being that winner, I came up with immunity tasks. What I loved about immunity tasks was that, while the money tasks promoted team spirit, the immunity tasks broke the feeling of camaraderie and made them stand against one another. Though I had all these ideas, the format I came up with left a lot to be desired, with money and immunity tasks sprinkled randomly through the journey. It was Janet who suggested that we have a consistent format where each episode had a money task and an immunity task, leading to a vote-out.

Next we had to decide the route. We settled on what later became one of my all-time favourite journeys: Jaisalmer to Leh. Exotic and adventurous. I was really looking forward it. But before that, the auditions.

Today, thousands—no, *lakhs* of people register online for *Roadies*, several thousands participate in *Roadies Battleground*—turn up for the personal interview, get selected. But back then, in 2006, I would actually send my crew out to discos, nightclubs and coffee shops to keep their eyes and ears open. If they found anyone interesting, they'd just ask them if they were interested in being on TV and that the *Roadies* auditions were happening at XYZ venue on XYZ day. I look at it fondly now. Yeh bhi karna padta tha.

◆

Actually, let's backtrack to a meeting before the auditions where MTV's top brass, because they were enjoying springing surprises on me this season, turned around and said, bro, let's put the auditions on air. I said no. No way. I didn't want potential contestants to be prepared, I didn't want them to be able to see what to expect; I wanted to maintain the secrecy, the sanctity of the auditions, so that I could take them by surprise. But now, MTV put me in a spot. They were pitching for more money from our sponsors, Hero Honda. One way of getting more money was to make more episodes. I fought, they fought, we exchanged words. I lost. If I'd won it, auditions would not be on air today. I still hate the fact that they are aired, by the way.

In fact, truth be told, I hate the whole process and I'd decided after Season 8 that I never wanted to do another personal interview. I'd rather work as a waiter at a dhaba than do these interviews. It's the worst feeling ever—don't ask me why, it just is! But airing it turned out to be the best decision for *Roadies*. Ah, well.

Now that we'd decided we were to air the auditions, who would be on the panel? Karthik, for sure. Anil Nair, Ashok Cherian (who was handling the marketing) and me. Me, well, because I speak Hindi. And secondly, I make the show so I know the kind of contestants I want. Today, I know everyone comes prepared for the personal interview; people even script and rehearse their answers. My job is to sit at that table, look this contestant in the eye, see through their act, strip it down, and put them in a spot. And when they're *in* that spot, how they act or react, how they choose to express themselves, *that* is what is of most interest to me. While interviewing a person, I am thinking of potential video diaries. Does this person express themselves interestingly? Cases in point: Season 5 winner, Ashutosh Kaushik, was a very interesting storyteller. I am sure many of you remember the story of how he ripped open his shirt to escape cops in Saharanpur. Then there's the Season 9 winner, Vikas. Contrary to popular belief, we did not select him because he abused us and returned, or because he had a *Roadies* tattoo. We selected him because the second time around, he told us such entertaining, kickass stories, I knew I'd found my man. *That's* what I'm looking for.

But the truth is, I hate the interviews. Really, really hate them. The only thing I like about them is that I get a chance to talk about issues that matter; it's a platform for me like no other. It was, and still is, the only forum for young people to talk about real issues that they face on a daily basis. If you watched or remember the auditions from Season 3, you'll recall me as unimpressed, deadpan for most part. Whenever I did start talking or questioning the contestant, the vibe in the room would suddenly change, the air would almost thicken. I also discovered that I had a penchant for making predictions about the people that came in for the interviews. I don't know how I did it, but I could. I guess it's because I have interacted with young people very intimately throughout my career. I would love to take credit for it, to call myself an antaryaami, and claim that I possess a great ability. But the truth—and let me warn you, it is a heartbreaking truth—is the young are damn predictable and subscribe to specific stereotypes. Anything from their dress to their attitude will tell me a lot about who they are. The other quality I'd discovered was that I could really make the interviewees uncomfortable without even raising my voice or changing my expression. I just could.

Only one interview stands out in this season. Laveen Bharadwaj from Chandigarh. You may remember him as this short, heavyset, long-haired guy wearing ripped jeans that had more holes than cloth, wearing a sleeveless denim vest, and a gym belt tossed over one shoulder like a WWE championship belt. Being interviewed by Rannvijay right before his interview, I could hear him saying the judges had better not mess with him. Main eent ka jawaab patthar se doonga. It seemed as if this guy was coming in to pick a fight, and I wasn't about to back down.

He came in, and in the course of the interview, I read out a question in the form: what was not so cool about India and Indians? To which he had written: 'Nothing is cool about India or Indians'. This got my goat. One look at him and I knew he didn't even have a passport, forget about having gone abroad. Now truth be told, I'm not a patriot, though I have spent a few Independence days sitting with my guitar at the Indo-Pak border, playing for the soldiers. But you know the tag line for Kerala, 'God's Own Country'? I'd believe that to be true for India, with one addition: Devil's Own People. I love India, I hate Indians for what they have done to it. That's okay, I can say it. But if someone says that to me, if someone criticizes India, my fists go up, I lose it.

Now, Rannvijay was sitting off camera but in the room during this interview. Since he comes from a family of army men who have defended the country through generations, gone to war for somebody like this fucker, my anger started rising and before I knew it, I was going full tilt, completely subduing him with my tone. He broke down, howled like crazy. Turned out, he had had an abusive upbringing because of which he was very maladjusted in life and his appearance was his defence mechanism. Inside he was very fragile. Which had all the makings of a brilliant contestant. I decided that it would be great to watch him. I later got up, apologized, hugged him and comforted him. And then I cast him.

This interview had gotten very intense: the screaming, the change in his attitude, the complete breakdown and the story that came out, and the final reconciliation. It was amazing, and it was television gold, the first time such a thing had happened on camera.

He came out from his interview saying, judges se kuch chhupa nahi sakte, woh sab jaante hain. The myth of the judges being all-knowing was starting to grow. Once this kid left the room, I remember everyone turned to me, saying, what happened, Raghu? I shrugged and replied, I don't know, I lost my temper. There was a silence and then a flurry of pleas: awesome, lose it more, lose it more!

I did.

◆

So anyway, bags packed, Roadies selected, the journey began. This time I had bid a (joyful) farewell to Alok, the old warhorse, and Akshay Rajput, a.k.a. Kaandi, had stepped into his place. I was *so* happy with him from day one because Akshay, despite not having a plan, despite making it all up as we went along, fucking got what Alok did not get in two seasons! Let the moment happen. If we get it on camera, great; if we don't get it on camera, then let's work harder next time. For the first time, I had a DoP who *got* me. The camera attendants who turned camera operators with *Roadies 3* are the guys I work with to this day. They are the guys most in demand in the television industry in Mumbai because they know their shit. Pakiya, Fanaa, Jimbo, Shanta. *Roadies* fans know them now. Getting them was another fantastic fucking move. Crucial, really crucial. The guys that work with me, they start working *like* me; something of me rubs off on them. The same held for Akshay's crew. It was like having ten Akshays at one go.

The first task for the Roadies was a treasure hunt; they had to find their way through sand dunes to their helmets. The previous day, I had traced out the entire path accurately using a compass, then set up directions and clues. That night, around midnight, I woke up wondering how the fuck this task was going to happen. Because the sands shift, leaving absolutely no landmarks. I had to do it all over again the next morning. Before the sun rose, I was at the desert, retracing the route. What I realized after this first task was that I was fortunate to have tried out the task again that morning. If I hadn't done that, we wouldn't have been able to carry out the first task. I could shoot it because I fucking knew it; I knew how the task would happen, what the problems could be. It was technically the first time I had tried out a task and I decided to keep doing it. I operate from a fear of failure and that makes me work harder. Anything that's nagging me I will go at again and again and again until it's sorted, and it needs to be sorted before the shoot. *Roadies 3* has had the toughest tasks

I have ever been a part of.

Why do I need to try out tasks, you ask? So that I can figure out whether the task is doable or not. Of course, I have an adventure crew I work with but they're professionals; their levels of fear and capability are very different from a normal person's. My levels are closer. Plus my philosophy has always been being in charge and leading from the front. I am responsible for everyone, and I take my job as a safety officer, very, very seriously. It wasn't even a studied thought, just an instinct that made me test the task myself that first time…and every time from then on.

◆

By the end of the journey, I remember Janet Price telling me, 'Raghu, I think you can do anything. I don't think you're scared of anything at all.' Was I? Not scared? This may a good time to confess that I was, in fact, SHIT scared. Of every single task. Every single time. There. I said it. But I found my ways to work around the fear. I used music. During Season 3, Rannvijay and I had gotten into this habit of listening to inspiring songs. Our favourites were 'Yeh Honsla' from *Dor*, particularly the line, 'Raah pe kaante bikhre agar, unpar toh phir bhi chalna hi hai.' That line fucking inspired me, told me, this is a shitty thing I have to do, but I have to do it! The other song was the title track from *Lakshya*. A couple of lines here go: 'Barse chaahe ambar se aag, lipte chaahe pairon se naag, paayega jo lakshya hai tera. Lakshya toh har haal mein paana hai.' Now, *that's* a line with an unreasonable demand; it's non-negotiable while being inspiring. We'd listen to these songs every day and while trying out the tasks, these lines would be playing in my head.

If the songs didn't work, I switched off my brain. The brain will tell you to stop, it will say, this is stupid, this is ridiculous, your feet won't move, you won't be able to do it. Fear paralyses you. I learnt how to switch it off just by not paying attention to my thoughts. It became a routine. Switch brain off, gear up for the task, play song in head, perform task. Over and out.

A fun, mad season, Season 3 was largely a pleasant journey until Akshay and I had our argument. It was minor actually, I don't even remember why we fought, but I all I know is that a routine was born that day. Akshay joined me as DoP in Season 3, and since then, all the way till *Roadies X*, Akshay and I have got to have one big brawl per season. It usually occurs by the end of the journey, and by the time we're done, neither of us can remember why we fought in the first place. The rest of the crew even waits for it to happen now; they consider it a fucking shagun, a good omen.

The finale happened, the journey ended, Parul Shahi was voted winner, when we received a call from Mumbai. It had been raining. Rather heavily. I shrugged it off, saying Mumbai mein toh baarish hoti rehti hai, big deal. Phone lines are down? Okay, that's fine! It was 26 July 2005, and while the porous walls of mine and Kuhu's flat in Andheri (we were living together at the time) were getting flooded with rainwater, I partied away in Leh. The next morning, we boarded a flight to Delhi and then waited for our flight to Mumbai. And waited. For three whole days, two of which we nearly spent at the airport. And here, another routine began. I pulled out my guitar, the crew gathered around and I started singing. I started doing this quite a bit from Season 3 onwards. Any time we had free, I'd pick some strings, sing some, everyone would make requests, I'd comply…and in the process, the whole team would bond.

I walked home on day three or four of the deluge to find an excited Kuhu waiting for me. She wanted me to meet some of her new friends: Mohan (Kannan) and Chinku (Arijit Dutta). They later formed Agnee along with Koko (Kaustubh Dhawale). So I came back from *Roadies 3* and made friends for life, friends who would soon turn into the musical arm of *Roadies*. Season 3 may not be a favourite but it was a very, very special season. It's when *Roadies* truly evolved, found its identity. We were not yet close to being the biggest youth show in India, but we were well on our way. And what an adventurous, agonizing road it would prove to be.

No, yes, vows and the Kerala connection

Kuhu would have never married me if not for that Diwali holiday after Season 3 which I was told to take because she complained I didn't spend enough time with her… and which I didn't because I spent day and night holed up with the edits of Season 3. Basically, Kuhu would have never married me if not for the long, impossibly gruelling hours of the Season 3 edit.

A word about edits. Several people believe (rather foolishly) that a show like *Roadies* gets aired as it is being shot. Ridiculous, because think about it: if that were the case, how would we show you a preview of an episode for the coming week?! What you watch on your TV screens isn't what is shot, it is the edit. Let me explain. The journey episodes on *Roadies* are ideally shot on seven to eight cameras. Each of these cameras records nearly eighteen hours of footage every single day of the shoot. We shoot every episode over three days, so every episode has a raw footage of approximately five hundred hours. This footage has to be digitized before it is edited, which means you have to take the camera tape and record it in the computer hard drive. Which takes you around five hundred hours as well. Then you have to pick the angles of the footage you want, put them all together, and finally an episode is made. Every step of it is time consuming as it is, and during Season 3, soon after the journey, the rains happened, delaying us further.

So we shook things up a bit. Janet decided that since we had four producers, Bumpy, Chhotu, Zulfiya and Debbie each would take care of one episode. If Rannvijay followed my brief completely and did exactly as was expected of him while anchoring, my producers did just that with the editing. They fully justified Rajiv's faith in them; after all, he had recommended them. The quality of the edit, the way they went about it, could only be compared to the Season 1 edit which, as you may well remember, dear reader, was done by yours truly. And which I am extremely proud of. Just as I am proud of Season 3's edit.

We had four edit rooms, four producers, and audition and journey episodes. Each audition episode took two and a half weeks to edit, each journey episode took four. My producers lived in the edit rooms for those months. And while each of them handled one episode over four weeks, I had one edit room to myself. Every time an episode was ready, I would access it in my edit room, fine-tune it, make it my own so that the overall look, feel and tempo of the series would be cohesive, consistent. I was the final check for each episode before it was sent over for telecast. Each producer had one dispatch a month but because I was the commandeering force, I was responsible for every weekly despatch. No matter whose episode it was, it had to go through me...and we were always behind schedule. We'd have to send the tape to Singapore (as was the policy then), and they would beam it back. For a Saturday episode, we'd have to send it on a Wednesday, which would get pushed to Thursday, sometimes Friday. It was worth it, though. The show looked awesome and was being talked about within the industry.

So yeah, Kuhu and I and the impending marriage. We were more or less living together by now, but my schedule was impossible, leaving me with hardly any time to spend with her. Things came to a head during the Diwali of 2005 when all she wanted was for us to go on a holiday. But I couldn't take even a day off. Kuhu broke down and I got mad at her, though the fact was that I couldn't see her crying and I didn't know how to deal with it when she did. And, strangely, this prompted her to look up at me and say, look, you know what, let's get married. And that was that.

Except that if you know me even a little by now, you'd have guessed that it couldn't have been so easy.

◆

So let's go back a bit. When the Season 3 shoot reached Delhi, I spent the night at my parents' place in Patparganj. Nanna was to drop me at the location the next morning. On our way there, Rajiv called to say he had great news: his wife, Susan, was pregnant. They were pregnant. We stopped the car, screamed, shouted; we were so happy, nanna and I. I went on road again and in a couple of weeks' time, the Roadies had reached Shimla. And this time I got a call from my sister, Tuppi. 'Guess what, Raghu?' she asked. What? She was pregnant too. I was really close to tears then, I was so, so happy with the news. I took my producers out that night to celebrate my double promotion as mama and chacha.

By the time I returned from the *Roadies* 3 journey, something in me had shifted. Both my siblings were married, both were waiting to become parents, while I, Raghu Ram, the oldest of the siblings, was sitting in an edit room making, not babies, but episodes! What do you want to do with yourself, your life, I asked myself and pat came the reply: I want to get married. I want to spend my life with Kuhu. So, in a tender moment, I told Kuhu, let's get married. She said no. I was taken aback and quite hurt. Why didn't she want to marry me? Kuhu said it was because she was just twenty-two and too young to get married. Round one: Kuhu. Well, if you're going to cite age as a reason, I retorted, I can too. I'm thirty, and I'm ready for marriage. Round two: Raghu. Then Kuhu said, everything is fine, why fix something that's not broken? I couldn't find a suitable reply. Knockout.

It made sense at the time, but I knew I wasn't going to be happy with it for long.

◆

So I emailed my mentor, Saul Nasse, from the BBC: Kuhu isn't ready to marry me, what should I do? Pat came the reply, crisp, curt, stiff upper-lipped Brit as ever: 'withhold sex'. Honest, no kidding. It was funny. I wrote back saying, it doesn't make sense. Instead of wanting to get married, she'll just end up feeling like a married woman. We laughed about it but I *did* try this approach.

I threatened to break it off with Kuhu unless she agreed to marry me. That put a lot of pressure on her and I am not ashamed to say that I became the girl in the relationship, telling her that if she wanted to be with me, she had better put a ring on it. (All those who criticize me for being against Indian culture, take that!) I knew what I wanted and I did what was required to get it.

And then Mrs Garg called me. 'Beta what happened, why are you breaking up?' I told her, 'Aunty, I want to marry Kuhu, she's refusing to, so I'm threatening to break up with her, but I don't really mean it.' Kuhu's mum got super charged and gave me the baap of all pep-talks: 'Don't worry beta, my daughter *will* marry you, dump her! She will cry. She will threaten, plea, but ignore her drama, ignore her pleas, make her suffer! I'll see how she doesn't marry you!' All this culminated in that Diwali when Kuhu finally said yes in the middle of a crying jag. And that was that.

I didn't really believe Kuhu even when she said yes. I demanded that she commit to it, call her parents tell them she wanted to get married. She called her parents, who were ecstatic, screaming our names over the phone.

Then I called nanna … and received a classic South-Indian, middle-class response. Dad, I said, I'm getting married. Okay, he said. It's November, I have many people to invite, so ideally it should happen within the next few months. I will be needing your janam-patri to fix the date… That's how the phone call went.

Now everything was falling into place, except that Kuhu had told me that whenever she had thought about the perfect proposal, it hadn't involved threats and tears but a ring. She wanted one, she said so two or three times. I picked one up with Manna's help. Not a very expensive one, just as much as I could afford. A little more than, actually. I began carrying the ring wherever I went, trying to find the right moment to give it to her. Ultimately, it wasn't quite as spontaneous as I had hoped. Vishal Sood, whom I'd worked with earlier at the BBC, told me about his brother's villa in Goa. So I took Kuhu to Goa for that vacation she had been begging me for. We went to Ashwem beach. It was a beautiful winter day, pleasant, sunny, but not hot. The sand was a pristine white, and there was no one around for miles; it seemed like we owned the beach. We walked around. Talked. I clutched the ring with one hand in my pocket, turned and went down on one knee, brought out the ring, and officially proposed. She wept, overcome with emotion, wore it. I don't remember much of it; I'm sure Kuhu can recount it in more detail. What I do remember is that she found it romantic as hell.

The wedding was set for 2 February, and I started thinking money. There were two basic problems: 1) We didn't have any, neither me nor my family. Not enough for a whole wedding anyway. 2) Kuhu's parents wanted to give me money, as tradition, but that would, in my mind, amount to dowry, and I absolutely refused. I applied for a personal loan of two lakh rupees.

A couple of days before the wedding, there was the mehendi function at Kuhu's place, and my boys and I were also invited. So I landed up with Rajiv, Rannvijay, Abbas Syed, Sharib Hashmi and Ranjeet/Chhotu who promptly came down with chickenpox and was bedridden throughout the rest of the wedding ceremonies. Mehendi was applied, songs were sung, the usual stuff. One lady from Kuhu's side got up and sang a song that took our breath away. The song ended and everyone from the bride's side started jeering at us, the 'ladkewaale', saying we'd been outclassed. I was ready for this; I had specifically learnt a song from a very close friend of mine, Sharib. It's a Marwari song called 'Chhoti Si Umar' by Ustad Nusrat Fateh Ali Khan from *Bandit Queen* about a girl who's being married too young, and her asking her father why she is being sent away. The point was that Kuhu's family is Marwari, and Kuhu was rather young when she got married.

I shut my eyes and sang like I always do…but had to stop after I finished the first antara because I could hear some sobs, and then a wail. I looked up. Everybody was crying. I wondered for a split second whether I had really sung that badly. My father-in-law came up, hugged me and said, 'What a song, beta, mazaa aa gaya.' When I said I knew more songs like this, he stopped and said, in all seriousness, 'Shaadi cancel kar doonga.' And we laughed.

But now it's become a tradition. Whenever there's a wedding in the Garg family, I am there, my guitar is there, as is this song.

The day after the mehendi was the sangeet and when it struck midnight, my wedding day…my sister promptly went into labour. Chaos ensued as I ended up being upstaged on my wedding day by an unborn child! My parents were going crazy; son's getting married, daughter's having a baby. It was in the middle of all this chaos that Kuhu and I finally got hitched. The day of the wedding was excruciating. I was woken up by 6 a.m., and the wedding finally ended at 11 p.m. I was giving the pandit dirty looks, threatening to walk out if he didn't hurry it up. The only bright spot in the entire day was Kuhu; when she finally came for the wedding, she looked like a Rajasthani princess, like an angel. I have never seen a prettier bride.

What does all this have to do with *Roadies*, you ask? I'm coming to it. For our honeymoon I took Kuhu all around Kerala, and it was the most romantic trip ever. I fell in love with the state, and it is for this reason that *Roadies 4* flagged off from Kerala.

◆

But before that, a quick backtracking to Season 3. By the time I'd reached Jaisalmer from Jodhpur, I found out that most of the top brass at MTV, including Cyrus Oshidar, Karthik Chintamani and Anil Nair, had quit for what seemed to be better opportunities. So there was a management change at the channel and rumour had it that I would be asked to step in as the next EP—which was everything I ever wanted to be. Karthik, over the last six months, had taken to calling me Mr Future EP and my colleagues had told me they'd be most comfortable if I took charge instead of some outsider. Sounded good to me. Didn't happen.

It didn't happen. Ashish Patil took over instead. Not as EP—that post wasn't quite filled—but Ashish was now the new man in charge. He had been heading marketing at the time and he turned out to be a very sweet guy. He never lost his cool, had an incredible amount of patience and has been a huge, huge support on *Roadies*.

◆

Anyway, with most of the team having quit, I recovered from my just-married bliss to the harsh reality that I had suddenly lost my panel of judges for the Season 4 auditions. Ashish then came up with this idea that I should have a VJ with me on the panel. We couldn't take Cyrus Sahukar because he wasn't perceived as a tough-talking guy, he was the funny guy! The same reason why we couldn't even consider Broacha. But then someone suggested roping in Nikhil Chinappa, saying he could speak excellent Hindi. Nikhil, of course, had been hosting *MTV Select* and he had this supercool persona on it. I agreed, but I had my doubts. I sat him down before the first audition in Bombay, told him his personality on TV was very friendly, very approachable, and that I wanted him to switch that off and become serious. His first reaction was to say he couldn't but that I shouldn't worry, that he'd manage.

And, oh boy, manage he did. By the end of the first day, Nikhil was frustrated, saying, I can't take this shit, these guys are talking crap! Within—and I am not exaggerating—*one* day, he went from being *MTV Select*'s approachable Nikhil to an ass-kicking animal! He even made efforts to change the way he was perceived. He barely smiled, dressed in crisp, full-sleeved shirts as opposed to the bright T-shirts he wore on *Select*, grew a stubble; his manner was very formal, a far cry from the multiple chain-toting guy who played you your favourite

Presenting… the 'monster' babies!

Inseparable through life's ups and downs,
Rajiv and I have always stuck together.

Getting ready for life on the road. It's almost as if Rajiv is looking into the future and saying, 'Uh oh!'

My early fascination with the guitar.

As a teenager at our Munirka house.
I can barely relate to this person now, though.

Passing out of D.T.E.A. Out of the frying pan and into the fire!

With the BBC crew after my last shoot for them at Sam Sand Dunes, Jaisalmer.

I remember shooting Roadies 1 *while battling constant rain. This was taken on a memorable truck ride during the hitch-hiking task.*

My favourite part of Roadies: *scanning a map to figure out our route for each season. This was for* Roadies 4, *with Sylvia, Vishal Sood, Chhotu and Debbie.*

Rannvijay and I posing on the stunning road to Leh during Roadies 3. *We had no idea then that we'd become such a great on-air team.*

At the Manvar dunes near Jodhpur with Janet Price during Roadies 4, *figuring out how to shoot a task in the blistering heat.*

Hanging out (quite literally!) with my buddy Rannvijay during Roadies 5.

Chhotu beating the ladyboys at their own game in Bangkok. This was during one of the first international tasks of Roadies 5.

At a Muay Thai training camp at Hua Hin, Thailand. This eight-year-old girl knocked us over with her cuteness.

Goofing around and pretending to shoot with crew members, Mushtaq and Fernandes (Fanna), at the floating market, Thailand.

When one is extremely tired, the whole world looks like a bed. Waiting for the cars to pick us up from Langkawi, Malaysia.

Riding an ostrich in Malaysia. I normally do a good job of hiding my fear, but you can see it clearly here.

Any place we go to, we have less than an hour to figure out where to place the cameras and how to shoot a task, especially since the action can happen anywhere. This was in Brazil during Roadies 8.

It's difficult to even think with the 'Behind the Scenes' camera in my face all the time. Their best case scenario is when I get badly hurt while doing a task.

The crew after pack-up at Rio de Janeiro, Roadies 8. So many years have passed but we still have the same feeling of elation after a shoot wraps up.

Brazil is a long way to travel to get hanged. This was taken in Poços de Caldas, Brazil, during Roadies 8.

At the iconic Christ the Redeemer,
Rio de Janeiro, just before heading to the airport.

In Karnataka before a task during Roadies 8. *The hulks behind us show no intention of hitting us, but I think the terror on our faces was real.*

I got burnt all over my back during Roadies 8 *when a task trial went wrong. I still have that mark on my shoulder.*

Posing with 'ghosts' at Death Valley, USA.

My head spins after being thrown like a rag doll by wrestling champion Sushil Kumar. It's in times like these that I consider doing a desk job.

No matter how fearful a task makes me, I'm more terrified of someone getting hurt if the task is not properly tested.

Monkeying around during the pole-dancing task in San Francisco. It's not easy, trust me.

With the director of Roadies X, *Udit, a.k.a. 'Filmy', sorting out some creative differences.*

Trying out my last task on Roadies, *with Rannvijay looking on anxiously.*

song. It was great.

We visited Lucknow for this season—our first time, and last. We did an average of twenty interviews a day but ended up rejecting the whole city! The thing is, the whole culture of 'tehzeeb', despite being sweet and very desirable in a person, was not necessarily an asset on a reality show. It would mean the person would always consider their manners and never quite speak their mind. Such a trait simply translates as *very* boring on TV. All I was looking out for was one person who, in their politeness, would be interesting. But I didn't meet anyone like that. And we've never gone to Lucknow since. Sorry, guys.

While that was the state at Lucknow, other potential contestants from other cities had started realizing that *Roadies* could be a platform for recognition. This was the season where people started coming in saying they wanted to become a Roadie to become famous. We also got Mika on the panel at Ashish's insistence, because he'd gotten this whole 'bad boy' image after his run-in with Rakhi Sawant at his birthday party. Mika, however, was quiet for almost all the auditions, not contributing much.

◆

I have to mention Chandigarh during this season. On day one, all of us had noticed this interesting-looking girl at the venue. She had on eyeliner, black nail polish, clothes, tattoos, and we nicknamed her Gothika. The day's auditions ended, the results with the names of the selected contestants were put up. Akshay was shooting the contestants' reactions and he passed by Gothika, noticed her looking rather put-out and upset. She was on her way out when Akshay stopped her, asked her what the matter was. Gothika shrugged, gestured to the list saying her name wasn't on it. A shocked Akshay did a double take, checked the list, went back and told her there had been a mistake, that she *had* been selected, but that we'd missed out her name. He asked her name, went back to the list and wrote it: Bani Judge. So if Akshay Rajput hadn't been shooting at that spot at that particular time, Bani would have probably gone back home and gone on with life. And the *Roadies* journey would have been very different today—a lot duller, actually.

Anyway, she came on board, the route was decided: Kerala to Rajasthan to Punjab to Sikkim. South. West. North. Northeast. We got to Kerala; the entire crew, along with Janet Price, and started to shoot. I was behind one of the cameras, taking on the fly reactions (OTFs) about other Roadies from everyone. Then something happened that gave rise to another tradition. Bani was very, very guarded in her opinion, and I remember telling her to open up a bit, to be herself, to not hold back. And what did Bani do? She turned around and, as only Bani could, snapped at me, asking me not to tell her what to say. In a manner of speaking, she was right, and in another manner of speaking, well, being anti-establishment, anti-authority is what makes Bani. I didn't argue further.

But later that evening, I sat all the Roadies down and had a chat with them. I told them they had made it to the show after several auditions and they now had an opportunity just waiting to be milked. Either they lived in the moment, did and said exactly what they felt like, actually used this opportunity to the fullest OR they could spend all their time here figuring out what image to project. I told them, in very clear yet non-threatening terms, that if they weren't being themselves, if they remained conscious of cameras, they wouldn't be as interesting, which meant they obviously wouldn't get covered as much and would make themselves redundant. I also added that the producers could be trusted with their thoughts, and that we would never repeat them to others. The chat worked, the first vote-out rocked. A fight broke out, Bani ended up slapping Shaleen Malhotra and the tone for the entire season was set. I was happy.

Akshay wasn't.

We wrapped up the vote-out shoot by 5 a.m. and we had to leave Kovalam at 7 a.m. Janet Price wanted a sunrise shot and asked the camera team to shoot it. Akshay lost it then. He called the entire crew and told us exactly what he felt: that his team wasn't a bunch of fucking robots, that we needed to get our fucking act together and make sure that the crew was a little rested. I knew he was right, so no one argued with him. He promptly walked out. It wasn't our annual fight, but it was day one and someone had lost their temper. It was a good omen.

It was already daylight by now, and I remember walking back to our room (Akshay, Rannvijay and I were put up together). I calmed him down, told him it was just the first episode. We should have ideally slept but instead Akshay and I sat on our balcony and downed whisky till 7.30 a.m. We chatted, laughed, and all was well again.

After Mika, Ashish Patil got the idea of getting another celebrity on board. Now since we obviously couldn't afford a Shah Rukh Khan or an Ajay Devgn and, well, since we were all about the twisted, messy side of people anyway, Ashish said we ought to get a villain on board. We decided on Gulshan Grover. I had another idea: he would claim to have a mole within the Roadies and they'd have to guess who the mole was and vote that person out. In reality, there would be no mole. The thought behind this was to make the vote-outs more unpredictable than they had been last season. My old favourite, the dinner-party dynamic would play out. Ah, the joys of teasing the human psyche!

A word about Gulshan Grover. Actually, no, a word about his house. It's as filmy as he is. A two-storied white house, it has a waiting room with a wall full of photographs of him with Hollywood actors, so you'll be sitting there going, 'Ooh, Steven Seagal!' 'Ooh, Goldie Hawn!' while you wait for him. And he *always* makes you wait for him. It's a smart ploy, one that probably helps him negotiate his fee—one that we couldn't afford. Now, I would never do this but I really pitched it to him, tried to sell *Roadies* to him saying, 'Sir we're young kids, we don't have the money but we have big balls and you won't regret it. I am nobody but I am confident that what I'm doing will be kickass.' I gave him some DVDs of *Roadies* and left.

I returned, negotiated again. I had to really work on him, and it was ultimately his son who helped seal the deal for us, because he was a *Roadies* fan and wanted his dad to be part of the journey somehow.

Aside from the bad man, this season had another very interesting occurrence. Bani would get voted out, Bani would stay back. Once. Twice. Thrice. When the show went on air, there was a lot of protest that it was rigged, that the makers were supporting and protecting Bani. This couldn't be more untrue, and I'd like to clarify it.

Gulshan Grover was too busy to come on the *Roadies* journey, so I had to shoot quick videos with him before leaving. The videos had him explaining the bad man twist: that he had a spy among the Roadies, and that they had to figure out who the spy was and eliminate him/her. Now about Bani's vote-outs. The first time it happened was in episode five, when the bad man's spy had to be voted out. Only after Bani was eliminated (and as was always the plan), Gulshan Grover's next video was played, in which he said that he didn't have a spy after all, and that he would grant a power to the Roadie who had been voted out (he got the gender wrong, because at the time of shooting, we had assumed that it would be a boy who would be suspected). Not only would 'he' stay back in the game, but the person 'he' had nominated would leave instead. So Bani not only stayed back, but her vote against Rishabh got him kicked out that day.

Vote-out instance No. 2: Episode eight. This episode, Bani and Roopali were both voted out. Only, they had to compete in an immunity task which involved rappelling and recovering a box which had a winning chit. As luck would have it, Bani recovered the box with the chit. Roopali left, Bani stayed.

Vote-out instance No. 3: In the very next episode, episode nine, Bani received a thumping number of votes. There were four contestants, she had three votes. But no one was supposed to leave that night. Rishabh had already been flown in and was waiting to re-enter the game. There would now to be five finalists, not four. Bani survived again, much to the frustration of the others.

I'd like to make it clear at this point that *all* of the twists and turns on *Roadies* are pre-decided, set down on paper, even before the auditions are held. We know exactly what the tasks will be, we know exactly what twist will be introduced at which vote-out. What we don't know is who will benefit from it. How would we know Bani would be the target every time there was a twist? Maybe it was her luck. Maybe it was the black she wore on every vote-out. Good for Bani. So that's that. *Roadies 4* will always be known for Bani and the controversy around her miraculous survival.

◆

It will also be known, in my head at least, for the season that gave birth to a new show—*Roadies: Behind the Scenes*. It all started when we took off for Patiala after Rajasthan. And the task here was at a fire station. Fire brigades have these really tall ladders, which seemingly have no support. So the Roadies were divided into groups of two: one had to climb the ladder while the other would be walking on the ground, lit on fire from head to toe. The burning Roadie would burn until the other Roadie could find a whistle suspended at the top of the ladder and blow on it.

Like all tasks, I was set to try this one out as well, especially since there was fire involved. Before the season had begun, I'd called some Bollywood stuntmen to the MTV office to ask them how it was done. How do you set someone on fire? They demonstrated it on me by setting my shoulder on fire—with all the protective gear, of course. I shot it, watched it later but I realized it didn't look scary. The fire looked completely under control. I wanted the fire to look daunting. So when we got to Patiala, I wanted to know how far I could go with it. (Of course I hadn't told Kuhu what I was planning.)

I tried it out again. I was given a jute fire suit to wear, and a helmet with a visor. There is something called a fire-retardant gel which you're supposed to apply on your body. I didn't know of it then (the fire safety guys had probably missed it), so I didn't have any on me. This was the first in the series of huge mistakes. They took a paintbrush and started painting fuel to the fire suit covering my arms, back, chest, feet. Once it was painted on, I had a discussion with the camera team, figuring out how it was going to be shot. Time passed. This was the second big mistake. The fuel they had painted on had dried up. Later, I got to know that once that happens and the material absorbs the fuel, it becomes harder to put out the fire. And then the third big mistake: not being sure whether the fire would be intimidating enough, I asked them to paint on even more fuel. But my biggest mistake was this new thing I'd developed since Season 3 and my very high success rate with task trials: my invincibility complex. I thought I could fucking do anything, and this was encouraged by my team telling me the same, and often.

So despite being nervous as hell, I was careless in my confidence. The brief was that if the fire got too hot, I was to lie down on my stomach and they would put the fire out. Simple enough. Not quite.

They set me on fire. Two seconds...three seconds...and I realized something was terribly wrong. No one could see my face or my expression; I couldn't talk and I felt all alone inside the suit, and I was fucked because the flames just engulfed me. I couldn't see anything but fire. I kept standing still and felt the heat increasing. Within seconds, it became unbearable. Then it got worse. I started seeing fire *inside* the fucking helmet. Now I knew my face was on fire, it was burning, and I couldn't breathe. I could also feel my chest hair catch fire. About ten seconds into the task, which seemed like an eternity in itself, I lay down on my stomach. And the minute I did this, my face was *in* the fire. So I instantly got up again...another huge mistake. The safety team was confused; they didn't know whether I had given up or not. They hung around and I remember having this sinking feeling in my stomach that this is it, Raghu, *this* is how you die. I knelt down and started banging my fist on the ground to communicate that I was in trouble. Outside, there was chaos. Janet was crying, Rannvijay was screaming but he understood my signal, grabbed a towel and came at me. And now everyone came by and started putting out the fire on my head, torso and, lastly, my legs. At which point my torso was aflame once again, because the fuel that had dried up and been absorbed into the suit now caught fire. After another eternity, the fire was put out and they finally pulled my helmet off.

Picture a huge kadhai burning on the gas, empty, and then you pour one glass of water in it. Steam gushes out, right? Furious, hissing, smoking steam. That was what happened when they pulled the helmet off. My nose was burnt, my forehead had burnt, my chest was burnt. It was not major, thankfully, but I sat down for a few minutes, completely winded. I called Kuhu; she sounded cheerful, happy to hear my voice. I didn't tell her what had happened, just that I was missing her and hung up. I then heard this murmur going around that we couldn't do this task. Impossible to shoot. Too dangerous. Can't—no, *shouldn't* do it.

I remember this being one of the first instances when I heard so many people saying, no, the task was impossible (it happened many times after that) and just like that, something clicked in my head. You see, my training dictates that when I go out to shoot something, I shoot it come what may. That day, I said I *will* do it, but with a few changes. No fire on the torso, only one application of fuel, use a fire-retardant gel (which everybody agreed by now was absolutely essential), and have a cut-off limit, say twenty seconds. It took a long time for us to figure things out, which is why the task was ultimately shot in the night, which worked well because the fire looked scarier.

When the journey had ended and we came back to Mumbai, MTV saw the footage of me burning and Ashish Patil had a brainwave. Why not begin a 'behind the scenes' section for *Roadies*? They had realized that since the auditions had been put on air last season, I, as a character, was really being talked about. And all the shit about why he is like this, is he like this in real life, what gives him the right to judge people, had started. They decided that if this guy is sitting and taking the auditions, choosing the Roadies, then doing the tasks that the Roadies are supposed to, AND getting hurt in the process, that was great content and justification. So Season 5 onwards, *Behind the Scenes* started. Now, the funny thing about *Behind the Scenes* is that their best footage comes from a task trial gone horribly wrong. In other words, they're praying every day for me to get hurt. So every time I would go to do a task, a crew member would come up to me, camera in hand, and gleefully ask how I was feeling. Do you think this task is doable? Bloody vultures! But jokes apart, *Behind the Scenes* went on to contribute a lot to the reputation of *Roadies*. Well, my nose is beginning to itch now, as it always does when I talk about fire. Let's move on...

◆

...to Akshay and my big fight this season. It was silly, like most fights are. We were nearing our final spot in the North East, and had just reached Kalimpong. I was sharing a room with Sylvia, the head of production, and Janet, both of who wouldn't stop talking; they had issues that apparently had to be addressed in the few hours that we would have liked to sleep. Hence, when I got out of the hotel room, frustrated, Akshay came to see me and said he had to talk to me about my producers. I lost it—for no rhyme or reason—and screamed at him right there in front of everyone, and then ran away from the hotel. The funny part is, Sylvia came after me to calm me down, which made me run even faster. Eventually, I walked it off, calmed down, came back. And now I called for Akshay in front of everyone again. See, it's very simple. Most people scream at colleagues or juniors in front of the whole office and, later, call the person to their cabin and apologize. Very civilized? Hardly. Such an apology doesn't count. If you've taken away someone's dignity in front of everyone, you bloody well give it back to them *in front* of everyone, in the same volume.

Shoots are tough, but the toughest parts are the beginning and the end. We got to Hanuman Tok in Gangtok for the final task, which gave me one of my most defining *Roadies* memories. There, we set up a see-saw, on one end of which a Roadie would be suspended, and on the other end, a water tank would hang, filled with just enough water to balance their body weight. The Roadie's hands would be tied behind them and there would be a noose around their neck. Then, a tap on the tank would be opened so that it keeps losing water, getting lighter, and going up. The Roadie's side of the see-saw would keep coming down, which meant the noose around their neck would keep getting tighter. They had to free their hands as soon as possible to avoid hanging. It was a dangerous task, and I knew it the minute I tried it that it didn't work properly. Keeping my balance on the see-saw was difficult. Also, I had to test the worst case scenario: what if the person slipped? I jumped off clumsily, taking the strain from the noose on my neck, and waited to see how long it was before the experts freed me. But by the time we had finished with the tests, it was 3.30 p.m. and since this was the North East, the light was already beginning to fade.

Akshay came up to me and said, Bro, I don't think we can do this task today. Something he never says. Debbie, Zulfiya, Rannvijay, Akshay and I had a conversation about it, and that was when something clicked in my head: I knew that I had to get the task done. (I attribute it to the Roadies Raghu, I think he had begun to manifest himself by then.) I said, fuck, no matter what, we'll do it. The minute I said it—and I think everyone was waiting for me to say it—we all separated at once, walking away in different directions. And then it went like clockwork. I was then a chanting Buddhist so I automatically chanted, 'Nam myoho renge kyo (I bow to the divine law of the Lotus Sutra).' Rannvijay walked off saying, '*Jo bole so nihaal, sat sri akaal.*' Akshay called out to Hanuman; Debbie, a Christian, crossed herself, and Zulfiya, a Muslim, also muttered a prayer. I am an atheist now, but this memory stays with me. Ultimately, light or no light, rain or no rain, we shot it.

Then there was the final vote-out; Anthony, Bani and Raj remained, and since Anthony had won the task, he got to pick who stayed. If you remember, Raj was Anthony's college friend while Bani and Anthony had become an item through the show. Friendship or love: which would you pick? Interesting dynamic, indeed! Well, we all know he picked Bani, and Anthony went on to win the season. Bani, who had been lucky all through the season, ultimately lost.

But that's not what I was thinking about after wrapping up the season at the Gangtok monastery. As I sat in the Maruti van all alone while being driven back to the hotel, I spoke to myself. Remember this feeling, Raghu, I said to myself. Remember it, remember how shitty you feel, remember how exhausting, how excruciatingly painful these days have been, do not dare forget this. The driver must have thought I was crazy, talking to myself, but I didn't stop. When you edit the journey, I continued, you will feel, good about it. But never forget this drive. Remember how fucked you feel, how tired, how stressed you've been from day one, how you almost died. You don't want to make another season of *Roadies*. You want to quit.

And then the edit happened, and I saw what we'd created. It was this season that *Roadies* actually took off. Rajiv came to me and said, 'Bro, awesome. Very well done. Now don't do it again. Quit while you're at the top.' And I looked at him long and hard... and said no.

The season of shocks, the armour of invincibility and some regrets

I had forgotten what I'd felt in that car drive from the Gangtok monastery, I had forgotten the misery; I felt kicked, and full of energy. I had another season in me and I felt I was on to something here.

Indeed, I was. All of us were. Season 4 brought in unimaginable ratings for MTV. Before the auditions ended on air, we had started scoring a rating of 0.7, 0.8, which was a lot for a non-GEC channel (GEC channels, or General Entertainment Channels include Star Plus, Colors, etcetera). And I started a practice around it. Every week, when the ratings would come in, I'd take a huge sheet of paper, get the rating printed on it in bold highlights and in the biggest possible font, staple it to my chest and back and walk all over the office. I'd go to every HoD's cabin; if there was a meeting going on at a conference room, I'd just walk in anyway, get on the table, not speak, just flaunt the sheet of paper, flaunt our rating. By the time the middle of the journey went on air, we'd started touching 1.5, and I added another sheet of paper, this one on my stomach with an arrow drawn pointing towards my crotch, saying, 'Suck here'. Mostly, I'd hop from table to table as everyone joined in with laughter and applause. I felt a huge sense of achievement. My team had done a hell of a job and I wanted the world to know that it was a big ass deal. And what was my team doing? They'd high-five each other when the ratings came out every week, and then promptly get back into their little pigeonhole editing rooms where they spent their nights and days. They had to keep working for the show to keep airing, keep rocking, you see?

2007 was also the year that MTV was acquired by Viacom18, which was basically Viacom (which owns MTV Worldwide and Paramount Studios in Hollywood) collaborating with TV18 which was now Network 18. I remember the merger being announced in the office in the presence of Raghav Bahl. Rajiv and I were so excited to see him again; he was the same, only whiter. We even made our way to him after the announcements—he didn't recognize us at first, but he had heard of *Roadies*, and that was huge. I felt proud.

◆

Raghav Bahl had only just heard of *Roadies*, but with Season 4, people were getting hooked on to the show. Youngsters slowly started feeling a sense of brand ownership, and it became a youth property; they took it online, because that was where they expressed themselves most. The die-hard fans were very active on Orkut (Facebook hadn't quite caught on then), and the social networking site hosted several *Roadies* communities. The biggest of these was one hosted by this college kid called Sehran Mohsin. Sehran was indirectly responsible for two very important developments in the *Roadies* journey: the first *Roadies* anthem and *Roadies Battleground*. More on that in just a bit.

Online communities made it clear that *Roadies* was catching fire not only in India, but other Hindi-speaking countries as well. Case in point: Pakistan. One fine day, I remember getting a call from Ranjeet, one of our *Roadies 1* contestants, Bani, and then Anthony, all asking me whether *Roadies* was doing anything in Pakistan. Bewildered, I said that we weren't. Apparently they'd all received invites from Pakistan saying they were remaking *Roadies* there. I knew nothing about this, so they forwarded the promo sent to them by a Pakistani network. Now, The Music, which was Pakistan ARY Network's channel had a show called *Living on the Edge* that was produced and hosted by this guy called Waqar Zaka, and he was 'proudly presenting' *Living on the*

Edge: Pakistan Roadies!

I showed it to Ashish and told him, hey, look at their balls, how can they! Ashish agreed wholeheartedly and then I said, well, we have to sue them, obviously. He went a bit strange and said, No, Raghu, we can't. Why? A tiny complication: we hadn't copyrighted *Roadies* as yet. Yeah, seriously. I gaped too. Apparently, this was because they never expected the show to do well, forget catch on in foreign countries! But I was livid. We were working so hard and I wouldn't let someone else pass it off as their work—that infuriated me. I went to the legal department at MTV and told them we had to copyright it. I was told it would take time; they didn't seem to take me too seriously. A week passed, I kept following up on it, but nothing. So I told Ashish, I am getting a lawyer and assigning the copyright to myself. Next time you want to make *Roadies*, I said, we'll talk. What do you know, it happened that very evening. The paperwork, at least. In order to copyright it, I had to make a booklet of everything we were copyrighting. So this was my routine from then on: I worked nights at the studio, editing and polishing my producers' edits. Days, I spent writing a big fat Bible— they actually call it that—that included every element of the show. How it's made, what the sections are, everything. Copyright in place, we made sure Pakistan and eight other countries could never touch our brand.

Pakistan's obsession with *Roadies* continues though. They recently bought the rights to telecast *Roadies 9*, and if you get on to YouTube and click on links that have titles like, 'Raghu called taklu in public', '*Roadies 10* theme song leaked' or 'Raghu exposed', they open up to *Living on the Edge*. The show rides on *Roadies* as a ploy to get its audience. It's okay, I guess. Waqar Zaka is now a friend though and keeps cajoling me to do a project with him. I don't know. I may never have had the chance to make that *Roadies* journey into Pakistan, but I'm glad *Roadies* itself has made it to the TV screens there.

Four seasons down, this is a good time to introduce you to some people who have a huge role to play in the success of *Roadies*. Vaibhav

Vishal, a.k.a. V2, was formerly a senior resource in marketing who then came on board shows. He introduced gyaan sessions that contributed immensely to the *Roadies* craze. The gyaan sessions were basically presentations that we took to schools and colleges and told people how reality shows were shot. The ulterior motive, of course, was to let everyone have a good look at me because V2 had decided that I was the best salesman for the show, and he was convinced that once people had taken a good look at me, heard me talk, they would go back and watch the show. Anyway, at the end of the gyaan sessions, we'd always provide one treat: a teeny, tantalizing glimpse into that weekend's episode of Season 4. I do believe that the reason our ratings started to skyrocket was these gyaan sessions, all thanks to V2.

Haresh Chawla, CEO, Network 18, said we had a captive audience online and we ought to engage them even when the show was not on air. Could we do an online *Roadies* for them? V2 and I jumped at the idea...and right after Season 4, the concept of *Roadies Battleground* was born. We decided to keep most of the elements of *Roadies* on *Roadies Battleground*. There would be tasks, immunity and vote-outs. However, we had to make sure that the tasks weren't risky because we'd be responsible if the contestants hurt themselves. So we decided to use embarrassment as a tool. We would dare contestants to do things they wouldn't do publicly for fear of embarrassment. It worked. No one has ever been hurt doing a *Roadies Battleground* task all these years. Every task would be recorded, posted online, people would watch them, vote for them. The popular ones would be immune, and there would be a vote-out among the bottom few contestants. V2 took over the execution of *Roadies Battleground*. The first thing he did was hire Sehran Mohsin and commandeer the Orkut *Roadies* community as the place where *Roadies Battleground* would happen. It was an instant hit. Fans could not get enough of *Roadies* online.

Sehran has musical tendencies and made us listen to a song that he had created on *Roadies*. Quite a few others in the community had also attempted writing lyrics for their own *Roadies* song. Since fans were showing such an interest in a song for the show, Ashish and V2 asked me whether we should ask the community to come up with an official song. I didn't agree, because we ought not to confuse what fans do with what we do. The next question was, could *we* then make a *Roadies* song? I said, sure, and instantly called Mohan, Koko and Chinku (Arijit), band members of Agnee, who had just launched their first album and who are the next most important people in the success of *Roadies*.

They already had a song in their album called 'Kaarwaan', which worked for me. It was a dark song about journey and seeking. Too dark for Ashish, though, who said he wanted an upbeat, peppy, canteen song. We agreed and in our excitement, ran out of the MTV office down to the ITC Grand Central, took up a suite there, and we worked on the song that very night. Koko came up with a basic riff and a tune that was peppy, sunshine, and to get them going, I wrote the first four lines: *Ghar se hum chale, bas ek backpack aur ek guitar. Paison ki fikar nahi, bike pe hum sawaar. Raahon ki hai khabar na manzil ka hai pata, phir bhi chal diye, jaane ab hoga kya.* They loved it so much, they asked me to write the whole song. And that's how the first track for *Roadies* was created: over one night between four friends, in the true spirit of the show. Later, when we recorded the track, Mohan and Koko kept saying something was missing and, finally, they got me to go into the edit to do my thing: speak, insult, intimidate. So if you listen to 'Jeet Lenge Yaar', you'll hear it peppered with my voice insulting contestants, saying stuff like 'you're just boring dude, personality nahi hai, filmon mein kyun nahi try karta? Achchi heroine banega tu.' That entire thing was done in one single take, on the fly. That was the high on which Season 4 ended: great ratings, a growing online brand, the *Roadies* anthem and another season to look forward to.

Like I said, I had forgotten all about that car drive from Gangtok and my promise to myself. I was kicked about the next season.

But before the fifth season could kick off, an incident took place that I've never ever spoken about, something that happened to Rannvijay and which still chills my blood when I think about it. Very late one night, I received a call from an unknown number. No, it wasn't a crazed fan, but a very irate policeman asking me whether I knew a Rannvijay. I said, yes, my heart suddenly in my mouth. He's been in an accident, I was informed. I felt myself go cold as the cop, not rude but short on patience and time, told me that before passing out, Rannvijay had given my name and number. I just wore my shoes and ran out of my house, calling out a quick goodbye to Kuhu and ringing Rajiv, who lived in Bandra back then.

Rajiv got to Holy Family Hospital before I did, and he called to tell me Rannvijay had had just a few scratches and he was fine. I relaxed for about three seconds. And then my brain started ticking. Why didn't he call me himself, then? And now Rajiv sighed and said, what do you want me to say, Raghu? It's bad, really bad, he's totally banged up. I didn't want you to hyperventilate, will you just come here? The auto couldn't go any faster, and I was shit scared. I finally reached the hospital, and there, lying on a stretcher in the corridor, all cut up, was my little brother. I looked at him and I couldn't believe it. His lip was bust open, his forehead was cut, his cheeks split, his nose was bruised and bleeding. He was caked in blood. He was wearing a sherwani, and he was conscious. I remember him looking at me, clenching his fists and saying, 'Raghu, you're here. I'm going to be fine now. I'm going to beat this.' Rajiv and I exchanged a look and I told him, as coolly as I could, 'Yeah, man, don't worry, it's not so bad, you'll be fine.' As it turned out, Rannvijay had attended a wedding where he had had a fight with Anusha, his then girlfriend. Furious, he had got on his bike and rode away into the night, as was his habit whenever he needed to clear his head or think. He was speeding that night, and was very distracted. To this day, he doesn't remember how it happened, but he was thrown off the bike and hit the road head first. He lay there unconscious for a while, and some asshole actually robbed of him of his wallet and cell phone while he was unconscious. The cops on patrol saw him and revived him—that was when he gave them my number, and passed out again. The irony was that Rannvijay never gets on his bike without wearing a helmet. And the one time he did, this shit happened.

Anyway, we waited as the doctor checked him. He was cut up bad, yes, but the cuts could be mended, the face could be stitched up and a cosmetic surgeon would make sure there weren't too many scars… but there was one complication. I looked at the doctor. His face was grave as he said they would have to check for brain damage. We (by now we'd called Bumpy and Akshay too) froze right where we were, the words sinking in. Brain damage. I was so scared, too scared to even think of it, as we waited numbly for the tests to happen. We called Anusha, and Akshay tried to convince me to call Rannvijay's parents as well. As is my habit, I wanted to protect his parents if I could. I was probably in denial, convincing myself that Rannvijay was okay. Then Akshay said, very seriously, 'Raghu, they are his parents. They have to know. If anything happens, who's responsible?' It was a big moment of reckoning for me; Akshay saying that something could go wrong made it very real. I couldn't take it and right there, out on the corridor of Holy Family Hospital I, who scorned tears, who thought they were weak, broke down and wept. I was shit scared for Rannvijay.

The MRI, CT scans, etcetera, all happened. You watch this sort of thing in a movie or on television, but when it's actually happening to someone close to you, it really sinks in: the possibility that there could be any damage to the brain. Finally, I called his mother and, despite my trying to convince her that he was fine, she broke down, too, and soon was on the next flight to Mumbai. The scans were clean, though, we were very relieved. Rannvijay recovered with such speed that he surprised the shit out of the doctors themselves. His favourite superhero is Wolverine from the X-Men, and Wolverine's superpower is that he can heal himself very quickly. I almost wish Rannvijay had taken his time getting better because we've never heard the end of him calling himself Wolverine after that. But even today, if you look closely under harsh lights, you can see the many, many miniscule scars all over his face from that night. Scary fucking night. For him, though, the biggest fear was that he wouldn't be allowed to ride a bike again. Initially, he humoured his parents and others who forbade him, myself included, but later...well, it's Rannvijay. Not ride a bike? Yeah, right!

◆

Rannvijay was fit and fine in a couple of weeks' time, and life went on. I had another season to plan. The usual questions were raised. Where? I knew I wanted to go abroad this time. After four seasons within the country, I wanted a change of scene; I needed new cultures, exciting pit stops for the journey, and for that I needed to step out of the country. MTV said, no, they didn't have enough money, and Hero Honda would never agree. Every season in the course of the journey, the *Roadies* contestants visit a couple of Hero Honda dealers, an aarti happens, the Roadies are welcomed, fed cake; we barely put this on air and even if we do, it's just for a couple of minutes. But it's a public relations exercise for the brand. If we travelled abroad, Hero Honda didn't have dealers out of the country to visit, so it would be a wasted exercise for them. Of course, the minute I heard the 'no', I felt the usual click go off in my head. I had to dig my heels in, make sure this happened, make sure we went abroad. I convinced MTV to not let the fear of rejection stop them from asking the question itself. Let Hero Honda say no, you don't say it for them.

We met Hero Honda in Delhi, and by 'we' I mean me and Aditya Swamy, who was then heading ad sales and marketing at MTV. (He currently heads the channel.) We all sat down: me, Aditya, Vivek Syal, General Manager Marketing, Hero Honda, with two or three people from Hero Honda and some from the advertising agency hired by Hero. The agency's job is talk to the production house, to dictate the positioning, the budgets, and how to go about it. And, yeah, they were like dogs. They would fucking lick Vivek Syal's ass and bark at us. Their main aim was to tell their client that, these guys are trying to fleece you, we'll save you. When we walked into the meeting, we felt rather confident that, since Season 4 had done well, we could demand a higher price and get it. This confidence disappeared within the first ten minutes. The agency guys taunted us, saying, aaj kal MTV ko ratings ka chaska lag gaya hai, that's why they're demanding a premium for the next season! I was seething inside but kept quiet. Negotiating money was not my job.

After we presented what we'd achieved with Season 4 and opened up our plans for Season 5, Aditya told them we should get more money. Everyone turned to look at Vivek Syal who paused, took a deep breath and when he opened his mouth to speak, it was to ask if anyone had Rajnigandha Paan Masala. Silence. No one had any. Someone was actually sent out to get some. Silence fell again. Until the paan masala had come to the table, Syal didn't say a word, and neither did anyone else. The tension was palpable. It was a master stroke, you see. Syal had taken the advantage away from us; he had told everybody, I am in charge, till the time I don't talk, nothing can happen. He leisurely opened the packet, popped some in his mouth as we waited. And then slowly said, repeat what you said. Aditya complied. Syal looked at him, calm as ever, and said, don't tell me that you've achieved something extraordinary because that is what I paid you for. If you hadn't achieved it, you wouldn't have come back in here.

It soon became an almost comical situation, with Aditya saying that, at least as a reward, we ought to be paid more. I was cringing; I wanted to throttle the agency boys sitting next to Syal. I finally opened my mouth and told Syal, 'Sir, I want more money because I want to go abroad.' There was an immediate uproar among the agency guys; they laughed, said it was ridiculous. I waited for it to die down, just kept looking straight at Syal. Why? he asked. I said India was becoming monotonous and going abroad would give the show a new lease of life. The next five years would be successful only if we went abroad now. Syal kept looking at me and asked, 'Are you sure, Raghu?' I nodded quietly, without breaking eye contact. It was intense. He paused, and then simply said, 'Okay.' The agency guys were outraged but Syal shut them up saying, 'This boy believes it and I believe in him.' He signed us on for more money, and that was it. I walked out feeling ten feet tall; I was going to kick fucking ass and how.

I flew back to Mumbai, met my team. While I had spent the past few months being involved in the gyaan sessions, *Roadies Battleground*, and writing and recording songs, my team had been living in the edit room, with no life beyond it. Their reward? Another season to work their asses off on. Their reaction: yayy, we're going abroad! Like I'd said, my team was mad. Thank goodness for that.

So, before we took off for Season 5, three decisions were made: 1) This season would air a behind-the-scenes segment. 2) This season would not have a special guest in the auditions panel, and 3) This season would see me participate in the journey, not just the auditions. The last was Bumpy's idea.

◆

This season, I started sensing a little something during the auditions: people were reacting very differently to me. It was weird, because I hadn't been on air for a long time—I was only one of three people sitting in the interview room, and that too a year ago. They knew my name, chanted it, the mobbing had begun. It made my life hell, and my job had slowly started becoming tougher. I was one of the moderators at the group discussions, and wannabe contestants wanted to come into my room for GDs; they felt I had the last call in choosing the final thirteen. And when they saw me, they'd become emotional as well. I remember this one kid who, when asked to speak at the group discussion, froze on the spot; tearing up, he said that I made him nervous and he couldn't speak in front of me. Something was shifting, something had changed. All this time, I had thought that my USP was that I was one of the guys; what I brought to the table was that I was an everyday person, which the others at MTV weren't, and which was why I could make this show better than anyone else. But with Season 5, I slowly started losing that. People stopped seeing me as a regular guy.

This was brought home to me time and again. Like this one time after a group discussion, when I was chatting in the room with Akshay and some crew members, we heard a racket outside. The security guards were stopping a girl from coming in; she was begging them to let her meet me. I told them to let her in. This girl ran into the room. I was standing beside the chair when she launched herself at me. She banged into the side of my face so hard, my earring fell off... and then she started sobbing. Akshay quietly backed off, indicating to the camera people to get the cameras—and this is why I loved this team; they knew this was a raw display of emotion, pure and unscripted. It's not about making people cry or fight, it's about breaking an emotional barrier, getting hold of raw emotions and then capturing them. *This* is reality TV, *this* is content! It was the first of something that is rampant now. I didn't know why she was crying, I didn't know why she ran up to me, but today, as it has happened many times with many people, I know why.

Today, when people tell me that they idolize me or look up to me, I already know one of two things is probably true: 1) They come from broken families and are craving a father figure or at least an elder brother figure, and/or 2) They have been bullied in life. They see me as a strong personality and that is one thing I find flattering, considering my past. But it's also made it impossible for me to ever sit in on a group discussion again, and this was one of the reasons why I never wanted the auditions to be aired. There is an intensity of emotion displayed by the contestants when I come into the picture, an intensity I cannot understand or explain.

MTV milked it to the fullest, though. I remember the public relations team telling me to be rude to the press at the press conference, because that was beginning to be seen as 'my thing'. Hell, this guy Sandeep Dahiya who headed licensing and merchandising, coined the name Raghu 'Rude' Ram; he said it would build my persona, build what I was. Apparently was, at least. I don't think any of the candidates within the interview room understood what I was actually about—

there are very few people in the world who do. But rude was the easy classification, rude worked for MTV, so I was informed that it was my persona and that I had to build on it. I didn't like it but I went with it.

During the journey, I made an appearance for the first time (as was decided by MTV), and I wanted to make sure I got the reactions I wanted. My entry into the episode had to be a surprise for the contestants as much as the viewer, so I had to hide until I actually came in front of the camera. I managed to, and I got the desired shocked reactions when I finally did appear. In subsequent years, I've had to pull off such crazy tricks just to keep the shock of it alive, it's ridiculous!

◆

I'd like to tell you a little more about some of the sacred rules during a *Roadies* shoot, and our interaction with the cast. It's minimal. Here's what happens:

The crew gets on location on what we call Day Zero, which is basically a day before the Roadies do. The crew briefing happens, and the rules are few but precise: there will be a crew member present in the Roadies' rooms at all times but crew members will not speak to them, neither will they speak of the Roadies in their presence. Crew members will not even speak of the Roadies over their walkie-talkies, because that runs the risk of the contestant overhearing our comments over a third possibly open walkie-talkie. Basically, the Roadies should, at no point, feel that we have an opinion on any of them.

Day One, the Roadies arrive, are shown to their rooms, our crew follows, stays put, cameras off. The camera within the room comes on only when the Roadies start talking about the show or each other. Meanwhile, we're away setting up the task, trying it out. Once ready, we call the Roadies. And this is when the dance really starts. The cameras come on. There's a knock on the door, the Roadies are given their scroll, they get ready, get on their bikes, follow a crew car, reach the location. There are cameras set up there as well. They get their mics on, and then we begin. Rannvijay introduces the task, we do our 'on-the-fly' reactions. The task is performed, the results announced, reactions taken again. The only interruption, the only interaction is when we mic them up. It's a brilliantly choreographed execution.

In all the years I've produced this show, I've made sure of one thing: that the Roadies' experience is pure, that they do not feel like they're on a TV shoot. They should experience a journey, obstacles, achievement, frustration. Real emotions. This I'd say is the most significant difference between Roadies and other Indian reality shows. Our focus is on capturing moments, not synthetically manufacturing them.

Season 5 was the time when I was growing fitter, I was trying out tasks better, I was getting used to feeling scared, I was able to deal with it. The feeling of invincibility was growing—a good thing, but then not such a good thing, as you'll soon see.

◆

Going abroad was exciting and anything but easy. But before I go any further, let me take you back a bit, to my BBC days. You remember Daman, Kuhu's co-host on *Haath Se Haath Mila*? I'd started receiving reports that, as the shoot went on, Daman would get annoyed when woken up for call-time; he even asked a crew member to come back in ten minutes and wake him up. I was concerned that this might be the beginning of 'presenter-itis', our code-word at the BBC for the tendency of presenters to throw starry tantrums.

Somewhere between Seasons 4 and 5 of *Roadies*, when Rannvijay started becoming really popular, I was worried that he'd start showing symptoms of presenter-itis. Back to this season, we were done with our first destination: Thailand. We next crossed the border to Malaysia and took a ferry to an island called Langkawi. At the time, we only had fifty members in our crew, and each member was allowed two pieces of luggage. In all, we had 100 pieces, not including the lighting, camera, adventure and sound equipment. We had to load all the stuff on the ferry and then unload it. Like clockwork, the crew made a human chain and kept passing the luggage and equipment, one after the other. And somewhere in the middle of the line was Rannvijay, just another crew member, also hauling equipment. I was so proud to see my little brother being one of the crew; he always was and even when his popularity soared even higher, he continued to be.

My dread returned during the task trials, however. After Langkawi was done, we made our way to Phuket. The next money task was at this location that seemed to be straight out of Peter Jackson's *King Kong*: mountains full of thick green trees surrounding a beautiful saltwater lake. The initial task was this: there were two storm fans (the things used to create storms in films) and a parachute. A parachute was to be strapped on to each contestant, after which they had to face the strong wind from the storm fans, to see how long it took for them to be thrown off their feet. Rannvijay wanted to try it out and he strapped on a parachute. The fan came on and we waited...the parachute didn't get blown at all. We tried twisting the fan this way and that but nothing happened. Suddenly, without warning, the parachute took off, taking Rannvijay with it and, instead of hitting the water as we expected, he went flying in the air and then dropped straight down to the edge of the jetty itself, landing on his head. The scarier part was that he didn't move. We all froze, but my head was in a tizzy. Images of him going into the CT-scan machine flashed in my mind and I ran to him, panic-stricken, and turned him over...his head was cut and bleeding. I lost it. The doctor on set is usually with the Roadies, so he wasn't around and we had to wait until he came. Rannvijay was largely fine but I was really worried. I made it very clear we weren't doing this task, and he wasn't to try out any other tasks, and that was that. We started thinking up an alternative. Looking around, we spotted a barrel around, and came up with the balancing-on-a-barrel task you watched in Episode 11.

Actually come to think of it, this season was one of the most eventful, and not always in the most pleasant way. Backtrack to India again. In the middle of the journey, we were someplace near Hampi when, one night, one of the contestants, Anmol, told my female producers that a couple of crew members were eve-teasing her. Debbie or Zulfiya (I can't remember which of them it was), came to my room right then and I was shocked. This was the crew I'd worked with for years, some of them even before *Roadies*. The other shocker was that, the minute Anmol said this, Shambhavi and Prabhjot joined in saying, yes, they had faced it too. I had to take charge; this was a grave matter, so early the next morning, I suspended the shoot and summoned the three girls, my four producers and Akshay. I broke the rules of not speaking to the contestants and I told the three girls not to be scared, to tell us exactly what had happened, take names. I made it very clear that the guys would be dealt with.

Two names popped up: one was a freelance production manager— the only guy who wasn't a permanent part of our crew, his name's not important. He would apparently whistle at the girls when they passed by, and sometimes even winked when they looked his way. The second guy was Shantaram, who has been a cameraman with Akshay for years now, a core team member. We sent the girls back to their rooms, asked them to relax, and now called the freelance production guy. We fired him...and that for him was the pleasant part. Bumpy was so mad, he became aggressive and almost hit him; we had to hold him back. We told the production guy he was not getting a ticket back, nor his luggage. He had to fuck off right then, and if he wasn't gone in five minutes flat, we would beat him up. He left.

Next, we had to speak to Shanta—and now Akshay chose to leave the room because it would destroy Shanta if it happened in Akshay's presence. Shanta was called in. He was initially calm because he didn't know what we were getting at but the minute he figured out what someone had accused him of, he got really worked up. Shanta swore on his wife that he wasn't guilty, and I wanted to believe him because we go back a long way. It was then that I realized that apart from two producers, I didn't have a single female crew member. The cameraman who stayed in the *Roadies* room at all times was always male, and when he wasn't shooting, he had been instructed to become a part of the furniture. Shanta has a very direct stare, and I figured that that was probably what was making the girls uncomfortable. I told Shanta that we believed him, but that to make the Roadies comfortable, we would be reshuffling the crew in the rooms. He accepted.

It was a huge setback for us, mentally, physically, and work-wise, but by now the *Roadies* crew had gotten used to rolling with the punches. I told the crew what had happened and also that we were not to speak of it to anyone. We haven't, till now. Why I am telling you about this incident is because I'd like to make my policy very clear: no matter how harsh I may seem to the contestants, their safety and security is as high a priority as that of the crew. It was the first and, thankfully, the last time anything of this kind ever happened on my show.

◆

Now let's talk about the finale of *Roadies 5*, which pissed me off simply because Ashutosh had made the cut. He reeked of a bad, bad attitude and I was regretting having cast him. Why? Easy—because he *wasn't* a Roadie, he was a mere bystander. He didn't perform, he played politics and yet he got to the top. The ex-Roadies returned for the finale and were divided into teams for both Ashutosh and Nihaal. They picked whose team they wanted to be in, and then I stepped in and swapped the teams. Each team had to perform five tasks to make either Nihaal or Ashutosh won. Four tasks were performed.

And then came the task that I regret to this day. It was a terrible mistake on our part, a task that was designed to fail but didn't. Felt like *I* had failed, though. One member each of Nihaal and Ashutosh's team had to volunteer to get slapped by the other. When we had sat down and drawn up plans for this season, we were sure nobody would volunteer for this task. They had absolutely no reason to. We even had a tie-breaker ready. But by this time, the ex-Roadies were falling over each other to prove themselves; they saw it as a last chance, so they did volunteer. Vibhor from Ashutosh's team stepped up and got slapped by Nihaal. All of us behind the camera, and Rannvijay in front of it, were stunned. It wasn't going according to plan. And now it was Nihaal's team's turn. When no one came forth from that team, we were almost relieved. Until Shambhavi suddenly stood up and volunteered.

We turned off the cameras and wondered what to do. To tell Shambhavi to back off at this stage would be unfair to Ashutosh, because somebody from his team had already been slapped. To tell Ashutosh to slap her softly would again be unfair, given the fact that Vibhor's cheek was still red. The level of the task needed to be the same for both teams. All we could do was ask Shambhavi if she was absolutely sure. She was. Rannvijay and I exchanged a look; there was nothing we could do except hope that Ashu would be sensible enough to not slap her so hard. The camera rolled. Shambhavi stepped up, all of us watching, hoping…and then Ashutosh swung his arm and hit her with such force that for a minute, Shambhavi couldn't move. Neither could we. We cut the shot instantly; Rannvijay ran to her, I ran to Ashutosh. Shambhavi hadn't been hurt as much as her pride was. I gave Ashutosh a piece of my mind but there wasn't much I could say. After all, it was a task we'd set up ourselves. True, Shambhavi did volunteer, there had been no pressure on her, but I had engineered such a situation where she *could* choose to get slapped. And this I will always regret. I did try and make up for it: I got her to slap both Nihaal and Ashutosh so she'd feel better, but still, it was something that ought not to have happened.

And so, all five tasks done, it still came down to a tie between Nihaal and Ashu and we went to the tiebreaker: Sonel. It almost felt like a throwback from Season 4, only there, Anthony had picked his love over friendship, and here, Ashutosh picked his friend over his girlfriend, and eliminated Sonel in the semi-final. We figured Sonel would choose Nihaal as the winner, but I seemed to have been saddled with stupid people this season: Ashutosh, who was stupid enough to slap Shambhavi, who was stupid enough to have volunteered, and Sonel who behaved like a lovesick teenager and picked Ashutosh. Ashutosh Kaushik won the season without doing a single fucking thing and irritating though it was, it was also an insight into human behaviour. Ah, well, another season done.

I screamed pack-up, went and congratulated every member of the crew, except for Bumpy and Rickinaldo, who had a tradition of getting on their bikes and riding off every time we packed-up a season. As I hugged everyone, I felt tears welling up. I had a sinking feeling that this was it, that I wouldn't be a part of another season. Because you see I'd... Hang on a minute, you do remember what happened during our pit stop in Chennai before we took off abroad this season, right?

I'll remind you. We'd stopped at the Golden Beach Resort in Chennai, which was incidentally where we had begun our *Roadies* journey exactly five years ago. Ashish Patil flew in from Mumbai, saying he wanted to be there considering we were about to go abroad for the first time. I was talking to Ashish when Rannvijay came by, asked for my phone. I was surprised but gave it to him anyway. He took it, walked away, and I continued talking. Suddenly, a bucket full of water was flung at me. I was bloody soaking wet, and the behind-the-scenes camera appeared. It was Rannvijay who had flung the bucket, which was why he'd taken my phone away. Before I could react, Ashish held out an envelope in his hand and said, beaming, 'Congratulations, Mr Executive Producer of MTV.' I stopped short, unable to register it for a moment. It was the ultimate dream come true—this was exactly why I'd come to Mumbai five years ago, this was my goal. And here I was, getting promoted on national television. I stood there, stunned, trying to take it in.

That last day in Malaysia, as I hugged the final crew member, I played this back in my head. I thought I wouldn't be so involved next season onwards since I was now the EP. Ah, well, you know better!

The asshole years

The first alarm should have sounded when Janet Price told me during Season 4 that I could do anything, a thought that was reiterated during Season 5 when my crew was cool, uncaring almost, as I tried out one of the underwater tasks. (The contestants had to be tied to a chair that was weighed down and then thrown into a pool. The task was to unlock themselves; I had done it despite not knowing how to swim.) They believed I'd do it, they believed I was invincible. I believed them.

The second alarm should have rung when I walked into Bumpy's edit of the Season 5 auditions. There was a shot of me appearing on stage and, all of a sudden, the music changed and my entry was switched to slow motion, making it look very heroic. I remember telling him that it seemed ridiculous to act so self-important. Bumpy said it worked. I let it go.

The third ought to have hit it home for me when Rajiv and I had our first ever full-blown fight. We had different ideas about how *Splitsvilla*—which we were brainstorming about—should be shot. I told Rajiv I knew what I was talking about because (and I quote myself), 'this [was] Raghu's next show.' Those were my exact words. I should have known then. Speaking of oneself in the third person smacks of pride, arrogance and believing your own myth.

It was just the beginning.

◆

I returned to India from Season 5 as the EP of MTV. We got to the edit stage but I was no longer just the producer of *Roadies*. People had started treating me like a celebrity. At a party, Nikhil Chinnappa, who had been seeing how people reacted to me, came up to me and said, 'Dude, I think you're bigger than Shah Rukh Khan!' He meant it in jest, of course, but at that time in the MTV universe, I was *the* man. And guess what, I enjoyed it. Like Kuhu says, for someone who had spent a big portion of his life being beaten up and had grown up feeling inadequate, this was suddenly a series of self-affirmations.

It wasn't all love, though. For instance, I was getting mobbed outside the HT City office in Chandigarh once, when out of nowhere, this lady, about fifty years old, came and accused me of spoiling the new generation. I asked her why she felt that way and she said I was teaching kids how to abuse—she had two kids of her own so she knew. I got to know her kids were in their late teens and I just told her that *they* could perhaps teach me how to curse because everyone spoke that way, really. They just never did it in front of elders.

I got it in equal measure: the people who wanted to put me on a pedestal, and those who wanted to burn me at the stake.

There were also some weird ones. The ones who would come up to me and ask me to abuse them, the ones who would pick fights for some strange, masochistic satisfaction. Once, at a club, I was just leaving the bar with my drink when three big guys accosted me, flexing their muscles, saying they wanted me to take their personal interviews. I just shrugged them off saying I wasn't working. Another time, I was at dinner with friends and, as is my habit, was sitting with my back to everybody else when I heard a heated argument start at the table behind mine. A drunk girl suddenly burst out at the top of her voice (to get my attention no doubt): 'Why is it called *Roadies* if there's no fucking road?!' I stiffened, and my friends told me to remain calm. They just asked for the cheque and we left.

When people stop reacting to your work and start reacting to you, the situation becomes strange. My first reaction was to lock down everything in my life that wasn't work-related: my marriage, my close family and friends. I had it very clear in my head that no one from the outside world should be able to penetrate this. I wanted the world to believe that I was the person they saw on the show; I was more comfortable being misunderstood because, that way, my privacy was intact. Kuhu understood this because outside of *Roadies*, our love, our friendship, was rock solid, but whenever we were in the thick of the public craze, Kuhu tells me that she didn't know *that* Raghu. And somewhere along the way, I was beginning to forget the real me too. The taller Raghu had elbowed his way into my life and, stupidly, I did nothing to push him out. I became Roadies Raghu. And the Asshole Years began.

One of the most defining moments of this period happened during the *Roadies 6* auditions in Pune. Kuhu was helping me with the casting (I often get close friends and family to help with casting, and just so you know, no one gets paid, they do it for me) and she had moderated a couple of the group discussions that day. I wasn't at the venue the whole time. I came by in the evening for a bit, and we stood, chatting. All of a sudden, this big bunch of about twenty or thirty Roadie hopefuls spotted me and came over. Kuhu and I were holding hands, and I remember she got a little nervous seeing the crowd. These kids came charging at me, saying, 'Sir one photo, sir we'd like to talk to you…' I wavered for a second, then let go of Kuhu's hand and walked away, leaving the boys looking confused and Kuhu deeply hurt. She recently told me about this incident and had tears in her eyes. She had felt abandoned then, like I cared only for myself and not for her. I know it certainly seemed that way. I had, at that point, had an overwhelming urge to remove myself from the situation, to get away from the boys or at least to get away from Kuhu, who might have gotten hurt had I been mobbed. But was it more to safeguard myself than Kuhu? I don't know.

Even now, when I think about it, Rannvijay is years younger, was as popular, but I feel he handled the fame much more gracefully.

Though, of course, Rannvijay had always been the poster boy, be it in school or college, so he was used to being liked. On *Roadies*, (Season 3 onwards), he had a very friendly, approachable image. So off screen, too, he was as loved. I, however, was beginning to embody *Roadies* for the world, so every opposing view, every weird reaction that *Roadies* inspired was directed at me. And since I'd shut everything else up in my life, I was also the guy they did not get, the big question mark. They wondered where I came from, who I really was. I didn't want anyone to know Kuhu was my wife, I didn't want it getting out that Rajiv was my twin, because the extreme reactions I'd faced had me worried for them. But even while I was shutting myself up, I was savouring the success without realizing how much it had affected me.

In the meantime, Rajiv had, after many attempts, finally quit MTV and started working as the creative director at a start-up company called Colosceum. You now know them as the guys who produce *Roadies* and *Splitsvilla*. Anyway, we were at the wrap-up party of Season 5 in Malaysia when Shilpi Gupta—part of the marketing team for *Roadies* and a good friend—and her husband, Ravi, asked me what plans I had for MTV now that I was the EP. At this point, I felt that *Roadies* had become popular, I'd created a brand, and it was time to do something else. 'Romance,' I said to them. 'I want to make a reality show based on romance.' I hadn't thought it through, except that it would be another social experiment, a research into human behaviour. When I came back, that show became *Splitsvilla*. I know people say love is a pure emotion but for me, jealousy is an integral a part of love, as is insecurity. They are what drive people to crimes of passion. I wanted to explore the dark side of love.

◆

I came back to Mumbai, told MTV about the romance reality show and told them Colosceum and Rajiv would make it. They approved, and Rajiv and I began developing it. As I had mentioned earlier, this was when Rajiv and I had our first and most unpleasant fight. I was in the MTV conference room with him, Ashish and a guy called Hitesh who would be directing the show and Rajiv said something to the effect that this show would have to be shot better than *Roadies* and I took instant offence without even hearing him out. I snapped, saying he couldn't say that *Roadies* was shot shoddily because my philosophy was to catch a reaction without worrying about the frame because *that* was what I considered important. Content overruled the grammar of framing. Rajiv explained that what he meant was that we'd have to differentiate it from *Roadies* in style—since it was romance, it ought to look glossier. I snapped back saying that by giving emphasis to the frame meant losing sight of the content which was priority. An argument ensued but soon turned into a lone screaming match—my voice the loudest, my comebacks cutting and bitter. I yelled at everyone; I don't quite remember what I said but I know it was very hurtful.

On our way home, Rajiv again tried to explain to me that he meant he wanted to keep the substance but up the style a bit. I still thought the approach was wrong, though. And then I said (and this part I remember clearly), 'Rajiv, ever since *Roadies* 4 and 5 have happened and I've been made EP, everyone's been asking me what next. THIS is my next show, THIS is *Raghu's* next show.' It was a simple statement, effectively conveying much. I. Me. MY show. Rajiv was quiet.

I stepped out of the car and went home. Sometime later, Susan, Rajiv's wife, called Kuhu and asked whether we'd had a fight because Rajiv was in tears. I rushed over; back then he lived in the same building in the apartment above mine. I found him sobbing uncontrollably. He told me it was the first time I'd ever hurt him and so much. I apologized, but added that there was just too much pressure on me to deliver. The reason for the success of *Roadies* was that there had been no interference from anyone, so it was my vision, my show. With a new show, I was worried that I'd be saddled with points of view that I didn't like but would be forced to consider. Also compounding my emotional distress was the fact that I wasn't sleeping. At all. As EP, I would be looking at new concepts, new ideas all day, and at night, I would tour the edit rooms to supervise the edit of the current season of *Roadies*. It was exhausting. But that apart, I still feel that even though television is a collaborative art, it is not a democracy but a dictatorship. The vision is singular. A team can work along with the person whose idea it is, if they all work at the same frequency. A committee can never paint the Mona Lisa or the Sistine Chapel. I have no respect for committees.

I, however, also had an unreasonable paranoia of failure. The paranoia was because I'd seen success, I'd seen the adulation in the eyes of my team members, in the eyes of the MTV office staff, in ways I don't think anyone has. Seriously. Don't believe me?

This one time, MTV was launching a new show (I don't remember which); I had taken a break and walked out through the office back door, near the studio where the press conference was being held. I just casually walked into the studio to see what was happening when, out of nowhere, the public relations team appeared and pushed me out, literally! They said I couldn't be seen there because if the press saw me, they wouldn't write about the new show but pounce on me instead.

◆

We were midway into the *Roadies 5* telecast, this season rocking the ratings even more than Season 4. And as a result, that year, like the previous, *and* the next, my team got the highest increment. I was as proud as a parent.

Then came the time for my appraisal.

Then in my sixth year at MTV, I went into Ashish's cabin, head held high, my face impassive, a piece of paper rustling in my chest pocket. Ashish sat me down and very cheerfully pushed a sheet of paper with a figure written on it across to me: my increment. I looked at him, at the figure…and then reached into my pocket, took out *my* piece of paper, slid it across the table to him. It was my resignation. I had actually taken a printout before going in because I knew this would happen, that I wouldn't get my due. Ashish read it, his smile fading, and then asked me point-blank what I wanted. Well, dear reader, I wanted to know what the fuck it took around this place for a guy to get respect. Why were the VJs paid so much just for a couple of days of work and the people making the show ignored? Did hard work and achievement count for nothing? What *did* it take?! Let me guess: a high-rated show? Uh, check that! A high-rated sequel? Check! Five years in a row? Check! Success on camera? Check! Ashish was silent. I went on. It appalled me that a creative person who gave his work all his sweat, blood, tears, time, family, everything, still had to make do with peanuts for raises while the guys in front of the camera walked away with the meaty cut! More silence. I was done. I got up, told him it was up to him, and walked out. This was me being assertive, which I hadn't been in my life up to that point. Apparently, Ashish later told the head of MTV HR that he thought I had gotten too big for my boots. I can understand his point of view. In my head, I *was* too big for this shit. Anyway, long story short, eventually Ashish agreed, and all was well.

◆

A few days later, I was partying at home with some friends and Rajiv. We were talking about a team of editors who had recently done a lot of work, were getting several projects and were referring to themselves as the 'dream team'. Now, at first I found this funny but as the night went on, I started to get very rattled by it. When Rajiv said they can call themselves whatever they liked, I lost my temper at him. Again. How dare anyone dub themselves the dream team, who the fuck are they, if there really is a dream team in this country, it's MY team. For some reason, I felt that my team was being robbed of their glory. My basic argument may have been sane but it was too silly a situation to get so mad about. And that apart, my attitude was hurting the people I loved; I was just obnoxious, even *I* wouldn't tolerate such behaviour. I made everything about me: my team, my show. In fact, Kuhu's sister, Snigdha, pointed out that it was impossible to have a conversation with me without *Roadies* coming up.

It proved to be quite a problem with my interpersonal relationships. Not just Kuhu, my whole group of close friends wasn't sure how to react to me anymore. I had started taking pride in my popularity even as I remained clueless about how to handle the press. If they didn't want to crucify me, they wanted to know all about my childhood: whether it was abusive, whether I'd ever known parental love—they drew their conclusions from my image. And wrote what they thought were sensitive pieces which spoke of how, *because* I'd had a bad past, I'd turned out this way—which basically insinuated that 'this way' was wrong. I reject that. I was not wrong. I *am* not wrong.

Around that time, I met this journalist called Jasmine who worked for *HT City*, Chandigarh, who, unlike the others, seemed nice. Her article was a breath of fresh air—sensible, insightful even. When I called to thank her, she said she found me fascinating and asked if I'd like to do a column for them. I agreed. It was a weekly column called 'Keeping it Real with Raghu Ram' and I was immensely proud of it, more so because amma is a journalist. Every week I'd get the paper and proudly show it off to Kuhu: look, *my* name, *my* column! She'd be least bothered. I'd be hurt. Every time. Years later, I found out that Kuhu and my close circle of family and friends had agreed that I was being consumed by my success and it was their job to try and keep me grounded.

The ploy didn't work. The more often Kuhu brushed off my popularity, the more desperate I became to prove it to her. The world was talking about me, I was a fucking God in my office, so when she ignored it, I thought it was because she resented my success. This wasn't so hard for me to believe then, because in our circle every one of us was an artiste in his/her own right and craved success. Unexpectedly but technically, *I* was the guy who had made it, who was popular. I thought she hated that.

It came up once again during the premiere of Kuhu's first Hindi film, *Jaane Tu Ya Jaane Naa*. We had just bought a car for this very occasion because I wanted Kuhu to drive to her first ever premiere in style. Anyway, we walked into the Reliance mall at Borivali, where the screening was being held. I was Kuhu's 'plus one'. No sooner had we walked in, however, that a huge roar went up. I saw that there were four floors full of people and a lot of youngsters had registered the bald head. They started chanting my name and Avantika, Imran Khan's then girlfriend now wife, turned to me saying, 'Dude, it seems like it's your film premiere!' I was petrified of Kuhu's reaction, so I just took her arm and started running to the elevator where I shut the door. The elevator doors opened on the fourth floor. I ignored the press and ran into the screening hall with Kuhu. We were right at the door when I heard a girl screaming my name, 'Please Raghu, please!' I doubled back, went up to her, kissed her on the forehead, and then ran back. I kept apologizing to Kuhu, though she didn't mind.

It was a vicious cycle where the more I would try and impress upon her that I had succeeded, the more she would ignore it and play it down. The more she played it down, the more I felt the need to spell it out. So much so that if we were out and I got mobbed, I would comply for autographs and photographs, even overdo it a bit just to tell her, *this* is what I mean, *this* is who I am. I was getting trapped in a vicious circle. For the first time in years I was actually becoming an angry man.

I even nearly lost it at nanna once. I was in Delhi, and though amma and nanna were quite removed from the circus of my success, nanna did gently broach the topic of my cursing on the show. I instantly shot him a stern look and said, don't interfere, stay away from it, that's my work, it will happen the way I want it to. Nanna, patient as ever, softly said, 'That's all fine, beta, but I just don't like it when people speak badly of you for it.' It was then that it dawned on me that my work, my attitude, was having an adverse effect on those close to me. I apologized to both amma and nanna, but there wasn't anything I could do about it. They were proud of me and, for most part, I have always kept them and my sister protected from what goes on in this part of my world and hoped that they don't have to bear the brunt of it.

◆

I'll go into a quick flash forward here. Right after *Roadies 6*, MTV hosted a huge offsite which is basically when the entire office takes off on a one to two day trip just to get together, think of new ideas, drink and party. We'd gone to Khandala that year. The idea was that all the MTV teams would be mixed and matched, and new teams would be formed. For example, a team would consist of members who were from production, marketing, on-air promotions, etcetera, and each team would have to come up with ideas.

I was forbidden from contributing since it was all my team and I had been doing. I'd come up with the concepts for *MTV It Sucks*, *Splitsvilla* and *The Fast and The Gorgeous*. So my team and I stayed out of it, the entire exercise happened, and the ideas that cropped up sucked. That evening, I got a little too free with the alcohol at the party and marched up to Ashish Patil. He smiled at me and I smiled back. And then told him, in the nicest way possible, that he was fucked. Ashish looked at me, confused, and I was sweet enough to elaborate: 'Without me, you don't have a single idea, a single person who can make a show. If I go, you're fucked.' He was probably as disappointed with Team MTV's ideas as I was, if not more. But again, my manner was anything but delicate. No wonder he thought I had become too big for my boots.

In 2007, the year before I quit, when my friends and family were all trying hard to keep my head firmly planted on the ground, my team, with whom I spent every waking minute, loved me even more. They didn't see me as an asshole; I was their leader, still fiercely protective of them, and in their eyes I could do no wrong. This didn't help matters because I'd feel validated by their attitude towards me, and just as betrayed by my friends and family who thought I needed a reality check. This *was* my reality, for God's sake! It's safe to say that I was not a likeable person at this point of time, although I was on the top professionally. In fact, the most popular season ever of *Roadies* was yet to come. Season 6: Hell Down Under. Prophetic words, one might say. In a year, I'd be quitting MTV, I'd be quitting *Roadies*, I'd actually be in hell. A hell of my own making? Perhaps.

◆

'Are you home?' Susan asked over the phone. I was. She came over and we were casually chatting when, all of a sudden, Rajiv walked in. Have I mentioned that Rajiv had a headful of hair? Well, he did. Only now he didn't. He had shaved it all off. I was stunned. He looked good, and spookily like me. He felt liberated, he said. He had had a haircut he didn't like, so he got it all off. Worked for me. Worked for us. Let me explain. As kids, Rajiv and I went along with the whole twin funda: we looked the same, wore similar clothes, had similar hairstyles, had glasses. Though I was fed up of people staring and pointing, I really loved the fact that Rajiv and I looked alike. Once I joined BBC and shaved my head, the hair became a distinguishing factor. But now, in the wake of his new 'hairstyle', we were back to being identical, and we loved it.

Kuhu came home, saw Rajiv, freaked out. We called Rannvijay over, who, after being appropriately shocked when he saw it, said on an impulse, 'You know what? For *Roadies 6*, we should get Rajiv on the panel! It'll be something else.' I don't think Rannvijay realized what a great idea he had given, and how much of a key it would prove to be in the continuing success of *Roadies*. I looked at Rajiv, he looked at me. 'Would you do it?' I asked. 'You think I can?' he replied. Rajiv was, in any case, conducting group discussions in earlier seasons and doing mock-up interviews with me and Rannvijay before the personal interviews. I had always loved his quick comebacks; we'd be in splits, and many a times I would use Rajiv's comebacks in the real interviews. Between us, Rajiv is the witty one and if anyone could come in and take *Roadies* to places I couldn't, it was him. It was the perfect idea, I told him. He agreed.

We called and conveyed the idea to Akshay Rajput (Kaandi). He freaked out, too, and the very next day, Rajiv and I, bespectacled, bald and purposely colour-coordinated in white shirts and blue jeans, walked into the MTV office. Everyone stopped working and got up to gape at us. Word spread, the entire office came to see us. (Incidentally, in the Season 6 auditions, Rajiv and I both sport zero-powered spectacles. By this time, we had both undergone the lasik surgery and no longer required glasses, but the spectacles were hung on to because wearing the glasses added to the twin-ness of our appearances.)

Ashish was damn kicked about it, all of us were. Since I had turned into the focal point of the show, bringing Rajiv on, well, was a no-brainer. By this time there were many wannabe *Roadies* shows on other youth channels, but bringing a twin on was something nobody could compete with.

For me, though, this was a huge leap of faith. As you may recall, I was very conscious about keeping my family out of the sudden spike in my popularity because I was worried that they'd not be able to handle the extreme reactions. For instance, my Orkut account had been hacked, photos from Rannvijay's birthday party had been leaked where Rajiv (then with hair) was seen dancing. The vicious circle spun on and on and on. I shut doors, people pried open windows, I boarded them up, but they continued to dig holes. And with *Roadies* 6, I would actually be opening up one door myself. It worked for me, and didn't as well. But more on that in a bit.

◆

Soon after *Roadies* 5, MTV's office in Australia was facing a lack of resources and they'd requested for mid-level employees from India who could come take over for a couple of weeks. Ashish offered to fly me and Kuhu to Sydney, so off we went. We stayed at a hotel for a day before moving to a service apartment. What I found most amusing, intriguing even, was a sign put up in the hotel room that said: 'Please look into your shoes before you put them on.' I asked the guys at the reception about it and they said I ought to take it very seriously because there could be poisonous spiders in my shoes. True to myself, this bit of information excited me no end…and it got me thinking. And when the two weeks were up and I was back in Mumbai, brainstorming about *Roadies 6*, I said: 'Australia, the outback, let's go there!' Because, in the outback, there were more things that could potentially kill you than the whole world put together. Scary? No, exciting! Of course, that's not what I told the Australian tourism department, who were informed that we'd be honoured to showcase their beautiful countryside.

I started reading a book by one of my favourite authors, Bill Bryson, called *Down Under*, which had an interesting take on Australia. Also around this time, Christopher Nolan's *The Dark Knight* had released, the second in the Batman trilogy. Now, I've always been a Batman fan, but this time around I was fascinated by the Joker. He was the Agent of Chaos, and I actually felt that the character spoke to me. I could relate to it. His philosophy, that civility or civilization is a mask, and that the minute things stop going according to plan, the mask of civility is ripped off and thereon it takes barely anything for man to reduce to animal, echoed my dinner-party theory. Season 6 was actually inspired by *The Dark Knight*.

◆

In true Batman-speak, I'd say Rajiv and I were the Agents of Chaos this season, but even if Nolan inspired it, the credit for the season's success goes only and only to Rajiv. It wouldn't have happened if he hadn't come on board.

And the idea of having a tag line for every season wouldn't have been conceived if it weren't for Piyush Raghani. In Season 5, I'd added a footnote, 'The Game Goes International', because it was our first time abroad and I wanted to emphasize that. But it would have been a one-off if, in the sixth season, Piyush hadn't come up with 'Hell Down Under'. After that, it became a tradition to have tag lines for each season. Piyush headed on-air promos at the time, and I knew him from my Channel [V] days. He's absolutely barking mad, which is why I suspect he was hired. It was he who came up with the name 'Splitsvilla'. I had originally wanted to call it 'Tough Love' but it didn't catch on. Splitsvilla was a smart name, and though I wasn't initially convinced, it has caught on now.

Piyush was also the guy who came up with the hoarding ideas for *Roadies 6*, which, if you remember, showed me as a shark and Rajiv as a crocodile. When I first heard of the idea, I was quite surprised. To start with, publicity for *Roadies* had never been about me but always about the contestants, but this season onwards, MTV decided that the one selling point they had was Raghu, and with Rajiv coming on board, it was a marketing bonanza. If I had any doubts that *Roadies* had become about me, this cleared them.

By now, with the audience reactions ranging from the sweet to the bizarre, I had a vague idea that this year's turnout at the auditions would be a bit more than what we anticipated. I remember telling Ashish that we ought to do one round of the auditions online but he thought it was unnecessary. It was early morning when we got to Kolkata. I headed out to the Swabhoomi auditorium before Rajiv to get the shoot started. The driver had been strictly instructed to get the car in through the back gate, only there was one little complication. The front gates hadn't opened, of course, but the queue was humungous. Starting at the front gate, it spilled out all over the street, and then wound around and reached the back gate. As a result, there were Roadie hopefuls at the back gate as well. We were in a Qualis, my driver and I, and he got confused and disoriented when he saw the crowd. He then drove in through the main gate. Big mistake. The Qualis didn't have tinted glasses, and I, the guy they loved to hate, was in clear view. The crowd lost it. They broke the lines, surrounded the Qualis, started chanting my name, hitting the glass windows, shaking the vehicle. The driver was petrified, shitting bricks, and I didn't feel any braver. But I had to make a decision; I didn't want the windows to break and anyone to get hurt, so I got out. I thought I'd calm them down, sign some autographs and then get into the venue. Simple.

Not. I got out of the car, shut the door and instantly regretted it. The mob's full attention was on me now. I was being pushed and pulled, at least twenty people had their hands on me at any given point, and I remember thinking, oh FUCK, what have I done?! I seriously thought I was going to get hurt. Thankfully, the security got in, pushed the crowd away, and guided me ahead. Now, there was a small barricade and a high podium built for the cameramen to get top angle shots from. Somewhere between coming out of the car, getting mobbed and then being dragged away to safety by the security guys, the switch happened. I was terrified and then I was not. I was being protected by Roadies Raghu. He got on top of the podium, and I suddenly felt taller, wilder, energetic, as he roared at the crowd, feeding off their madness, and they roared back. This was flamboyance at its most vulgar; I was not only accepting the adulation but revelling in it, encouraging it even! And that's not me, that's him.

◆

The crowd was quelled, Rajiv arrived at the venue well-protected, the auditions began. Earlier, the contestants knew Nikhil and though he tweaked his personality for the show, he still remained the familiar one for them. With Rajiv, however, it was the ultimate magician's trick. He was the Joker in the pack (thank you, Christopher Nolan)—no one knew what he would be. Even we didn't know, for that matter. We just decided to go with the flow and see what happened. People wondered whether he'd be the good cop to my bad cop, or maybe a worse cop. Rajiv turned out to be none of these. He had a knack of taking their confidence away with just an amused smile or a witty crack. I would hate to face him in the audition.

Another thing that happened was, the contestants took us more seriously now. Gone was the comfortable familiarity of Nikhil—they were now faced with two unpredictable guys. Now we are from MTV, yes, but Rajiv and I are also from Munirka, D.T.E.A. and Deshbandhu College. All in all, a formidable combination. I very calmly explained this to a goonda contestant in Ahmedabad who said he 'uses and throws girls' every few months, that dude, we're sitting behind a table, are regular decent guys and that's what you're counting on. But get the table out of the way and let us rip off our jackets, and we're bigger goondas than you can even imagine. The goonda freaked out and confided in Ayushmaan outside the room that he was actually scared.

By *Roadies 6*, the audition episodes had started being intimidating. It was a conscious effort because I'd figured that everyone who walked into the interview room would have a plan. In boxing, there's a saying that every boxer has a plan until he gets hit. Our job was to hit fast and hard. It was only when things didn't go according to their plan that the candidate would start fumbling, floundering and I would get an insight into the real person.

When these kids fill their forms, they think they're telling us about themselves. Well they are, but they're also providing me with ammunition to turn their plan on its head and then observe what they do. Aside from wanting to figure out what lay beneath an aggressive contestant, sometimes Rajiv and I would simply take on the bully just to show him who was boss. And we were the bosses. After all, we were trained at Munirka.

◆

I really, really regret casting Ashutosh Kaushik in *Roadies 5*, not just because all he did was play politics and not perform (and still won), not just because he slapped Shambhavi, but also because this guy coming in made others feel that all they needed was a history of fighting to get through and win. So this time around when we got to Delhi, there was an overwhelming number of kids from villages around Delhi who could be called bad elements.

The day of the Delhi auditions, the madness began even before it was actually light. It was barely 5 a.m. and the gates at the NCUI

Auditorium in Hauz Khas had already been broken—some assholes had jumped over them when someone had started the rumour that the forms were being distributed early. When I reached, I was smuggled in from the back gate and things were already very tense. Once inside, we started the auditions, trying to dismiss the commotion outside. I was sitting in on a couple of the group discussions with the moderator when someone came in from Fountainhead, the event management company, and said we can't go on because there was pandemonium outside, a near riot. The crowd was going berserk, destroying property. I was stunned. The other moderators were informed, the contestants within sent out safely. Everyone from the crew gathered, all of us were scared. But I am of the opinion that if you've gone out for a shoot, the shoot has to happen, come what may. I was still thinking of how to go on when a bunch of cops entered the room, asking who Raghu Ram was. I put up my hand. They said the crowd outside was chanting my name, asking for me, and whether I'd consider going out to talk some sense into them. I had thought of this already, and I had managed it to an extent in Kolkata. But one of my producers, Aien, stopped me, told me there was no way I was going out; she was sure I'd get lynched. I argued but I was overruled, so much so that everyone was putting their heads together and trying to figure out a way of getting me out of there safely instead. The cops left the room. Reports started pouring in: people within the waiting area, caught up in mob mentality, had now started breaking stuff and were chanting, sloganeering. One of the event management guys grabbed a mic and told the Roadie hopefuls that if they didn't behave themselves, we would be forced to cancel the auditions. No sooner had he said this that a chair came flying at him. It missed his head but triggered off more madness, more chaos. It was mass hysteria.

What you watched on air was barely a glimpse of what actually happened.

Later I watched the videos on YouTube and was horrified by what actually went on outside that day. People were out on the street, doing wheelies on their bikes; traffic was blocked, buses broken, autos overturned, stones pelted at passing vehicles. To this day, I don't know why it happened. We hadn't shut the gates, we hadn't rejected any of them, we were just holding the auditions, just doing our job. There was no reason, no logic to their actions. It was scary.

The first thing I did was round up all the event managers, the promoters, and got them to wear their *Roadies* T-shirts inside out to make sure they weren't identified as the crew. Second: the girls on the team were all sent out with these guys to the cars via the back gate. Next, my male producers also left via the back gate; I was scared for them as well because the behind-the-scenes segment had also made Chhotu, Bumpy and the others well-known. I called Rajiv, told him not to come. Finally, only I was left along with V2, the gyaan sessions brain and our cameramen, Kamal and Shanta, who had refused to leave without me. We were on the first floor, and I could now hear over the walkie-talkie that the mob had flooded the ground floor and was breaking everything. The lift was disconnected and some of these fuckers climbed the lift cables and got on to the first floor! We instantly clambered to the stairs to get to the second and top floor. Once again, I could hear them thrashing the first floor through the walkie-talkie.

We entered the conference room on the second floor and V2, Kamal and Shanta made me sit down and stood all around me. This was my own personal snap moment. Outside, there were kids vandalizing, burning my posters, screaming abuses and calling out my name—the fury was very clearly directed at me. And within, my crew, my colleagues were literally standing up for me, not caring for themselves, ready to take on whatever came my way. This was what I'd become. I didn't understand it but I remember it being overwhelming. There was also a conflict in my head because I felt like a huge dickhead considering I was the safety officer and I was the one who ought to be making sure no one got hurt. This was not was they had signed up for, this was *my* job. But they wouldn't let me stand up, they were very protective of me. This lasted an hour—sixty nerve-wracking minutes. Slowly, we thought we heard the noise decibel go down. There seemed to be more cops on the road, and we thought, okay, if the second wave of madness happens, we had to get out before it could escalate.

Two cars were brought out near the back gate and I felt overwhelmed again. These guys formed a circle around me and moved as a unit down to the first floor and then to the back gate. I got into the boot of the car and hid under a very stinky pile of clothes that belonged to the driver. We got back to our suite at Hotel Vikram in Lajpat Nagar only to be informed within thirty minutes that about a hundred people were outside, asking for me at the reception. And just then, Aien came to me, handed me a ticket to Mumbai and said, Raghu just take the ticket, fly back. I protested as I didn't want to leave these guys behind but she argued that the mobbing, the madness, the chaos wasn't for them, it was for me, so with me gone, they'd be much safer. I couldn't counter that. And as it turned out, Raghu 'Rude' Ram was (against his wishes) driven to Delhi airport in two cars with eight bouncers. They were the real deal, these guys—about seven feet tall, hefty, menacing. They saw me all the way to the airport, and waited till I had checked in. I flew back to Mumbai and the auditions in Delhi were scrapped for the moment. They happened again a few days later, but this time Ashish agreed to follow my conditions. We shortlisted forms online, emailed and informed a limited number of contestants individually to appear, and that's how the auditions finally happened.

I was glad when the chaotic auditions were behind us and we had started the journey from Manesar, near Delhi. But this time there was one difference: I couldn't be on the journey with my crew. I had to go back and be the EP at MTV. It was a strange, sentimental night for me. Now if Kaandi had come out and said, motherfucker, I'm so glad you're leaving, you're the reason why we get paid so little and still have to do this show, I'd have been so happy. But he actually turned to me and said, 'I'll miss you, bro.' I looked away. I couldn't handle it.

Later that night, after getting hammered, I told an equally drunk Rannvijay that I'd miss the curious mix of thrill, fear and unexplainable calm before trying out every task only because I had my little brother with me. Poor Rannvijay started sobbing. We had a good run, I said, five years, and it's not meant to be anymore, but I want you to know that of all the things I'd miss about *Roadies*, this—you and me—is what I'll miss the most.

And so it came to be that *Roadies 6* was flagged off the next morning by a hungover Rannvijay still smelling of the night before. Meanwhile, I returned to Mumbai.

◆

I will always remember *Roadies 6: Hell Down Under* for its amazing ratings every week. For Palak, one of the most reactive, provocative contestants ever seen on reality television. And for the fact that it was the season during which my relationship with MTV deteriorated.

When I got back to Mumbai, I was approached by Miditech who had just launched their own channel, Real. They were making a show called *Sarkar ki Duniya*, which was basically a bunch of people on an island with one guy in charge: an overlord called Sarkar. They wanted me to be him but I refused—it was too close to what I was doing on *Roadies*. The other show they called me on board for was *Sitaaron ko Chhoona Hai*, which was a singing reality show involving an academy of sorts and I was to be the dean of the academy. I liked the offer, the money was good, too. I went to Ashish—as was my habit with such matters—and told him straight out what the deal was. I told him I never got paid for appearing on *Roadies*, anyway (I was only paid as an employee of the channel), and that I had equity outside that I wanted to monetize. It was not in the same space as *Roadies*, so there was no conflict of interest here. Furthermore, we were only going to shoot on weekends when MTV was shut, so I would not be taking any time away from my work. I could see no problem with this arrangement. Ashish heard me out, then said, 'No, bro, this doesn't work for MTV.' I was very hurt, but all I said was, 'Well, bro, in that case, *MTV* doesn't work for me.' I felt inside my pocket for the familiar rustle of paper, and out came my resignation. The date was 12 December 2008. Ashish read it through, the same resigned look on his face as he said I'd have to sign a special contract. Sure, I said. And waited.

Fast forward to New Year's Eve. Kuhu and I, her sister, her husband and friends, were all driving from Delhi to Corbett when I received a panic call of sorts from my team. Something had been happening for a couple of weeks now—after I was done checking the edits of the season, Ashish and V2 would come in and make changes. They would knock some stuff off, stuff they thought was too edgy. I agree that it was a violent season, and in parts very unpleasant (mostly credited to Palak), but all the same, re-editing after I'd been through the episode, was, frankly, unacceptable.

It was obviously a power tussle and I refused to take it lying down. I instantly called up the human resources department at MTV and told them I'd given in my resignation on 12 December and since there had been no response, it was to be counted as accepted. My last working day at the channel would be 12 January 2009. I hung up, determined. Within minutes, V2 called me to ask what had happened. I gave it to him; I was rude, hurtful. I was hurtful to Ashish as well and I remember sending an email to HR that said: 'It seems as if random people think they know the show better than me. Congratulations, obviously you now have a second-rung team who can take the property and grow it further. Obviously, I am no longer needed, so I am out. All the best to you.' Now, while I'm aware that I did end up hurting these guys, guys who were more than just colleagues, I am also equally aware that if such a situation were to arise again, I'd react in exactly the same way. If they had an issue with the edit, they ought to have told me about it instead of making changes behind my back. They may be the bosses but *Roadies* was mine.

The clock struck midnight, the new year had arrived: 2009. It was going to be quite a year. When I returned to the office in early January, my contract was waiting. And such a ridiculous contract it was. It basically said that I couldn't work outside, I couldn't quit MTV. I had to recognize that my contribution to MTV and *Roadies* was stuff that couldn't be measured in money. If I worked outside, MTV had the right to stop me and sue me, and so on. It was basically bonded labour! I sent a reply to Ashish saying, 'You could have sent me the contract you did, or you could have sent me a single line: Tu karega, tera baap bhi karega.' MTV doesn't own my ass and never has. I told him I was quitting right then and there. And since they had threatened me with legal action, I dared them now. Sue me. See if I care. I'm out.

Ashish called me, tried to sort the matter. I was still livid, but the contract was brought in, deliberated over, the clauses changed and ultimately signed. I went back to work, but something had shifted in the equation.

A few weeks later, I was working on the concept for *Splitsvilla 2*. Rajiv was in a meeting with Ashish about the show (since Colosceum was making it), and he said we ought to get Rannvijay to host it like he did with Season 1. Ashish instantly said, no, he can't host it and Raghu can't make special appearances either. Rajiv was stunned because it had worked in the first season, and this rejection made no logical sense. At least not then. Now, however, I get what was happening: Ashish was trying to sideline me. If he had let me have my way with *Splitsvilla 2*, I'd really have MTV by the balls. Two of their successful properties/ shows would depend on me, and as a company, they couldn't afford that. Technically, they weren't wrong. No channel wants to be at the mercy of a single person. I only had a problem with how it all played out. The equation worsened. It was almost like a replay of what had happened with Rohit: the more they tried to rein me in, the more rebellious I got.

But I'd signed the contract, so I stayed on, unpleasant though it all was. I took care of two more shows, *Teen Diva* for *The Times of India* and *Fast and the Gorgeous*, a hunt for pit-stop girls for Force India, Kingfisher's F1 racing team, but the shit was flying by now. I was barely home, and if I was, I was snappy, rude, sleep-deprived and short-tempered. Kuhu felt it wasn't fair that I was working day and night through the week, shooting in Delhi over the weekend, then coming back and going straight to work. It was taking a toll on our marriage.

In the middle of all this, we had to shoot the finale of Season 6 on 14 April, the eve of Rajiv's and my birthday. The shoot wrapped up, and Kuhu and Susan came by to surprise us. It was all very nice—only, I felt numb on the inside. I remember telling Kuhu, 'I don't think I can do this anymore.'

I flew back to Mumbai, this time having made up my mind about certain things. I went to Ashish and for the umpteenth time, I told him I was quitting. My personal life was fucked and I wasn't okay with that. I needed a break, I didn't know whether I'd come back, but I knew I needed to go. And this time Ashish must have seen something different in my eyes because he didn't protest. I quit *Roadies*. I quit MTV.

Complete lockdown

But it wasn't easy to walk out of MTV. I had commitments to fulfil. I went back to Goa to wrap up the *Splitsvilla 2* shoot which Nikhil was hosting that year. As soon as that got done, *The Fast and the Gorgeous* began to be shot, also in Goa. And *Sitaaron ko Chhoona Hai* also ended exactly a week after, in Delhi. When I would fly back to Mumbai in mid-2009, I would be free from everything. I wasn't looking forward to it, though. I wasn't dreading it either. I was just numbly going about my work.

Days went by and soon, my last day at MTV was upon me. I went through the day like any other, shooting till sunset, and then retired to the crew villa, called for food and sat down, a cloud settling over me.

I was feeling horrible, really, really unwanted. At MTV, a farewell party was tradition, even if you were fired. I'd been to numerous ones, but there had been no talk of one for me. Forget that I had made *Roadies*, forget that I'd given the channel their highest-rated show, I was the fucking EP and I was quitting but here I was, not even in the office on my last day but at a bloody outdoor shoot. And never mind a farewell party, not a single person from the channel thought to pick up the phone and call me. I didn't even know if they remembered. I sat outside the villa, completely alone—no Kuhu, no Rajiv, no Rannvijay. I was picking at my food when, suddenly, a plate was plonked on the table.

I looked up. It was a cake for me, and there stood my entire shooting crew, the same bunch of guys who shot *Roadies*, *Splitsvilla* and *The Fast and the Gorgeous*. Kaandi, Shanta, Pakya, Fanaa and Chawda had all come to say goodbye. I nodded in acknowledgement, then abruptly got up, excused myself. I walked into the washroom, shut the door, and broke down. This was what I'd been looking for: validation, the feeling that I would be missed, that it mattered to someone. And it wasn't the management or the cool office gang at MTV, but my crew that managed to convey it to me. I came out, and I remember that night to this day. Just hanging out with my crew by the beach. I was giving up my dream job but these guys had made it better. It was more than enough for me.

I flew to Delhi, finished up the last week of *Sitaaron ko Chhoona Hai*, and now I couldn't wait to get home. At the Delhi airport, I was so exhausted that I fell asleep sitting by the boarding gate. Hours later when I woke up, I was duly informed that the flight had taken off. And now all the pent-up frustration within me, my anger at everything and everybody, came bursting out. I turned red in the face and created a huge fuss. I told them I didn't fucking care if they had made announcements, it was *their* responsibility to make sure I got on the plane. To cut a long story short, I was put on the next flight, landed at Chhatrapati Shivaji Airport, took a cab to Yari Road, knocked on my door. When Kuhu opened it, I told her, in all seriousness, 'I'm home. For you. And I'm not going anywhere.' And I didn't go anywhere. My home became my fortress. Here on began a strange period of my life. The asshole years were drawing to a close. But I still had miles to go, months to go before I was fully healed. Fifteen, to be specific.

◆

I stayed home for the first couple of months, not doing anything, just vegetating, just being a zombie. Kuhu was right there, anytime I needed her, but she knew what I'd been through and that I needed to be by myself. She let me be. There were too many questions in my head, too many contradictions. I was never supposed to be on television. But I was. Being on television, I ought to have been paid for it. But I wasn't. MTV was supposed to love me for all that I had done. They didn't. In fact, they didn't care! There were so many VJs on MTV who were supposed to be popular, but they weren't. I was not supposed to be popular, but I was. And that meant I shouldn't have been hated, right? But I was! When I walked out on the street and someone approached me, I didn't know whether they wanted an autograph or an argument. Nothing in my life made sense. I had a lot of time to think about what I had become, and was scared by it. A drastic change took place in me, and I went from revelling in the adulation to being repulsed by it. I felt like a shadow of the man I used to be, and Roadies Raghu was nowhere around to rescue me.

It took a couple of months for me to step out of my self-imposed house arrest. I had begun to enjoy the routine of having no routine. I didn't have to set an alarm; I would wake up and the whole day stretched in front of me: broad, sunny, and full of glorious nothingness. I loved it, I cherished it. So much so that I began to resent it when people would call and ask to meet outside. Because that meant making a plan, which I didn't want.

Three months passed and Kuhu told me I couldn't be this way, I had to pick myself up. I said, okay, let's leave Mumbai. Go away for a while. I didn't want to be in the city. Remember my burnout at Miditech? This was maybe a few times worse than that. I couldn't bear to look at the television or a camera, and you'll understand this emotion only if you've ever suffered from a burnout. This time, though, I had money, thanks to *Sitaaron ko Chhoona Hai*. So I decided I wanted to go away to the Himalayas. Not just because I prefer mountains to beaches, but also because I had Goa coming out of my ears! So Kuhu called her dad, who, since he was a chief engineer at PWD, organized accommodation for us at Kanasar in Uttarakhand. It had been an army base till 1965, after which it was opened to the public. After a pit stop at Chakrata, we would make our way to the forest reserve up in the Himalayas.

We took a flight to Delhi and then a train to Dehradun, and I was shit scared that I'd be recognized on the train. I give Kuhu a lot of credit for dealing with me during that time in my life. She was playing three roles simultaneously: she was my best friend, my mother and my bodyguard, all rolled into one. Thankfully, the train journey was uneventful. We reached Dehradun, took a car to Chakrata. And all the calm I felt after the train journey evaporated as soon as we entered Chakrata. Because this little town went MAD as soon as they realized I had arrived. My presence there started something of a carnival; everybody had to meet me, *everybody*. Wherever I went, there were people following me. It was worse than being in Mumbai.

We left Chakrata as soon as we could and headed to Kanasar. And after the mind-boggling madness of Chakrata, Kanasar was a huge, huge relief. We stayed at a beautiful wooden cabin facing a lawn surrounded by a white picket fence and overlooking the ranges. It was primitive, minimalistic and beautiful. This was where I needed to be: in a complete state of isolation. Peace, at last.

◆

While on my way to Kanasar, I'd gotten a call from writer-director Abbas Tyrewala, saying he wanted to cast me in his next film starring John Abraham. It would eventually be called *Jhootha Hi Sahi*. I told him I couldn't act but he said making me act was his headache. Apparently he needed a certain personality for a character in the film, and I had it. I said okay.

It was in the span of these fifteen months that I shot for two films, *Jhootha Hi Sahi* and Farah Khan's *Tees Maar Khan*, in which my dream to work with Akshay Kumar came true.

Anyway, at the end of this delicious isolation, I returned to the real world ready to take on the film project. But before I took off for London to shoot *Jhootha Hi Sahi*, I received a bizarre call from MTV. Shahzad Bhagwagar, who was heading production now, casually asked me, 'So can we crack a deal about the auditions?' I wasn't sure I had heard right. 'Auditions?' I asked, 'What auditions?' Pat came the reply:

'Roadies, bro, Season 7!' I was quiet for a moment and then I said that since I had quit, if they wanted to 'crack a deal' it would have to be for the whole season, not just the auditions. 'Bro, I've just been asked to talk to you about the auditions,' he said. I was silent for a while and then said no, I won't do it.

Jhootha Hi Sahi was on a two-month schedule, and it was my first time ever on a Bollywood film set. It was really fun. It was only whenever I would get in touch with Mumbai or even get any kind of update from the city that I'd lapse back to feeling low. This was around the time I received an email from Ashish saying, bro, why don't you come do the auditions? I saw this as part of a gradual process of removing me from Roadies. And I wasn't going to go with the plan. I replied saying that reducing my presence on the show would be a step down for me and I wasn't going to help anyone make me redundant in a property I had helped create. It would have to be everything or nothing. Also, they'd have to pay me. Since I was no longer an employee of MTV, they would have to engage me as an artist. I would rather not do Roadies than negotiate on these terms. Ashish replied saying that it was unfortunate I felt this way, but that if I couldn't do it, it was okay, we'd work on something else some other time. I should have been happy. I wanted to be free of Roadies and, finally, I was. But it hurt. A lot. Ashish seemed only too happy to let me go. And even though I had said no to Roadies, I felt rejected. Disrespected.

By the time I came back, it was mid-August and MTV had announced the launch of Roadies 7. It was all over the papers—not the launch of the new season, but my absence at the press conference. Every article was headlined: No Raghu on Roadies?

Ashish told the press: 'There was one season where we had Gulshan Grover as the bad man, then we had Raghu Ram introduced in the interview rounds, then Raghu and Rajiv. So it's just that now we are going to come up with something different and unpredictable. Raghu has been with the show for many years. People know the kind of reactions to expect from him. In fact, having said that, we haven't yet revealed who will be interviewing the contestants. There's a huge surprise lying there.'

This hurt on many levels. By equating me with Gulshan Grover, they had reduced me to a paid artist with very little involvement with the show. They had positioned themselves as the brain behind the show, as the people who took all the decisions. By using the excuse that I was becoming predictable, they tried to say that I was no longer relevant to *Roadies*. It made me look like a has-been. I felt like shit.

It didn't end there. Irrfan Khan was brought in to replace me—he was the big surprise. And what hurt the most was that they paid him exactly the same amount of money I had quoted to be a part of the show. They had the money but they preferred paying it to an actor who had nothing to do with the show at all.

But somewhere, even as I say this, I know I can't hold it against Ashish. They had announced a new season, and the viewers and the press were obviously asking them about me. What else could Ashish have said? That Raghu has quit and we're going to try and make another season without him, we hope you like it? Obviously they would want to downplay my absence, right? I understand that bit. I just wish there had been a better way to do it, to convey all this without making me feel like a loser.

There was a huge uproar on Facebook with fans starting communities like 'No Raghu, No *Roadies*' and 'Bring Raghu Back'. But MTV had to go ahead without me. And I don't hold it against them, not really. I dropped by the MTV office one day to chat with Ashish, and he told me that it was going to be great this year: 'Seventh season, we're going with the seven deadly sins.' I didn't like the idea at all, because in India there's no concept of seven deadly sins, it's a very Western thing. It's something that will look good on paper and you can sell it to sponsors but viewers are not going to get it.

The season began, the journey began, and I was told by my team (it was still the same team shooting the show) that it wasn't a good experience at all. Sometime before the season ended, I was hanging out with Rajiv when Bumpy called and asked whether I could make an appearance at the finale. I asked him why and he said he just wanted people to know that it was still my show, which was sweet, but when Rajiv shook his head, I said no. Rajiv's reasoning was that I was being asked because the season wasn't working and they wanted me to come because my presence would bring some credibility back to *Roadies*. 'Let this be their season, Raghu,' he adviced. He was right. It wasn't fair on me. I had nothing to do with the season, and I couldn't stand by it.

Roadies 7 blew up in MTV's face. They threw everything they had on it: VJs, actors, former Roadies, and still they failed. In spite of trying so hard—or maybe *because* of it.

As for me, I'd like to be very honest about one thing: I felt nothing about this season of *Roadies*. I did not feel like they took my baby and they ruined it because, you see, it was made very clear to me that it wasn't my baby to start with! I distanced myself from this season, I did not watch it at all.

To say that *Roadies* 7 flopped because Raghu wasn't there would be oversimplification. I felt bad for my team because they had worked just as hard on it as they had on the other six, but because it had flopped, they'd lost some of their invincibility. *Roadies* 7 is a season rife with mismanagement—something my team and I laugh about today. But back then, it wasn't so funny.

If it had succeeded, I would have felt very proud and a little bad. Proud because, well, the crew shooting it was still my crew. And bad, well, because it would prove that what I brought to the show wasn't that much after all.

Back on the road

'Kya ho gaya?' he asked. I looked at him blankly. It was 2010 and we were at the Delhi airport. I had just walked out of the security check to the boarding gate. The guard at the gate asked me to step aside, brushed my ticket away, looked me in the eye and repeated, 'Kya ho gaya?' I shrugged and now he elaborated, 'MTV ke saath jhagda ho gaya?' I was taken aback as he continued, his tone almost accusatory now: 'Aap *Roadies* kyun nahi banaa rahe iss saal?' Finally it made sense. Actually it didn't. Because this guy was in his forties, a security guard at Delhi airport, and I would never have considered him to be an audience for MTV or *Roadies*. But, clearly, he was. I told him there was no fight, all was fine. I was just not making the season. And even as I turned to go, slightly flummoxed at what had just happened, he touched my shoulder most understandingly and said, 'Agar hum kuch kar sakte hain toh bataa do!' I smiled. 'Nahi thank you, it's all fine.' And now he hesitatingly said, 'Achcha lagta hai... aap, aapka show...' I walked away, my head reeling. How random! How utterly sweet.

It was to happen much more over the next few months. Wherever I went I was being asked why I wasn't making *Roadies*. And when the initial surprise of it wore off, I was left with the same thought: when I was *on* the show, making it, appearing on it, I would get abused, I would be asked why the *fuck* I was doing this. Who do you think you are?! And the one season when I had stepped back, the very same guys were again yelling at me. Why the fuck are you not making this season?! Basically, my audience is like a difficult girlfriend. There's no making them happy. They love to hate or maybe hate to love me. And I'm still trying to figure that one out.

◆

While I was figuring out life, so was MTV...in their own way. Even as *Roadies 7* was airing, MTV changed their working model. They wanted to stop producing their own shows, and outsource them. It definitely made better financial sense for the channel. Producing their own shows meant that MTV had so many more people on their rolls: producers, editors, cameramen, etcetera. By outsourcing shows, they would save a lot of money on salaries and production budgets. It would then be the production house's headache to produce a show within the given budget.

And so MTV drastically downsized its staff—true, with excellent severance packages, but at the end of the day, they were fired. Ashish Patil was moved to the films division but had been given a three-month window to find other work. I remember feeling quite bad for him, seeing that he'd been sidelined, shunted to one end of the office that was once his. He went on to co-found Y Films, a youth constituent of Yash Raj Films, and is going great guns today.

The MTV I walked into some months later felt alien. The *Jerry Maguire* speech had been long forgotten: less wasn't more. MTV wasn't—isn't—the same any more.

When *Roadies 6: Hell Down Under* rocked the ratings, MTV became confident. Cocky, even. So now, when MTV went to speak to Vivek Syal, the baap of *Roadies* at Hero Honda, they told him, in no uncertain terms, that he had 'better' double the sponsorship. Or they'd find another sponsor. Seriously.

I was in Mumbai when he called me and asked me to come to Delhi. I booked my ticket for the next day. Syal was furious with MTV. He sat me down and vented about how had funded *Roadies* for six years without demanding ratings. The man was right. He had supported the show wholeheartedly, seeing it as a long-term investment, and now that the show had become a hit, he obviously expected the investment to pay off. What he did not expect was for MTV to show *him* attitude. I agreed wholeheartedly and now Syal came to the point. 'Fuck MTV,' he said. 'I'll get you a GEC, and you make *Roadies* for me!' I was quite taken aback by the intensity of his anger. I let him cool down a bit, and then I told him I was willing to support him but I couldn't possibly take *Roadies* away from MTV. It wouldn't be ethical. What they were doing wasn't ethical either, he snapped back. I couldn't, I insisted, it would be copyright infringement. His enthusiasm didn't die. Fine, he said, let's make another biking show with you as the face. Let's KILL *Roadies* if we can't remake it. I heard him out, but eventually had to say no because it wouldn't be cool. I offered to make him any other show he cared to produce but Syal wasn't kicked about that. Eventually, he did produce *Roadies 7*, he did pay a higher amount, though not as much as MTV had asked him for.

When *Roadies 7* flopped, no one had the balls to go look Vivek Syal in the face. Word was out that I was the only one who could actually face him.

◆

This was around the time I got a call from Ali, who took care of digital content at MTV, specifically *Roadies Battleground*. 'Have you had enough of fucking around?' he asked me. 'You wanted a break, you got it, now would you like to come back and do some real work?' I paused for a while and I asked him what he had in mind. He wanted me to come on board *Roadies Battleground* as he was having trouble finding sponsors for it this year.

I stuck to what I'd told Ashish: I wouldn't just be part of one aspect, especially not something that was merely an offshoot of something I had created. If he wanted me to be a part of *Roadies Battleground*, I'd have to be a part of *Roadies* in its entirety. And on my terms. Ali said he'd speak to the Viacom 18 CEO, Haresh Chawla. Now, Ali is quite shrewd and he knew for a fact that, since Haresh was a businessman and I had the temperament of an artist, chances were that any dialogue would turn into an argument if I felt I was being given attitude. So he spoke separately to Haresh, separately to me. It was a good move. I was duly informed that MTV did want me back on *Roadies* as a whole.

So one evening, Rajiv and I sat down and talked about MTV's offer. When he asked me how I felt about it, I admitted that I had missed *Roadies* and I would love to do it again but I wanted to make sure they paid me. Rannvijay called at this point and suggested I tell MTV I wouldn't come back on *Roadies* unless they let me produce it. I immediately called up Ali and told him the same. My idea was conveyed to Haresh Chawla who agreed but also said that they'd be more comfortable if I co-produced it with Colosceum, since Network 18 had a stake in the company. I wasn't too keen because, by now, I had thought of forming my own production house with my former colleague and friend, Vishal Sood (from BBC, remember him?). With Colosceum, it would be a fifty-fifty deal, and with Vishal, it would be 100 per cent my own.

Rajiv sat me down and told me why Colosceum would be a better deal. You could argue that he had a personal interest considering he worked at Colosceum and, ideally, he'd want me to work with him. But Rajiv was completely honest and fair in his explanation. For their end of the deal, Colosceum would take care of the commercial part of it, and I would be free to do what I did best: handle creatives. And the money paid to me would go straight into my pocket, it wouldn't have to be invested anywhere, which would be the case if it were my own production house. It made perfect sense and I agreed. But I resented the fact that this decision was being forced on me by the channel. It seemed to me like they were not asking me to make *Roadies*, they were *telling* me to make *Roadies*. I didn't feel in control; in fact, I felt disrespected, taken lightly. I became extremely sensitive to how I was being treated.

The disastrous meeting with Colosceum didn't help. The top three people at Colosceum—Lalit, big boss Ajit Andaare and, of course,

Rajiv—and I were to meet at Tian, a restaurant in Juhu. The monsoons were on but I reached at 7 p.m sharp. These guys were delayed by a couple of hours, thanks to the rain. And I lost it. It felt like they were taking me for granted as well. So I called Rajiv and Lalit and let them have it. They ultimately arrived, we spoke and everything was okay… Only, Rajiv was really hurt. Again. This time he let me have it, telling me that if this was my attitude, he didn't want anything to do with *Roadies* 8. He said that he'd never do such a thing to me—as his brother, I ought to have understood that he wasn't fucking me over. I was flabbergasted. Anyway, it went on for a while, him ranting, me apologizing, Rannvijay (who had joined us later) playing referee. Finally, we made up and all was well. I was making *Roadies* with Colosceum.

◆

Everything sorted, I went to meet the new guy who had joined in Ashish Patil's place. I'm just going to call him Mr Creative. He was rather sweet to me and quite excited that I'd come back for *Roadies*. He had some radical ideas for Season 8. Really radical. He had been watching this reality show called *Man vs Wild* and had also just seen a documentary about Mumbai, so why not do Man vs City this *Roadies* season, and make contestants do all the tasks in Bhendi Bazaar? He looked at me expectantly. Very frankly, I didn't know whether he was serious or yanking my chain. He was serious. I said, yeah, sure let me get back to you, and I almost ran away. When I told Ali what had happened, he laughed like crazy and then said I was required to come for another meeting with Mr Creative, but this time, thankfully, Aditya Swamy, the head of sales and marketing, would be there, too. At least I could turn around and roll my eyes at someone in the course of more 'radical' ideas.

Adi and I braved a meeting with the man and I survived this one. I presented my idea and he loved it, an idea that had taken seed when I'd read *The Devil and Miss Prym* by Paulo Coelho. Even though I'm not a Coelho fan, I found this book interesting. It's about a stranger who walks into a remote village and befriends the local bartender, a Miss Chantal Prym. He takes her to a forest, digs a hole which has a gold bar in it and tells her that it's enough to set her up for life. You know where it is, so you can come here, dig it up and take it. But if you do take it, you'll know you would have stolen, you would have sinned. He then walks further, digs a bigger hole, and now reveals ten more bars of gold, tells Miss Prym that he's taking the ten bars of gold back and adds that it's enough gold for the whole village. But if the villagers want it, he has one condition. In the next thirty days, someone from the village must be murdered. It couldn't be a death from natural causes, it *had* to be a murder. The basic funda of the story was that the stranger wanted to tear human beings down to their basic emotions to see what they naturally are: good or evil.

This story appealed to my opinion of human nature and made me think, if the wrong way was the easy way and the right way very difficult, what would people choose? And, by now, my faith in human nature was pretty much absent; I knew people would take the easy way out. Human beings aren't scared of sinning, only of getting caught.

So at the meeting with Mr Creative and Adi, I laid out my idea and said that I wanted to call it 'Shortcut to Hell'. Both of them loved the tag line: they thought it symbolized what *Roadies* was about. But that's not why I named it so. For me, every season's tag line isn't just a cool-sounding line, it has to be justified by the content of the show. In this season, we'd have tasks where you could choose a shortcut but if it went wrong, you'd have hell to pay. All the twists would involve a shortcut, too, which would lead to either victory or hell. In short, I would make it difficult for the Roadies to make the right choice; I'd make it easier for them to play underhanded games and then see what they would choose. I would be the devil.

◆

So, I was playing the devil all right but the ferocious lion was still Vivek Syal, and a wounded one at that. And I was still the only guy who could look him in the eye and ask him for money to make this season. I flew to Delhi with this guy from sales called Jaideep (JD for short). And the lion was in his cave, waiting. As it turned out, Vivek Syal spoke to me with great familiarity and affection and completely ignored the rest. Whenever JD said something, Vivek Syal would turn around and say, 'Well, I'd like to hear Raghu say that. I'd like to know whether he believes in it, because I think it's pretty clear why you guys haven't been asked to leave yet. If not for this guy, you wouldn't be allowed into my office.' Now, while I was happy about his undying faith in me, I also felt bad for my team.

There was a little hiccup at this stage: a woman, who shall henceforth be referred to as Her Highness, represented the agency for Hero Honda this time. I had met her at one of the meetings and remembered her as being extremely obnoxious. She wanted to go back to the drawing board, question everything that was being done; basically, she behaved as if she were running the show, that we needed her approval before things were finalized. That pissed me off to no end. When we came out of the meeting, my team was fuming. I wouldn't have half-minded if the barbs had come from Vivek Syal because it's an ongoing relationship and, technically, he had the rights. But for this girl to spring out of nowhere and act so uppity? Not in my line of work, no sir! I had to set things straight.

We were called for another meeting, this time by the agency. They wanted us to take them through the *Roadies* creatives, JD informed me. I nodded. Creatives? We'll just see about that. Just make sure it's in their office, I said. This is something I have learnt from Munirka. There is nothing more intimidating or satisfying than busting people's balls in their own area. Doing it on your home ground is wimpy, anyone can do it. You have to be a real badass to take people on when on their turf. JD and I walked into the agency's conference room where Her Highness was holding court at the head of the table. We took our seats on either side of her. I kept silent as the meeting went on in the glass-walled conference room. Whenever JD explained something to her, she'd turn around and ask me a question. And whenever she was talking to me, I'd start by looking at her and then by mid-sentence, I'd calmly swivel my chair around, look outside the window and contemplate. Her voice would trail off, she'd wait for my answer but I'd remain quiet. I'd take my time, swivel back, turn to JD, and talk to him about something entirely unrelated.

I did this again and again and again. I was just making it very clear that I didn't owe her any answers. The conference ended, I came out of the office and called up Vivek Syal, asked him if he had faith in me. He said yes. In that case, I said, Her Highness is never to come for a meeting again. In fact, no agency person will. If he wasn't okay with it, I told him, I didn't do *Roadies* the previous year, I'd be happy not to do it this year either. But I would not be told by outsiders how to do my job. He said, don't worry, she won't come to another meeting. And she didn't. Now this doesn't usually happen. In this equation, Hero Honda and the agency are clients, and vendors like MTV don't get to dictate terms. Unless you are Munirka Raghu.

◆

Getting rid of Her Highness was a small but significant victory and helped me feel a little more in control. Next up, I wanted to talk commercials, which is channel-speak for 'money'. I told them, point-blank, that in the previous season I'd asked for an amount that I wasn't given—one that was given to Irrfan Khan when he made an appearance. I'd take double that amount now, because I was worth that. It was non-negotiable.

Finally, I spoke to the head of commercials, a very powerful man at Viacom 18. He's the guy who talks to Salman Khan and Amitabh Bachchan when they do *Bigg Boss* for Colors. Anyway, he was going to talk money with me and I was very clear in my head that I was not backing down this time. He'd made someone else call me to say that I ought to consider a middle ground with the money, and I said, in that case, why don't you just get Irrfan? Pay me what I want or I walk. Finally, I was told, bro, at least take off a token amount because it's someone's *job* to negotiate you down. I paused for effect and then said, 'You take away five rupees from what I asked for, and I quit right now.' I meant it. They backed down. I got what I asked for plus 50 per cent of the producer's margin. I had a good deal, I'd played hardball and I'd won. I felt respected.

◆

Now that everything else was in place, I had to start putting together a new team. My old guys had quit, moved on to other channels (Zulfiya, Chhotu) or were directing movies (Bumpy). I would be thinking up the *Roadies* journey soon and needed people for research. If there was anything worth knowing about the places I picked, I wanted to know it.

Colosceum sent me a thick file stuffed with resumes but I didn't even open it because I've had instances where kids lie about their experience on shows they have no inkling about. Resumes don't matter, I told Rajiv. You recommended my previous team to me, do the same now. Rajiv recommended a guy called Mandesh Shetty who had worked on *Splitsvilla*, another guy called Rishabh Soin who was a trainee at the time of the show. Mandesh is hardworking, and you know Rishabh better as Chikna. He is one of those guys who not only understands a brief but also executes it perfectly. The third addition was Harman, Rannvijay's younger brother, who used to be in the Merchant Navy but desperately wanted to do something creative. Rajiv had hired him when Colosceum produced the first season of *Masterchef India*. Along with Rickinaldo, these were four kids who had emerged from our very own pool of talent: they'd worked with us, they'd grown and now they were perfect to come on board *Roadies*.

I also brought back on board, Jonas—whom you know as Romance Rambo. Jonas looks like a goonda and, to add to the image, has a tattoo of Rambo on his shoulder, but he's really a very sweet, sentimental guy. The other person from my old team, Udit, a.k.a. Filmy, has been on board Seasons 5, 6 and 7. So Filmy and Romance Rambo were the veterans of my new *Roadies* team. I also remembered one guy called Ankit from the crew of *Sitaaron ko Chhoona Hai*—he was the only guy who had any knowledge among the clueless crew, and he was a team player. Even if there were fuckups in other departments, he'd bear the brunt from me, apologize on their behalf, then go back and give it to them. I liked that he protected his team. It showed character. So I called him, he said yes, and moved to Mumbai with his wife and daughter to join *Roadies*. I had two freshers as well: Yamini and Zoravar (who was Rannvijay's cousin, the poet in their family). The team was made.

◆

As the team was being finalized, I also decided to come up with another Roadies anthem. Agnee, the band, comprising Mohan, Koko and Chinku are pretty much the unofficial sound of *Roadies*. But at this point, Chinku had broken free from Agnee and formed his own band called Airport which was struggling quite a bit. But since he had sung the first *Roadies* anthem, 'Jeet Lenge Yaar', I wanted him to create this song too. I wanted this song to equate the journey with life. Like there is both good weather and bad, good roads and roadblocks in a journey, similarly one faces good times and hardships in life. My philosophy was that they're both welcome; opportunities and obstacles both have their significance and the journey, like life, has to be enjoyed. I wrote the lyrics, Chinku composed a kickass tune for it, and the song became 'Yahaan'.

MTV was totally supportive, and even approved my request for a budget of twenty lakhs to make the video. I asked my old friend Manu to direct it. I'd first met him when he was a cameraman on *Roadies 2*, and at the time Manu didn't speak to me…because he was observing a maun vrat. Seriously. Anyway, he was a director of photography by now and hadn't really directed anything but he agreed. He asked me what I had in mind, and I said, just Rajiv, Rannvijay and me on a road trip, with various elements of our *Roadies* experience thrown in: fun, adventure sports, bonding. The budget of twenty lakhs was barely enough to afford three days of shooting in one location with a crew, equipment and adventure sports, which were very expensive to organize.

I told Manu he'd have to be producer-director for the video. I'd give him the twenty lakhs and he could spend as much as he needed to on the production. The rest (if there was any left), would go to him. Manu refused and said he'd spend all the money on the video. So, for 'Yahaan', Manu wasn't paid a penny. The video was shot over three days in Wai and they were the three most exhilarating, exhausting, scary days of my life—it was during this shoot that I nearly lost Rajiv again.

Back on the road, volume 2

Now would be a good time to tell you something about me. A well-kept secret. I don't know how you'll take it, dear reader, but here's the deal: I have owned one, I have been on one, but I don't know how to ride a bike.

Rajiv and I both. Really.

When we were kids, our parents were paranoid, so they never let us ride bikes. Dad had a Maruti 800 when we were younger, and later, when we turned twenty and started working, dad bought another Maruti 800 so we kids got hold of the old one. That blue-coloured car was the one in which Rajiv and I, as well as our friends, learnt to drive. And it was the unofficial date car as well. Years later, when I was working with the BBC, I bought a Maruti Esteem, but somehow never got around to riding a bike.

On my thirty-second birthday in 2007, Kuhu and I took a walk around Bandstand, where I remember spotting a lovely Bullet, admiring it and then Rannvijay springing up out of nowhere and before I could realize what had happened, Kuhu pressed the bike keys into my hand and said with a grin, 'It's your bike. Happy birthday!' It was a lovely surprise, my first ever bike; only since I couldn't ride it, I went back home riding pillion behind Rannvijay. I learnt the basics of riding over the next few weeks at the ripe old age of thirty-two. But as luck would have it, the very next year, the day I turned thirty-three, in fact, I had a little accident on the Bullet. I was riding behind a friend's car in the middle of the night when, suddenly, a car zoomed in between me and my friend's car. I banged straight into it, flew over the car, but like Spiderman, I landed on my feet, unhurt. The bike had no such luck, though. It was quite mangled, and I never got around to fixing it. So I can somewhat manage to ride a bike but I'm not comfortable doing so. And Rajiv is even worse than me!

And now back to Wai where we were shooting the music video for 'Yahaan', which involved a bloody road trip...on bikes! Manu told Rajiv he'd have to learn how to ride one. He had about a day's practice, as did I. On reaching Wai, we realized that we didn't have enough budget to put the crew up in hotels. And Manu had made it very clear that, despite the fact that Rajiv, Rannvijay and I were the 'talent' in the video, it would be unfair if we were the only ones shacked up in rooms. Fair point. So everyone, the cast *and* the crew, camped out for the three days. We pitched our tents on a cliff and it was so bloody beautiful. Just as much as the shoot was tough.

We started the next morning. One of the montages had all three of us parking our bikes off the road and running down a slope. Rajiv started having a problem while trying to park the bike. Because it wasn't a road, just a path with overgrown grass, he hit a huge stone, lost control, the bike fell over his leg and he was injured. It was upsetting because he was limping a bit, but we also thought, chalo ek accident hona tha, ho gaya, no problem. We finished this montage, went on with the shoot.

Then came the bungee jump, which was another sequence in the video. There was an industrial crane that was brought in, and we were to bungee jump from a height of 140 feet. Now, every time a wannabe contestant feels cocky because he's done bungee jumping, I instantly put him down by saying that kids *pay* to bungee jump. But that's not what I really feel. I respect people's courage in facing their fear of heights, mainly because I am terrified of them.

And I was shit scared that day, which is why I went first—I didn't want to keep feeling scared. The fear of doing something is worse than actually doing it. The terror is short-lived, but the fear can take hold of your head and heart and make you feel really small. As I stood there while being strapped into my harness, my heart in my mouth, I looked at Rannvijay and Rajiv. I don't think Rannvijay ever realizes how scared I am. No one does except Rajiv. They've all seen me only after my transformation from bullied to bully, but Rajiv has been there right from the beginning. And he and I are the same, so if he's scared, he knows I am too.

Anyway, to compound my problems, I was made to wear a helmet which had a camera inches away from my face. So not only would I have to face my fear of heights alone, I had to do it without letting even a flicker of the terror that was flowing through every inch of my body show on my face. Oh and just to add to the fun, I was supposed to jump multiple times, both forward and backward. I stood on the platform, 140 feet up in the air, turned my back, and before my brain could paralyse my body, I just let myself drop. That is among the first shots of the video. Can you tell how scared I really was?

◆

But the scariest part of the shoot was yet to come. It was day two and Manu had arranged for a jib, which is basically a mechanically-operated camera on a crane. The jib was mounted on the back of a truck which would be driven ahead of the three of us riding our bikes. The camera would capture top-angle shots of us. Now, the roads in Wai are ghat roads—they have hairpin bends, a sheer drop on one end of the road and rocks on the other. I was on the side of the road that was bound by rocks, Rannvijay in the middle, Rajiv on the other, open end. Rajiv and I were managing as well as amateurs can, following the truck. All was going well when something went wrong. Deadly wrong.

A hairpin bend came up ahead of us and the truck went around it first. Manu had told us we couldn't ride in a line, we had to stay together in one row at all times. So we did, even while going around the bend...but there was a slight problem. The truck went a bit faster than we anticipated and was soon far ahead of us. We had to ride faster to catch up with it because if we didn't, the camera would be too far away to get a good shot. We sped up... and as we took the turn, a huge rock appeared on my end of the road—I realized I was riding straight into it. So I swerved to my right, towards Rannvijay. He, in turn, swerved towards Rajiv. And Rajiv swerved right... off the road and down the cliff. For a second, none of us realized what had happened. Rannvijay rode off ahead and I did, too, and then it suddenly registered. My fists abruptly closed on the handlebars, trying to stop the bike, and since I'm not so well-versed with riding, one of them was the clutch. The front tyre of my bike jammed, the bike skidded and I was thrown off too. I landed on the road, broke my fall with a roll, and in one motion was up and running towards Rajiv, my heart in my mouth.

It wasn't a sheer drop, thank goodness—there was a ditch right below the road, and then the cliff. The bike was thrown into the ditch, and because of the impact, Rajiv was thrown off the bike but remained on the road. It must have been a funny visual, with two brothers toppling off bikes within moments of each other. But, of course, it was anything but funny.

The visor of his helmet was smashed, his eyes were shut, he wasn't moving. I sprinted to him, and for a minute I thought he was dead because he was so still. I remember holding his head in my hands, screaming out his name over and over even as Rannvijay and the others came running. He wasn't responding. I have never been so scared in my entire life. And then, after what felt like an eternity, Rajiv slowly opened his eyes and said he was okay. He slowly sat up as I checked his arms, legs, head for blood or fractures. He tried to stand up but couldn't. His right leg was sprained. As with *Roadies*, we were shooting the behind the scenes of the video and, just as it is with *Roadies*, one of us getting hurt was great content for them. They instantly picked up the camera and started shooting us. But I shot them such a threatening look that that they cut the camera feed and backed off.

And now my panic gave way to rage, and I directed it at everyone.

I screamed my head off at Manu, asked him if he was happy now, and whether these shots were worth it. No more riding shots, I thundered. You know we can't ride well but you don't care. But I *did* fucking care because *my* Rajiv could have died! Manu took it silently because he understood that my rage had come from fear and concern for Rajiv. A while later, Rajiv calmed me down and we managed to shoot another chunk which didn't involve riding or Rajiv moving around much: the dhaba bit with Rannvijay arm-wrestling.

Anyway, the day went on and soon it was sundown, the sky was spilling over with this rare, beautiful blood-red colour. Manu got really excited; he was sure that if he tried, he could capture it. He did exactly that. That silhouette shot you see in the video of us on the bikes is *exactly* how he shot it—no colour correction, no tweaking on edit. It was Mother Nature in all her glory.

◆

With the video shoot nearly done, I sat down with my new team to decide important matters. My team needed nicknames!

So Rishabh became Chikna (well you've seen him, you know why anyone would call him that!), Ankit became Sweetu (who always, always smiled, no matter what), Harman became Little Harman (because he was the little brother of my little brother), Zorawar became Zorro, Yamini became Bhatakti Aatma (she was the junior-most and was forever wandering from producer to producer and later, editor to editor), Ricky christened himself Rickinaldo (he was a huge fan of the Brazilian football team), Mandesh, the emotional guy, became Senti Cutlet, Udit was Filmy (well, because he *is* very filmy), Jonas became Romance Rambo and, finally, Lalit of Colosceum became Mukhiya, after the guy who wouldn't really take any decisions in *Lagaan*—and no, he didn't mind.

Then I explained *Roadies* to them: what it was, how we shot it and why. Most importantly, how tasks weren't an entity within themselves, nor were they only about performance. Tasks on *Roadies* are a setting for human drama. For example, if it's a shooting task with Olympic champion Lajja Goswami, it will be about the Roadies being able to match up to her shooting skills, but the background drama is that the Roadies divide themselves into pairs, and since there are an odd number of Roadies, one person will be left out—a great window for drama.

Once they were clear on this, I asked them to come up with ideas on what would be the dream scenario for *Roadies*, how we could absolutely change the game. They thought it over for a while and the mutual consensus was 'India vs Pakistan'. I was thrilled. If you remember, I had wanted to go to Pakistan with *Roadies* since Season 2, and this seemed like a great time for it. Indian Roadies versus Pakistani Roadies. The two teams would travel, perform tasks and somewhere along the way, the teams would be shuffled, changing the entire dynamic. Basically, this was what later became *Roadies X* where, instead of India vs Pakistan, it was Raghu vs Rannvijay. Back then, we were all so kicked with the idea and its possibilities that I went straight to MTV. Aditya Swamy and Mr Creative were equally excited... and then sat me down and calmly told me, no bro, not happening. There is no doubt that there cannot be a better concept but we can't air it. The political climate is just too volatile.

We were crushed; we had our hearts set on this and nothing else sounded good enough. Just when we were at our most despondent, I came up with an option which we all liked: we'd go to Brazil and bring in four ex-Roadies there who wouldn't compete with the Roadies but would have special voting powers while the rest couldn't vote them out. We soon got quite excited about it as we felt it would be very interesting to see what happened to group dynamics within the Roadies with this kind of outside interference.

Next, we had to come up with tasks. I have to say, if one ever eavesdrops on a *Roadies* brainstorming session, they'd *never* understand what the hell was going on. Before any season takes off, I encourage the team to expose themselves to books, movies, video games, music—

anything but TV shows. And then we'd sit and chat. We'd swap stories of stuff that we'd seen, that we had found interesting and from these stories would come our ideas. With the new team, however, I hadn't yet found a similar level of comfort. They were mad all right, but becoming a cohesive team takes time...

...until that amazing night when Sweetu, Zorro and I sat down and chatted and chatted and before we knew it, we were in the zone. Tasks and twists were just tumbling out, one after the other like clockwork. We were on such a creative high that I decided no one would leave the room till the entire season was done. And so it came to be that all the creatives, all the tasks, all the twists for *Roadies 8* were thought out over one single amazing night with the door locked. Only cigarettes, chai, three mad men and their ideas. What a rush!

◆

Next up were the auditions. The one big twist this year was that Rannvijay would be on the interview panel with Rajiv and me. I don't know what it is between Rajiv and Rannvijay! In Season 2, getting Rannvijay as host was Rajiv's idea, in Season 6, getting Rajiv on board was Rannvijay's idea and now, again, Rajiv had suggested getting Rannvijay on the audition panel. I loved the idea. If there had to be an addition to the audition panel, it could only have been Rannvijay—he had credibility, he had been a contestant in Season 1 and then a part of every single season as the host. Hell, he knew the show better than my producers did. Rannvijay was very excited but also nervous because he felt Rajiv and I together would be a tough act to match up to. We reassured him that we would take care of him.

This was around the time I was giving press interviews and being asked about my comeback. Yes, I had been out of sight, but it had never felt like I'd been out of mind. For instance, once, right after my London schedule for *Jhoota Hi Sahi* and before *Tees Maar Khan*, Rannvijay called me and told me to come to Pune. *Stuntmania 3* was being launched with a rock concert and some bike stunts. The whole

MTV gang would be there, he said, come, we'll hang out, it will be fun. I agreed (I had a lot of time on my hands) and drove down to Pune. The concert was well on its way by the time I reached. I got out and called up Anna from MTV, asking her to come fetch me—since I was no longer an employee and had no tickets, the security would probably not let me in. Anna met me at the parking and we began walking towards the back of the stage, but through the crowd. I thought it wouldn't be such a problem anymore. Boy, was I wrong.

Two or three guys at the back of the crowd spotted me and started running towards us, screaming my name, drawing the attention of the entire crowd...and it soon turned into a mobbing from hell! Abdul, my driver, got scared and backed off; I also told Anna to get away from me because I was afraid she would get hurt. People were all over me—touching my head, tugging my clothes—and I was just engulfed by the crowd.

Through the jumble of limbs, I saw Suvro from Fountainhead—the event management company that takes care of *Roadies* auditions and who were in charge here as well—running towards me through the mob. He dragged me away, the crowd following, but ultimately we got to the booth where the sound system was. There was a walkway from the booth to the stage. We got to the sound booth and, since I was scared, well, you know the drill—*he* emerged. He jumped over the booth, started walking really fast towards the stage, screaming Rannvijay's name. The whole crowd saw Roadies Raghu now, and there was a huge cry that went up, drowning out my words. I gave the crowd high fives as I ran to the stage. Rannvijay, who was standing on stage, mic in hand, thought I was actually angry, that's how aggressively I ran to him. I got to him, hugged him, the crowd roared its approval.

Anyway, just as my exit had caused a furore, my comeback received an overwhelming response as well. In every city we auditioned, Rannvijay would get on stage, speak to the crowd and ask them, 'Guess who's back?!' The entire crowd would scream my name. And then I'd walk out with full attitude, wearing my stud glares, because, well, I was being Roadies Raghu. The crowd would erupt, start chanting my name. It was so emotionally moving for me that I had tears in my eyes. Every time!

Finally, in Pune, I decided that I had hidden enough. I was ready. So I stripped out Roadies Raghu, took my shades off, and decided to show them what *I* was feeling. I didn't want to hide anymore. They went madder, if possible. This is one of my most special memories of this season: there were no masks between me and the *Roadies* fans anymore.

And I haven't worn my masks since. You know about my masks, right? No, not the figurative one, the *actual* ones. During Seasons 4, 5 and 6, when people's reactions were tending towards crazy and I couldn't handle it, I had taken to disguising myself. At airports, during the hour between check-in and boarding the flight, I would spend the entire time locked up in a cubicle in the loo. When I was out in public, I wouldn't feel safe till I was wearing a mask that covered my entire face. It was silly because people would stare at me anyway because I looked like an idiot but at least they didn't know who I was and I would therefore be left alone. Once, Rajiv and I were in Darjeeling, and before heading out, both of us slipped on masks over our faces and stepped out. Within moments, a whole crowd had gathered, screaming, *Roadies, Roadies*! What gave it away? Umm, we weren't wearing caps. And two men, same height, same build, same bald head…that kind of was a giveaway. Funny, crazy times!

✦

But funny, crazy times would be too mild a description for the Season 8 auditions. One year of having stayed away had changed something in me. I found that I no longer had the patience to listen to the same crap audition after audition. As a result, the interactions this season became much more violent—even physically so. The contestants included several guys who had come with the sole intention of picking a fight with me. Why, I fail to understand, considering they also wanted to be a part of *my* show. They wanted the fucking fame that my hard work could give them but they would not even acknowledge, let alone give the respect due to me. So was my anger at their attitude justified?

These kids would walk in with shit written in their forms like 'Rannvijay Gandwaa' and 'Fuck you, Raghu'. Did they expect me to be a nice guy and counsel them about their low self-esteem? Okay, let me try to explain why I do what I do again. In order to pick the Roadies, I need to test the candidates. And it's only fair that I test them based on their own claims! If the candidate was to tell me, 'I am a failure and I want to prove that I'm tough', I will test him on his toughness. And if someone comes to me claiming to be a goonda and threatens me, I *will* test that as well! It's only logical. I am to people exactly the way they are to me. So it's rather unfair that once the contestant is out of the interview room, *he* gets to be the victim, and I'm called the bad guy.

All the same, in hindsight, I do regret my outbursts of violence. As a casting director, I have been asked whether I have the right to physically throw someone out. No, I don't. Is it something that part of the audience enjoys, and even expects? Yes, it is. Does that make it right? No, it doesn't. If you were to take right and wrong as absolutes, then my actions aren't completely right. I could have calmly told people to leave if I found their behaviour offensive, if I found their views disgusting, or even if they poked fun at me or the rest of the crew. I needn't have roughed them up—and *that* is what I feel bad about for the auditions this season. When I thought about it after the auditions, I couldn't justify my behaviour to myself.

And, on this sour note, I started the *Roadies 8* journey.

Resurrection

The promos had shown me rising from the dead, meaner than ever, coming back to kick ass. That was nowhere near my state of mind as the Season 8 journey took off.

I flew down to Bangalore where we were supposed to start the journey. In the flight, I couldn't stop one thought from nagging me: Did I still have it in me? For most people, having done something once or twice before is a source of confidence while doing it again. Not for me. Because I need to do it better than before. And I had killed it in *Roadies 6*. Would I be able to match up? I operate on a weird combination of cockiness and nervousness. You can tell, right? Nervous: me. Cocky: him.

Anyway, when I landed, I met the whole team and started feeling a little better. Just as we were loading our bags into the car, Akshay looked at me and impulsively said, 'Raghu, let's shoot in 16:9 this time.' Now, there are two aspect ratios for TV. One is 4:3, which is the usual format. It means that the visual will cover your entire TV screen. The other is 16:9, in which the visual will have two horizontal bands of black—one on the top and one at the bottom of the picture. This is how films are viewed. Right up till Season 6, I had insisted on using 4:3 because I wanted everything to add to the sense of realism. But when Akshay asked me to change it to 16:9, I instinctively said, yes, let's do it. I felt we were ready to make it more cinematic. All seasons after this have been shot on 16:9.

Right from day one, I knew I had a winner with 'Shortcut to Hell'. The cast, the tasks, the locations—everything just fell into place in the most amazing manner. Brilliant content just seemed to generate itself. The human drama I spoke of to my new team? *Roadies 8* was the best possible example of it. Two of the contestants, Avtar and Dev, had been trying to make it for many seasons now. They'd struck up a friendship during the various auditions they had been to, which we didn't know about. And for those of you who've watched *Roadies 8*, you'll know that Avtar and Dev pretended to be enemies but they had an ulterior motive. We did catch on eventually, but it made for great content.

But that's not it. What was most fascinating about this season was that it had taken seed in *The Devil and Miss Prym*, which was about the good and evil within human beings, and most uncannily, what had started evolving on *Roadies 8* was, in fact, a good guy vs bad guy story. On one side were Suchit and Mohit, while on the other side were Dev and Avtar. Now, Suchit was rocking the tasks, as was Mohit but since Mohit was quieter, Suchit was in the limelight a lot more. They were both really popular and favourites to win. This threatened Avtar and Dev, and they started bullying Suchit—Dev even hit him. But Suchit maintained his dignity and didn't let it affect his performance.

◆

Rannvijay said he wouldn't be around for the shoot on New Year's Eve that year as he had been signed on for an event. I assured him it wouldn't be a problem; I figured Rajiv and I could take over for a day. We'd shoot the task in the day, party the night together and then Rannvijay would shoot the vote-outs the next night. I had summoned Rajiv along with Susan, Kuhu and Noah, Rajiv's son, to join us for New Year's Eve. I woke up that morning and Kuhu and I went over to the location to try out the task. If you've watched *Roadies 8*, you'll know this was the very eventful fire task. It was going to be Raghu vs Fire: Round two. Kaandi wasn't happy I was trying it because he remembered what had happened the first time around, four years ago.

But I had to try it anyway, and this time I felt I knew exactly what to do, like get painted with fuel just before getting lit up, and putting on fire retardant gel on my face. I remember Kuhu being nervous; I myself was shit scared but I couldn't show it. I had a bad feeling about this but there was no way I could back down now. And the bad feeling wasn't ill-founded.

Like always, I had to test the worst case scenario. The fire professionals advised me not to go beyond twenty-five seconds. I said let's try forty-five. They said they should only set fire to my arms and legs. I asked them to put fire on my torso and back as well. I need to clarify that I didn't do any of this out of cockiness or bravado. I had only one shot at the trial. I was okay with reducing the time and the fire for the Roadies but there was no way I could increase them. So I would have to go to my limits in order to set theirs.

Heart in my mouth again, I was set on fire. Flames leapt up and I started walking. But the minute I did that, I realized the fire was really *on* me, and within two seconds, I'd started feeling really hot. So I started running, which turned out to be a good idea because now the flames were behind me. I again felt all alone inside the suit and wondered how much fire was actually on me. But the moment I turned around for the first time, I knew. I could see nothing beyond the visor but huge golden flames…and I knew no one else could see me either. I was just a big ball of fire. And, at this moment, I felt really, really scared. Suddenly, however, things became clear in my head: I knew what I had to do. Keep running.

I ran and ran to figure out how long I could go. And by the third round, the fire had reduced quite a bit, but it had burnt through my clothes, the white fire suit was all blackened, I could feel my back getting burnt. I ran another round and when I couldn't run any more, I lay down on my stomach…and started screaming—my back burned with pain and it was agonizing. My crew came rushing, started patting blankets over my back to put out the flames which only served to hurt me further. The red hot blankets fused to my skin, peeling it right off my back. Kuhu was absolutely freaking out as they took off my fire suit and my helmet. I clearly remember howling in pain, trying to indicate that my back was on fire. But the minute I saw Kuhu, sobbing with her hand over her mouth, I instantly changed my tone and said, 'I'm okay, I'm okay.' I shot a glance at Kaandi who understood and promptly went over to console Kuhu. Of course, because of this, we reduced the amount of fire and the cut-off time for the Roadies to twenty seconds. I had to go back and change for the task. The pain was bad, really bad. I couldn't bear to wear clothes over my body but I had to. I did that entire shoot in so much pain, it's hard to describe. And I was petrified for the Roadies; in fact, I had told Romance Rambo that he didn't have to look at a camera or anything else for this task—he just had to be in charge of safety. I would give Romance Rambo a cue at fifteen seconds and one at twenty, and to jump in, come what-the-fuck-may, and just put out the fire at that point. Even if the Roadie was not lying down, tackle the person down and make sure the fire goes out. Thankfully, nobody else got hurt and I felt like I'd earned my New Year's Eve party.

It was a lovely night, all the crew's families had come down, there was an open bonfire, music, alcohol flowed, we danced, sang...while the Roadies sat cooped up in their respective rooms, boys locked in one, girls in the other, no alcohol for them, nothing. I have this distinct memory of Mohit peeping out at us from his room window. I paused, called one of the production guys, asked him to go upstairs and draw the curtains. It's very simple: I really do want it to be a hardcore experience for the Roadies. I don't know how it functions on other reality shows but on mine, the Roadies would NOT see us, the crew, with our guards down. To them, we are machines, robots, quietly doing our work, nothing else. I don't want them looking at us and feeling a bit of familiarity the next day. That would lead to comfort and I cannot justify that on the show.

2011 dawned, a beautiful morning and that night we shot the vote-out. Rannvijay was waiting at the location when the Roadies walked in, and when they saw him, they beamed. Rannvijay asked them how the experience of meeting Raghu and Rajiv was, and they said it was intimidating. And now he asked, did you guys miss me? And boy, *did* they miss him! They begged, pleaded with him to never take off again, because they didn't want to meet Raghu and Rajiv, they *only* wanted to meet Rannvijay. Standing behind the camera, I could hear them over one of the speakers and I did feel a little tinge of hurt. I had literally burnt myself just to keep them safe, and yet here I was, completely rejected by the Roadies. Then I decided it was okay. In fact, it was better this way. It meant I was doing my job well!

◆

Next stop: Brazil. Rickinaldo was very, very excited because, in his words, 'I'm in MY country, you fucking Indians are on my home ground!' *cue evil laughter* The recce, which I hadn't gone for, had been quite eventful. My team had landed smack in the middle of a gun fight between the Brazilian armed forces and the favelas—the slums of Brazil which are a law unto themselves. Rickinaldo, with the help of the local Brazilian line producers, convinced Mukhiya that he looked Brazilian and would get shot in the gang fight. Barking mad, I tell you!

It was also in Brazil that I lost my temper on my crew for the first—and last—time. We were in Sao Paolo during the third day of the shoot. Rannvijay and I woke up bright and early, got ready and came downstairs to the hotel reception for call time. No one from the team was around; we were informed they had left about an hour ago. I was surprised because no one had informed me. Eventually, after much trouble with Portuguese and a smattering of English, I was informed that Akshay had decided the night before that since we didn't have enough shots of the Roadies riding from the airport to the location, he'd prepone the call time and get those shots done before the task. So everyone had left, except for the presenter and the director.

I didn't say a word in the car when Rannvijay and I left to join the crew. I should have been kept in the loop, I should have been informed.

It smacked of disrespect and I wasn't used to being treated this way. Least of all by *my* team! But I was open to logical explanations.

By the time we reached, a part of the crew was shooting the Roadies and the rest were setting up for the task. The minute Rannvijay and I walked in, Senti Cutlet, who was hanging out outside with Chikna, saw us, grinned and said, 'Oh, aa gaye superstars!' Now, anyone in my team can say anything to me or anybody else, but this was the wrong time for such a statement. I stormed in, and despite my anger, I managed to patiently ask the whole crew to gather. Everyone came and now I let go—if these guys were not as hard and tough as nails, they would have been in tears because I ripped them apart. The Brazilian crew also stood around, shell-shocked. It ended, everyone walked away and finally Akshay came to me and asked me what the fuck had just happened. I was much calmer now, and I asked him why I hadn't been informed. The explanation, ultimately, was a simple one: Akshay had taken the call late at night and he didn't want to wake us up, thinking they'd be done by the time we arrived. Perfectly understandable. I think what had gotten my goat was the fact that I wasn't informed, coupled with Senti Cutlet calling us superstars. I have always, *always* hated the 'star' label and made sure Kuhu, Daman and Rannvijay were always punctual and professional. So imagine my anger when the same was attributed to me! Well, it was silly and Senti Cutlet meant no malice. Akshay told me, very firmly, that whatever the provocation, I couldn't speak to the crew like that. I agreed. True to habit, I gathered the whole crew again, including the Brazilian guys, and apologized to all of them.

We moved on to Ribeirão Preto and heard that there were floods in Sao Paolo and Rio de Janeiro—so we were actually travelling from one flood to another. We saw footage of many cars being washed away by the floods on the news, but we had no option other than to press on and hope for the best. Luckily, we escaped the floods. Very soon, the floods were the least of our problems—we were concentrating on a task that *no* one thought would ever happen: the naked portrait. It was my idea, of course, and was happening inside an auditorium. The idea was this: the Roadies would think they had come for a rock concert. A band would be playing on stage, there would be men and women among the audience, and a painter. The male Roadies would come in a bathrobe, strip it off and stand on the stage, naked, to get their portrait painted. Suraj instantly backed out. And in my head, I had a Plan B if all the guys refused: I'd gotten special thongs made with the cartoon of a cockerel in front and a donkey on the back. Cock and ass, get it? But then came the two awesome kids who'd been acing all their tasks—Mohit and Suchit said what the hell, we're Roadies, we'll do it. I was shocked but happy, although, even as we set up, I was on tenterhooks. Shit, was it really going to happen?

Because, see, they had agreed but it was only at that point on stage when they would untie their bathrobes that Mohit and Suchit would really know what they were in for. How was this a *Roadies* task, people have asked me. Because being naked in front of people is everyone's worst nightmare, literally. We've all seen it at some point or the other, a dream of being in the nude, either in school or any other public place. And to do this task, you had to face your ultimate fear. That's why it was a *Roadies* task! So the minute Mohit dropped his bathrobe, I, who was standing behind the camera, caught his attention and gestured that he look at me and me only. Forget the audience, forget they had binoculars in hand, forget the artist who was sketching him. Have faith in me. I did the same with Suchit. I have so much respect for both these boys. Of the crazy things that one can do in life, this one's pretty much up there as the craziest! What? Me, do this task? I'd rather be set on fire again, thanks!

◆

As soon as we landed in Mumbai, I headed straight for the edit rooms. Soon, the auditions went on air and the minute people saw the Pune auditions, the response was tremendous. At first, it was all about how a boy from a little known village near Hyderabad had inspired everyone all over the country. That boy's name was Suraj. Rannvijay, Rajiv and

I had really liked him, and along the journey, he proved to be an okay contestant. A couple more days passed and now the response was a bit different. People started posting his photos online, his friends and acquaintances claimed he was a hotel management student and a bartender. And the first time I heard it, I instantly believed it to be true. It all fell into place. When I thought back to his audition, the details he had given us hadn't quite added up. He had made several mistakes during his interview, and even during the journey in a segment called Kadwa Sach. We couldn't use this in the edit for lack of duration, but I clearly remember Avtar had passed a comment saying that Suraj had had it easy in life. Rannvijay had stepped in and told Suraj, what the hell man, tell him what you've been through, what you told us at the interview. And Suraj had looked confused; he didn't remember all the lies he had told us. We should have known then, but I'll tell you why we didn't work it out: we *wanted* to believe him. We wanted someone like him to come on national television and be a success, be an inspiration for others. We *wanted* Suraj to be real so, unconsciously, we were intentionally blind to the glaring loopholes in his story.

He hesitated to come to the finale but did finally make it. We confronted him with the truth in front of everyone and paid him back by bringing a donkey named Suraj to the location. A lot of people on the Internet were delighted that someone had fooled the *Roadies* selectors, but here's the deal: when we audition, we're casting personalities, not people. For example, in *Splitsvilla*, by default, we have to cast girls and boys who are single. If there's a boy who says he's single, I'm not going to do a background check. Because it's not a job interview. And in the course of the show, if it comes out that he does, in fact, have a girlfriend, well, that's a story as well!

I'd like to make it very clear that Suraj was not cast for his background story. We hear plenty of sob stories every year. He was cast because of the way he expressed himself brilliantly in chaste Hindi. Even if it had turned out that this guy was some Tata/Birla's son, it wouldn't have changed the reason why he was cast. And it most definitely does not make his casting 'wrong'. I need people who are reactive, expressive and interesting in their expressions. As a director, everything is a potential story for me, so even if his secrets had come out earlier, it was a win-win situation for me. Given a second chance, I would still cast him.

The only thing I have against Suraj is that he gave hope to a lot of people who felt heartened by his presence, his story. He initially made people feel that nice guys can win. And later, when the truth was out, it felt as though lying was the formula for success, that it was good to be shrewd, to not be yourself if that can get you places. While *Roadies* is not a moral science lesson, I definitely was answerable to all those watching who felt cheated.

◆

The day of the finale dawned. We shot it close to Bengaluru, in Ramnagar, incidentally in the same spot where *Sholay* had been shot … and the location was Gabbar Singh's adda! By this time, though, Avtar had gone around bad-mouthing *Roadies* all over the Internet, trying to reveal the twists and turns and claiming that it was scripted. Avtar, like Suraj, initially refused to come down for the finale; he was scared I'd beat him up. Ultimately, he did come. And we didn't show you everything that happened during that shoot.

Avtar is the first and only Roadie who, despite having been voted out, was still kicked out of the finale. Renee and Pooja had both mentioned that Avtar had spoken badly about them on social networking websites, called them sluts, said they were easy. Behind the camera, I could feel my anger building. And, finally, when Rannvijay told him to leave, he slunk around and didn't go. Mohit from Season 7 and Shaleen from Season 4 were asked to escort him outside; they were doing so when my anger had reached its height and I snapped, cut! As everyone cut their camera feeds, I started walking, making it obvious that Avtar was going to get it. He had sullied my crew's name, he had spoken badly of the girls on the show, he had bullied Suchit all through, he was *asking* for it, and I was going to oblige. But the others got a little worried now, even as my kameena crew restarted their cameras and began shooting.

I walked right up to Avtar, raised my hand to slap him, but when it was an inch from his cheek, it was stopped by another hand— Rannvijay's. He had stolen up behind me, knowing what I was going to do. Meanwhile, Mohit grabbed Avtar and told him to leave while Shaleen and Rannvijay held on to me. After Avtar had left, I screamed at the Roadies, saying that they dare not bad-mouth the show, and that if any of them had a problem with it, they should have the balls to say it to our faces. Silence. I walked away, calmed down a bit, and then, by force of habit, turned around and apologized. I couldn't have shown this on air because, at that moment, I had entered the *Roadies 8* story as a crew member, not as Raghu. I'd crossed a line.

◆

The shoot went on.

The black box was brought out and given to Aanchal, who had the power to eliminate either Mohit or Suchit or herself. She would have to drive an open jeep into one of three frosted glass cages, one for each contestant. Suchit and Mohit would each pick one cage and wait inside it. If her jeep rammed into the enclosure with Suchit's cage, he'd be out; if it was Mohit's cage, he'd go; if it was the third empty cage, Aanchal would go. Aanchal, of course, didn't know who was in which cage, and Mohit and Suchit obviously didn't know which enclosure she'd break. Aanchal sat in the jeep and made her decision: the extreme right one. My heart sank. I could see Suchit standing behind that glass. I felt he deserved to win, but there was nothing I could do about it.

It was an elimination based purely on luck, and Suchit was the Karan of the Mahabharata. He had given his all to every task, and no one could beat him—except his own luck. Aanchal smashed through the glass enclosure, and Suchit had to go. Mohit was jubilant at first, pumping the air and then slowly the smile slid off his face when he realized that his pal was leaving.

Suchit's goodbye was one of the most emotional moments on *Roadies*: there was not one dry eye on the set that day. Then something happened which stunned me—two things, actually. Dev looked at Suchit and said, very emotionally, 'It's okay, bhai hai tu.' This was the same Dev who had bullied the shit out of Suchit, had called him 'Chuchit' the entire season. The second surprise was to see Suraj, the big fat liar who had hated Mohit and Suchit all through, also quietly shedding a tear.

I'm going to tell you a secret. My opinion of human nature, though similar to that of the Joker in Christopher Nolan's *The Dark Knight*, differs from him on one crucial point: Hope. I still believe in goodness. The whole point of creating the fucked-up world of *Roadies* is to look for that one guy who will justify my faith in humanity. And, finally, here was Suchit, who had refused to play dirty, focused on his performance and was walking away with everyone's respect. So when Rannvijay asked whether anyone thought Suchit deserved a bike and everyone's hand went up, the feeling was so intense, so pure, that I couldn't control myself: I started crying. You can't script content like that; if you've done your job with honesty and dedication, it just comes out of nowhere, and really hits you.

Season 1 will always be special because of the fun of the journey and the friends I made. *Roadies X* is also something I will always hold close to my heart but in terms of intensity and story, *Roadies 8* will always be *it*.

Which takes me back to the time before the night we cracked the season's tasks and twists. I had been really, really nervous about my comeback. I wasn't getting the tuning with my new team, I'd been off *Roadies* for a whole season, gone into my shell, my confidence completely deserting me. I thought I'd lost the plot: if not for my confidence and attitude, who was I anymore? I had to be better than Roadies Raghu and I didn't know if I still had it in me. When we wrapped Season 8, though, I knew I did.

The season that would have never been, volume 1

So the crazy fame had happened. The asshole years had happened. The complete withdrawal from the world had happened. I had finally returned to the real world. And then this shit happened.

The year was 2011. *Roadies 8* was on air, rocking the ratings, the auditions had all been telecast when I received a call from Pune. There was a store opening the next day and the owners wanted Rannvijay and me to be there as chief guests. I agreed, and as the next day was a Saturday, I woke Rannvijay up and we drove down to Pune. We got there and the owners wanted to make a big noise that we had come. They had organized an open Gypsy that they wanted us to stand in and be driven to the store from a distance of barely five hundred metres; there would a convoy, and people would be lined up on either side of the road. We hadn't been informed of this earlier, but we went with the flow.

Rannvijay and I got into the car and were slowly driven to the store. There was a girl among the crowd who was walking along seemingly uncaringly, a bottle of Thumbs Up in hand. Suddenly, without warning, she shook it up, flung open the cork, turned around and started spraying the liquid all over herself. It splashed all around, some of it hitting us too. Rannvijay instinctively ducked, but I didn't initially register what had happened—I thought someone was throwing water. Then I took a look at the owner of the shop who was standing next to me and had been closest to the girl's line of fire. It was then that I realized that there wasn't fizzy cola in the bottle, it was ink and there were big streaks of it on all our clothes. I ducked, too. I knew some mischief was going on but I didn't know what it was.

It was soon made clear to me. Around fifteen to twenty people suddenly emerged from the crowd with banners that read 'DOWN WITH ROADIES' or 'RAGHU GO BACK'—clearly, it was all organized by a political party. There was also a TV camera that materialized out of thin air and started shooting all this. I've always known that political goondaism exists but I've never faced such stupid behaviour and, truth be told, I was fascinated, almost mesmerized by the situation. Especially when one of the guys got on to the bonnet of the car. I didn't know who this guy was, what his problem was and why he was behaving like this, and I kept staring at him. I'm sure it seemed like defiance to him but it was just a morbid fascination. I couldn't tear my eyes away. He stared back at me for some time, shouting slogans. But after a while, his voice trailed off; he lowered his eyes and stepped down from the car. Finally, I snapped out of it; I had my little brother with me and my protective instincts kicked in. I wanted to make sure he got out of there safely. There were a couple of other cars in the convoy and we both got into one. The TV camera rammed itself against the window pane but we ignored it. Rannvijay was fine, I was fine, our ink-riddled clothes the only indication that something untoward had happened. The owner also got in with us. By this time, the cops had come; they took the sloganeering guys away, made way for our car, and we drove to the owner's house.

It was only when we reached his house and encountered his sobbing wife, heard accounts of what had just happened, that the gravity of the situation sunk in. It had been a planned attack by the youth party, Akhil Bharatiya Vidhyarthi Parishad (ABVP). It was obvious that these guys wanted to position themselves as moral guardians and a great way to do that would be to take me on, make me the enemy of morality and then pretend to fight with me. My first thought was, damn, it *was* politically driven, which meant it was the real deal. These guys have no soul. No ethics. No morality. They'd do whatever it takes to get attention, and I immediately worried for the safety of my family. I made calls to both Kuhu and Rajiv. I didn't delve into the details with Kuhu but when I called Rajiv, I told him all about the ink, the sloganeering and that Rannvijay and I were both fine, so he mustn't panic if the press called him for a quote. I also told him to stay put wherever he was so he'd be safe. I hung up, and dialled another number.

'Hey, Raghu,' said the friendly voice of Aditya Swamy, who had now taken over as the head of MTV from Mr Creative (thank goodness!). 'Hi Adi,' I replied and then went on to say, 'I just became too expensive for you!' I told him what had happened. 'I didn't sign up for this shit,' I said. 'I'm making a youth show commissioned by MTV, and if that show is compromising the safety of either me or my family, bro, you can forget it! Or in the very least, you'll now have to afford me.' It was true, right? I had hit the big league, I'd really pissed some people off, and they thought they'd get some headlines out of me! Which, technically, they did, through the press statement they issued in which they claimed: 1) They had attacked Rannvijay, Rajiv and me. Not true. 2) They had blackened our faces. Untrue yet again. 3) They had told me to leave and banned me from entering Pune. About that in just a bit.

Now this would have blown up into a really huge story as they even had a TV camera at the scene. But one little problem came their way—that very TV camera. As it was rammed against my window in the car, I noticed the name of the channel on the mic: IBN7. Parent company of IBN7? Viacom 18. Ha! The poor devils had barked up the wrong tree. During my phone call to Adi, I also told him to make sure that the footage got lost. He did. That tape never saw the light of day. So, ultimately, there is no official footage of the event, no photographs, nothing.

On my way back to Mumbai, I went on Facebook and clarified that the news that would soon come out about the 'attack' wasn't true, and that we were fine. I called up my parents and told them I was absolutely okay. I felt better. But the ridiculous press statement had still been issued, and that was gnawing at me.

When I returned home that evening, Abbas Tyrewala came over and we sat and had a few drinks together. I was troubled and asked him whether I was doing anything wrong, because the people with the banners, the girl with the ink bottle, they were the youth. I made my show for them. Abbas looked me in the eye and said that the day a right-wing political outfit opposed you, it meant you were doing something absolutely right. Also, there were just fifteen kids in the crowd; they did not represent the youth in Pune or the rest of India. All I needed to do, Abbas said, was to be careful, be safe. I nodded, but before that, I needed to do something else. The very next day.

◆

Early next morning, Kuhu woke up and left for a shoot outside Mumbai. Coincidentally, Rajiv left the same morning, as did Rannvijay. I'd called my driver, Abdul, at 7 a.m. He came, I got into the car, and told him, 'Chalo Pune.' Abdul turned to me incredulously and said, 'Pune? Really? Now?' 'Yeah, really. Now,' I replied. I made one call to Koko, a.k.a. Kaustubh Dhavale, the lead guitarist of Agnee, who was based in Pune. I gave him a crisp Munirka-ized account of the events: Pangaa ho gaya. I am apparently banned from Pune. I want to make a point that no one fucking bans me from anywhere. I am driving to Pune. Alone. I need you to come with me, take me places where I'll be seen. Koko heard me out and said, great, come over.

When I reached, we drove to Vaishali, an iconic restaurant in Pune. There are two colleges near it and, coincidentally, *The Times of India*'s office is right opposite the restaurant. I walked in with Koko and we spent nearly four to five hours there, just standing outside by the entrance, sipping coffee, chit-chatting with everyone who approached me. Being seen. Soon enough, *TOI* realized we were there and a journalist came down to talk to me. I was only too glad to give them a byte. I have been apparently banned from Pune, I said. But here I am, to say that ABLP (Akhil Bharatiya Loser Parishad) are nobody to ban anybody. I am not going to get bullied. A picture was clicked, Koko and I drank some more coffee, and eventually went back to his place.

The next morning, I was in the newspapers of Pune. They said I'd come back and was at my cheekiest. Point proven, I drove back to Mumbai on Monday with Abdul...and received a call from MTV: I had security waiting for me at home. Okay, I said, slightly taken aback as I hung up.

◆

When my housekeeper, Arjun, opened the door for me, my jaw dropped. There were bodyguards in my house. My living room seemed to shrink as I went in and counted them, head reeling. Twelve. There were *twelve* bodyguards in my house! I sent two of them to stick with Rannvijay, two to be around Rajiv, two guys to protect Kuhu. Two guys would stand below my apartment from 9 a.m. to 9 p.m. Two would take over from 9 p.m. to 9 a.m. And the last two would be with me.

This was still a bit much, but the truth is, I *had* gone back to Pune, I *had* been defiant and I *had* been seen. It was not just my safety that was important, but the safety of those close to me as well. MTV wanted me to know they were taking it very seriously.

It was annoying but I put up with it, because there was one unforeseen advantage—no one could come to me for photographs or autographs! I was getting used to the bodyguards but two were still one too many for me. So, by the end of the *Roadies 8* telecast, I said goodbye to one of them. The other guy had said that if I'd have him, he'd like to stay, because he liked me and the agency he freelanced with didn't pay him much. I liked him, too, so I let him stay. That's Sadiq; he's paid by MTV to keep me safe, he stays with me all the times, and has now become indispensable to me. Those of you who've watched *Roadies* will have seen him in any audition that goes wrong, especially ones in which I'm throwing someone out. Sadiq is now family; everyone at home and my friends are comfortable in his presence, and he loves me to death. With him around, the fame is easier to handle. I can actually wait for my flight in the boarding lounge, bury my face in a book, and Sadiq will be constantly muttering to anyone who comes close, no disturb, no disturb, no disturb, and everybody backs off.

◆

While we were still in the edits of Season 8, Sweetu had suggested going to the United States for *Roadies 9*. I loved the idea and USA had been on our list for a long time, anyway, almost like an elusive destination because, of course, it would be the most expensive to produce.

Later, when the thought had solidified, MTV said they'd be okay with it, mainly because they were so pleased with how *Roadies 8* had turned out. The next logical step was to find a unifying theme around the season, and figure out the journey.

At the time, Rajiv, Rannvijay and I were rather crazy about this one James Bond PS2 game which we would spend nights together playing. This game was called *Everything or Nothing*, and that's how *Roadies 9* got its tag line and theme. I also like this tag line for another reason. The common belief among MTV and my team is that, okay, don't put all the good ideas you have into one season; space them out, save some up for the next. But I don't subscribe to this thought at all. I feel that one shouldn't hold back, one should actually put *everything* one has into each season. The place from where these ideas are coming will also be the place from where other ideas will come the next time. I actually believe that. So, 'Everything or Nothing' worked for me on many levels. I knew for a fact that it would also work for the youth. Just like 'Shortcut to Hell' had. I have facts to back up this thought. MTV keeps doing these youth researches, and one of them had revealed that the youth did believe that struggling was for losers. Working hard was stupid; they'd rather work smart and get to the top faster. Similarly, 'Everything or Nothing' had reminded me of another insight the research had thrown up: the kids of today indulge in high-risk behaviour, be it their careers or their love lives. They don't mind the fact that they stand to lose a lot if there was a lot to gain. The stakes are high, the rewards are, too.

I brainstormed with my team and we designed the tasks in such a way that the theme came through in every episode. For instance, a money task always let the Roadies earn according to performance. So if the maximum money they could earn was a lakh, they could even go back with five thousand. In Season 9, however, we worked it out in such a way that the Roadies *had* to earn at least seventy-five thousand rupees to qualify for a lakh. If they earned anything less, they'd get zero. It was literally everything or nothing.

For *Roadies 9*, I took on one more guy on my team: Chulli, a.k.a. Rishabh Sudan. He's called Chulli because he's very naughty and keeps provoking everyone. But there's much more to him than that. An army kid, he's also a cancer survivor. He has survived five cycles of chemotherapy and come out stronger than ever before. He's second to none in terms of energy or capacity for hard work.

◆

It was time for auditions and the panel was repeated for the first time ever on *Roadies*. Our roles and positions were clear: I was the aggressive asshole, Rajiv was the witty one who would make candidates laugh even as he stripped their confidence away, while Rannvijay was the friend, the comforting presence. Only this time, something had shifted within me. (I'd like to think that, in some way, it was because I had Sadiq around now.) I no longer had to deal with fans I didn't understand; I was a happy recluse and I was at peace.

It wasn't all sweetness, though. I was also, by this time, beginning to loathe the auditions more than ever, especially because of the listening to the same bullshit over and over again: sir, I can do any task; sir, I have attitude; sir, I can play mind games.

Then there were the death threats: the guy who had worked so hard to edit and morph photos so it looked like he was holding my bloodied, severed head. He had also made a tombstone for me with the epitaph, 'RIP Raghu Ram: Don't disturb, Raghu is sleeping forever.' It wasn't funny, it was a fucking death threat and to top it, this kid who wanted me dead was at the auditions trying to become a Roadie. I repeat: I. DON'T. GET. IT. Did he?

In Kolkata, during one of the group discussions being moderated by my friend, choreographer Gaiti, one guy came really close to her and started speaking very loudly, his manner threatening. She asked him to leave; when he wouldn't, Gaiti got up and left. She met me in the crew room, told me what had happened. I got the crew to find this kid, and then, in front of Gaiti, I beat him up. I wanted Gaiti to feel secure and know that we were there to protect her, that we had her back.

Then there was Vikas who didn't agree with the form, who didn't write his real name, only 'Roadie', who cut out questions and said this was not the same *Roadies* he had been watching for years. Who Kuhu insisted I call for the personal interview. I was dead against it but the one person who could disagree with me disagreed with me. Kuhu didn't let go and, finally, Vikas was called. The way he spoke of my show, of the form, pissed me off. Criticizing the form meant criticizing my hard work, my crew's hard work. He had sat home all these years and *watched* the show while we had gone to hell and back making it every year. He had no right. I lost it and went at him, guns blazing. A lot of it was censored; Vikas got quite roughed up, and before I knew it, I actually hit him. Rannvijay held me back after that, and Vikas was sent out. Later, it was decided that someone needed to go speak to him, make sure he was fine. Filmy did the needful. And Vikas returned, this time in another city, with a better attitude, the form duly filled. He turned out to be quite an interesting guy, and a fun storyteller. This time, he was not only selected but went on to win the season. But that was the only violent instance of this season's auditions.

I remained in my happy place for most part.

But this wasn't appreciated. Even Rajiv and Rannvijay couldn't understand what had come over me. During Diyali's audition, when both of them were putting increasing amounts of pressure on her, I could see her retracting into her shell. I wrote 'STOP' on the pad and showed it to both of them. They stopped. I made her comfortable. And she turned out to be a very interesting girl. She was selected. But Rajiv and Rannvijay gave me an earful about this new sweet me. And they weren't alone in their disbelief. Barely one or two audition episodes had gone on air (we were yet to leave on the journey) when the research team at MTV came back with their findings. The kids were rejecting my softer avatar. They were asking questions like, 'Why is Raghu not torturing these guys, why is he hugging people! This is Roadies not Huggies!' Seriously, those were the words.

And then there came a landmark audition. I can't tell you the name of this kid, but you will remember him. He came in, spoke of his ex-girlfriend who was now his stalker and, suddenly, on a hunch I blurted out, 'Do you want to talk about your sexuality?' He was stumped. Eventually, he admitted to being gay. He was the first guy to come out of the closet on national television. It was a touching story, and while I can't say I've been through exactly the same thing, I do know what it feels like to have low self-esteem, to feel persecuted, afraid, rejected. The minute he confessed he was gay, I wasn't sure if I wanted to put him through this. We sent him out for a few minutes while Rajiv, Rannvijay and I debated. They were confident that we could blur his face completely because we needed to have this conversation. People needed to hear it. And if you remember it, it *was* something. We called him back, he spoke at length, we encouraged him and he left, a bit more heartened I think.

Later, when I came back from the journey, this boy sent an email to one of our production people saying that his father had figured out it was him despite his face being blurred out, and that he was really low and down and felt like dying. That sentence set off an alarm in my head and I instantly decided to meet him. I picked him up and we went to an empty café where I counselled him for two hours. Who you are is your problem, I told him. Your father's acceptance or rejection of it is *his* problem. I told him to go out into the world and prove himself and *then* make his father proud. I'd like to tell you, too, dear reader, that just because a man has fathered you, it doesn't make him automatically right. He may be your father but you do have a responsibility towards yourself, too. You have a responsibility to reject the intolerance that the previous generations have been seeped in, be it on the basis of religion, social standing or sexuality.

The last candidate I must talk about is Rohit Batra, the boy who suffered from thalassemia and came in during the Chandigarh auditions. He claimed to be a real-life Roadie because of the trials and tribulations he faced in his everyday life, and Rajiv, Rannvijay and I couldn't agree more. It was an inspiring interaction; we even gave him our trademark Roadies salute. When I'd returned from the journey, I came to know Rohit had passed away. I visited his Facebook page and it was overflowing with newspaper articles about him, wishes and tributes. Of course, it was a tragic end but, in some way, it was heartening to see how he had gone from being the boy who was battling an incurable illness with a smile, who had been bullied and had lost in love, to being someone who had been watched on national television by lakhs of people who had then reached out to him via social networking websites. He'd made friends, been praised, been commended for his courage. I'd like to believe Rohit passed away a happier man, and that a little bit of that was due to *Roadies*.

Now, back to the post-audition, pre-journey stage of *Roadies 9*. My new soft image was just not working for the audience, and if research wasn't proof enough, there were articles to the same effect in the press. And then I realized something: I couldn't please everyone. No matter which side I was facing, I'd still have my back to half the world. That has been my mantra throughout, anyway, but since MTV insisted on sharing all their research findings with me, I was more and more conscious of this shit. Now I decided that if I wanted to stay within my cocoon (and, boy, I did), I had to stop knowing what people thought of me. For my own good.

The *Roadies 9* journey began.

◆

We were thrown slightly off-course this time. We usually shoot *Roadies* during December-January, but since the US would be most expensive in those months, we shifted our travel to February. The auditions were done, and MTV had decided that they had to go on air in this very financial year, so the season would have to launch in January so that we could have the journey on air by March. This meant that the auditions would have to go on for ten weeks, a decision that cost both MTV and *Roadies* dearly. Ten weeks is more than two months and gets exhausting for the viewer, but we had to go ahead or else they'd be too much of a gap between the auditions and the journey.

So we got to Jaipur, where we kicked off the journey. And Adi called.

Adi: Hey, Raghu.

Me: Hi, Adi.

Adi: So, bro, research tells us this soft side of yours isn't working.

Me (thinking oh no, not again): Adi, what do you want me to do? This *is* me. I don't know what your research says, who these people are; even if they represent the youth, I don't want to be something I'm…

Adi (cutting in): I'm not asking you to beat people up, bro. I don't want you to get aggressive just for the ratings. All I'm saying is, if you feel angry, *don't* hold back.

Me: You're actually saying this?!

Adi: Anger will come. It's bound to happen. Just don't hold back.

Me: Adi, be careful what you wish for, because if I go out with this thought at the back of my mind that you *want* me to do this, you can't come to me later and say, Raghu, how could you do this.

Adi: No, no, I won't!

LATER:

Adi: Bro, this was just *too* much, how could you do this?!

Me: Ah HA!

The season that would never have been, volume 2

But before we get to that, let me tell you about the deep shit we were in even before the journey began. The shoot was not going to happen. In America, I mean.

To start with, the rupee fell against the dollar. Whatever budget we had now translated to lesser money. It was a stupid fucking situation which was under nobody's control, and we were screwed. Colosceum and MTV were talking but I already knew what would happen. They couldn't give us any more money and Colosceum wouldn't be able to pull off this season, and at the end of the day, I'd have to change the tasks. Which I did.

And as if the money problems weren't enough, it was time for the Great American Visa Dance. We needed thirteen Roadies on the show, so we had selected twenty-five: the twelve extra were backup, because when it came to visas, especially the American one, there's no guarantee who would get one and who wouldn't. On the first day of the visa interviews, half the crew, the top thirteen Roadies and I, went to the American embassy. And eight out of the thirteen Roadies were rejected because they came from weak economic backgrounds. Some of my crew didn't get visas either for the same reason. I came out, stunned, devastated, clueless, but determined. I spoke to all the Roadies; they were obviously crestfallen, and I admitted it was a bad situation but I wanted them to hang on, I would do something about it.

While driving back, I spoke to Adi, told him this had happened but not to worry, I already had options. Obviously, I couldn't force or buy the visas, so I figured we'd have to do this journey within India. It was next to impossible but, well, this was me and my mad crew, and I was sure we'd pull it off. When we got to Jaipur for our India leg of the journey, some of my crew would simultaneously start a recce up to Kashmir. This would be a near impossible situation. If anything went wrong with the recce, we'd have to stop the journey midway. That was the promise *Roadies 9* began with: the odds against us, our continued exhaustion (we'd had just twelve days off after *Roadies 8*) and constant change.

And then—since this is *Roadies* where one comes to expect the unexpected—something else happened. Two days later, we received a call from the embassy. We went back, surprised. We were greeted by the officials, and then something was thrust into my hands. I looked at it in shock. They were our visas, all of them. No interview, no application. I know, right? How the fuck?!

I was puzzled and relieved as hell, and as I hugged Mukhiya, he said, 'Brother, you take me too lightly.' I did, oh, I did, and Mukhiya had pulled off a miracle! You see, Colosceum was also producing *Masterchef* Season 2 at the time, whose main judge was Vikas Khanna. This guy owns a big Indian restaurant in New York called Junoon, and has been awarded a Michelin Star by the White House. He *knows* Barack Obama; in fact, a newspaper article mentioned that he was to give Obama lessons in Indian cooking. So Lalit called up Vikas Khanna, who called up the—wait for it—WHITE HOUSE, who, in turn, called up the American embassy. And our visas were done! And *that*, dear reader, is how we shot *Roadies 9*: courtesy the White House itself!

◆

While this was the happy note *Roadies 9* began on, the season itself sprung up one huge surprise for the contestants: its patently unfair situations. Survival was a bitch this time, especially for the boys. In any case, there were more girls than boys this time around: seven girls to six boys. And four of those six boys had been voted out by the time we had reached America.

So now it's time to tell you another little secret, one which can be quite explosive. It starts with a word we coined at *Roadies*: Incepticon. My team came up with the word, I came up with the concept, inspired by Hollywood films, *Inception* and a term used in *Transformers*—decepticon. Inception + decepticon = incepticon. What is it? Well, it's a seed of thought planted in the head of a Roadie.

Let me explain. See, the crew is obviously privy to backbiting and secrets, but we can't tell any of the Roadies what's going on. We can't say stuff like, 'Bro, someone's screwing you over, watch out,' because it's against the rules.

For example, the boys were clearly getting a raw deal during every vote-out in this season. This was bad for us, because all the tasks had been formed making certain assumptions. None of those assumptions included an all girls' or all boys' cast. An uneven sex ratio is always disastrous for a show. We had to save the boys but couldn't do so directly.

Which is where the incepticons came in. They are basically questions we ask the Roadies during their video diaries, questions which are designed to plant a suggestion in the minds of the Roadies. For example, a boy can be asked, 'The girls have the power and you're being protected, but once the rest of the boys are gone, the power is completely in the girls' hands, how long do you think you will survive?' Here's the deal: incepticons do not tell anyone what's happening, they do not ask Roadies to plot or vote against anyone, nor reveal game plans. That's entirely the Roadies' prerogative. Incepticons only encourage the Roadies to think along certain lines which may not strike them otherwise, because they are too close to the situation. We, on the other hand, have a fucking aerial view of events, and we can see exactly what is happening where. All the same, incepticons are a grey area because we do push the boundaries of what's permissible. I was extremely careful about the questions being asked; I couldn't have any Roadie saying or even thinking that he made a decision based on our suggestion. I would frame the questions, write them down, and my crew would ask them verbatim to the Roadies. This way, we were not breaking any rules, only bending them slightly.

No one knows about incepticons. Not Colosceum, not even MTV. Only me and my team. Well, until now.

◆

Speaking of bending, let's talk about the journey now. If I was Mr Sensitive during the auditions, I was Mr Ruthless Asshole during the journey. In fact, things came to such a head that I only had to make an appearance and the Roadies would go absolutely quiet. They were sure that if any one of them volunteered to speak, I'd fuck them over. Well, normally, I would rectify such a situation, make them comfortable, let them know I was on their side. But I'd been told not to hold back. So I didn't.

In Delhi, one of the last pit stops before America, I was asking the Roadies questions, but no one had any answers. So I summoned one of them to come ahead and made him bend over. I had a stick in my hand. I'd asked the Roadies questions again. Every time they kept quiet, didn't answer, *this* guy would get a whack. I asked another question. Silence. *Thwack.* This kid would get it again. The next question would get a hurried answer, because if the guy being asked the questions still kept quiet, he would be painting a target on his own ass. The kid getting hit would become the victim and the guy who didn't answer, the bad guy. Ah, mind games. Messed up, unjust and yet in some warped way, not really, because the violence was a result of their choice to keep quiet. They could choose to speak and the stick would not swing.

Now, being Mr Ruthless Asshole had one huge advantage: for every ten times a Roadie got whipped (literally or otherwise), the one time I did praise them, they were over the moon. So much so that all the Roadies began stepping up their performance just so they could please me. And that was quite a tall order considering the tasks in this season were very, very difficult. *Roadies 9* will be remembered by many as the season in which several people backed out of tasks. It wasn't entirely their fault.

So, incepticons planted, impossible tasks nearly done, seven girls, two boys and the crew flew to America. When we got to San Francisco, the first girl, Dimpy, was voted out. Usually on *Roadies*, vote-outs are shot at night, but this time, because we wanted to show the scale, we shot the vote-out during the day with the Golden Gate in the background. This meant that our next episode had to be shot right after, while it was still day. We'd just battled the long, long flight to the USA and now this? As if we weren't tired enough! We shrugged, though, rolled up our sleeves and got down to preparing for the next task that night.

◆

While I was prepping for the task, I got a call. Rishabh Soin, a.k.a. Chikna, had met with an accident. The person over the phone added that it wasn't serious; apparently he was crossing the road when a car hit him but he was just a bit stunned. He'd have to skip the shoot, though. I said okay, get the doctor to go look him up. Then I went back to work. The shoot wrapped up that night and only then was I told what had actually happened. It was bad, really bad. This was the first time during *Roadies* that someone had really, really gotten hurt.

Earlier that day, the crew bus had been waiting outside to take them to the location. Soin was just heading out when he realized he'd forgotten his walkie-talkie in his room. He went back in, grabbed it and rushed back out. The crew bus was across the street. Now, in America, the cars are driven on the left side of the road, and since we'd been there for barely two days, he hadn't registered this yet. He was crossing the road while looking in the wrong direction when a big SUV came by and...no, it didn't just hit him. It *crashed* into him. He flew into the air and fell, first hitting the bonnet of the SUV, bouncing off and hitting the windshield, cracking it, and finally flying ten feet away, hitting the ground with full force. By now, the car had braked and swerved…and just as Soin was getting up, the car rammed into his head so hard that the SUV's mud guard actually had a dent. Soin lost consciousness and, to this day, doesn't remember what happened.

But thank God for small mercies. Within ten minutes, the cops had reached the scene and the ambulance had arrived. Lalit went to the hospital along with a part of the crew; the rest left for the location. They decided not to tell me exactly what had happened until we'd wrapped up the shoot for the day. We couldn't meet him that night as the hospital had no visiting hours so we came back to our hotel to spend a sleepless night. It was scary.

The next morning, I rushed over to the hospital. Soin's left ankle was smashed. His left hip was crushed. His shoulder was—and there's no other word for it—crushed. He also had a skull fracture. He had no recollection of where he was and he was talking strangely. I was taking in this information when, suddenly, Doris, one of my crew members, said she couldn't take this, got up and left the room. It was then I realized that she had meant my state. She couldn't see me crying and I had been crying without even realizing it. It was Rannvijay's accident all over again, this time with Kaandi telling me we would have to tell his parents. I felt the same hopelessness and despair. No one knew whether to console me or let me be—they had never seen me cry before.

As it turned out, Soin's girlfriend lived in San Francisco. We informed her, informed his parents, booked them tickets, booked them into a hotel, and a part of the production crew stayed back in San Francisco. We were short-staffed, but there was no way I would let this boy be by himself.

Before we left San Francisco for the next pit stop, the whole crew went by to meet him. We joked with him about how hot the nurses were and then, just as abruptly, I felt tears in my eyes again and walked out. They were going to screw metal rods into his arm to support the bone, do the same with his ankle, and operate on his hip. And I held myself responsible.

To start with, I was the safety officer and I hadn't been around; I couldn't shake the feeling that this might not have happened had I been there. And I work these guys to such a state of exhaustion, delirium even, that if they had ten minutes in hand, my crew members would sleep standing up. This accident was waiting to happen. I was tired too, but the fact is, my work by *Roadies 9* had become more mental than physical. It was these guys who had taken over a lot of the actual execution. And while I have done this in my day, I couldn't take for granted that everybody could. I've always had a special corner for Soin, so this felt worse. He was bedridden for six months, he had huge medical bills to pay, and after *Roadies 9*, even before I signed up for the next *Roadies Battleground*, I personally hired Soin and paid his salary out of my pocket for two months until the project took off. But no matter what I did, I cannot shake off the guilt or the feeling of responsibility for what had happened to him.

◆

Next up was Las Vegas. Now, Vegas is where, along with an amazing night life, they also have the Strong Man Competitions. And one of these 'Strong Men' is a guy called Chris. He's *huge*. I was told that Chris had more calories in his breakfast than we do in the course of two whole days! And like all big men, Chris was a sweetheart; his wife was also competing in the Strong Women Competition—you can see her picking me up like a baby in the behind-the-scenes segment.

The task was really difficult, a kind of tug of war between the Strong Man and two Roadies. Unfair, you might say. I won't disagree. But it wasn't just about strength; there was obviously a drama angle to it. You see, by this time, there were an odd number of Roadies, so they'd have to pair up and one guy would be left behind—one who would have to pay the price if the Roadies lost. That guy was Arsh. Before the task, I wanted to convey to the Roadies, as well as to the audience, how strong this guy was. So I decided that as soon as Rannvijay introduced Arsh to Chris, Chris would pick up Arsh and fling him over his back.

Chris agreed, but like all tasks, I had to try it first.

Chris asked me if I was sure, and when I nodded, he picked me up, lifted me over his head (Chris is about 6'5", by the way) and flung me. I landed on my feet but not properly, and there was a sudden sharp pain in my back. On camera, I made a joke of it but the minute the camera feed was cut, I froze in place. I couldn't move. And the whole shoot was still to be done. This backache stayed with me through the season, and is the reason I couldn't do any more tasks. The task went on anyway, and the Roadies gave it their all, but they couldn't win. And since this was everything or nothing, they had to pay the price.

That night, they were called to the terrace parking where there were two guys waiting—one an ex-Marine, the other a veteran bouncer. Their job was simple: beat up Arsh every hour for ten minutes until morning. If he took the beating, the Roadies would get all the money, if he didn't, they'd get nothing. Of course, this task had to be safety-officer proofed as well. Since I had to moderate the impact of the punches while still making sure they sounded loud and threatening enough, I had to be punched too.

Hence, by the time I could give my go-ahead for the shoot, my shoulder was hurting and my back was heavily bruised. Arsh didn't look like he could take the pounding, though, so we changed the task. He just had to stay awake till morning while being completely comfortable. We wrapped up the journey in Los Angeles, the finale was done, and we jumped straight into the edit.

◆

Did I mention that I began drinking almost every night during the *Roadies 8* edit? Well, I did. The edit rooms we lived in were tiny, and we spent weeks and months in there. So we got into the habit of working some, drinking for a bit, then getting back to work. So I started drinking in April 2011, and I didn't stop till February 2012, which was when we left for the *Roadies 9* journey. I'd drink almost every fucking night. Not because I'd turned into an alcoholic but because here I was, working night and day, Saturday and Sunday, through festivals, other holidays, and I felt I deserved a break. And when I'd sit with my team, drinks in hand, the alcohol became a symbol of a break. It made me feel like I was hanging out with friends, like I had a life. This continuous drinking, coupled with exhaustion, the lack of a break, and another season that had lasted a year was the reason I was in my worst state of health all through *Roadies 9*.

◆

Before the journey was aired, I had decided I needed a theme song again, and this time around, I returned to my trusted composers, Agnee. I had absolutely no budget this time, though, but Agnee, being the rockstars they are, agreed to make a song anyway. I requested Abbas Tyrewala to write the song for me, and even he did this for free because he has followed *Roadies* for a long time and was glad to be associated with the show. The song was in place, as was the music, but something didn't feel right. Be it 'Jeet Lenge Yaar', the first ever *Roadies* song which had come out during Season 5 or even 'Yahaan' that was composed for *Roadies 8*, there may not have been the word 'Roadie' in either song, but it belonged to the show as I'd written both songs. With 'Manmaani', the song composed for *Roadies 9*, I was missing from the mix, and so this didn't feel like a *Roadies* anthem...which was when Mohan suggested I sing it.

I had many qualms about it, mainly because it is not the Roadies Raghu who can sing, nor is it Fun Raghu. It's me, the real one, the one none of these kids have seen. Singing would be an immensely personal part of me to make public. Writing lyrics is still okay; the words are yours, yes, but you can still hide behind the vocalist or the music. Singing, on the other hand, bares you. But Mohan was adamant. We recorded 'Manmaani' in YRF Studios, Mohan paid for it and my pal and first roommate in the city, Melly, who was now a cinematographer, shot the video, which I paid for. Mohan came up with the 'manmaani' chant while I came up with the line, 'chahiye sab kuch ya kuch nahi', since the *Roadies* 9 theme was 'Everything or Nothing'. The song was recorded before we left, but we shot the video after I came back from the journey.

During the journey, I heard about a controversy that had erupted: my *Indian Idol* audition video had gone viral and was out in the papers as well. It was being shared by hundreds of people on Facebook and YouTube. Well, I'm sure you've seen it and you also get the irony, as, in the video, *I'm* telling the judges to not be rude. That's right, that was the outrage now: I, Raghu Rude Ram, didn't think judges should be rude to contestants. Many even thought it was a genuine audition as opposed to what it really was: a prank I'd played because Nivedith Alva had requested me to. I am pretty sure *Indian Idol* released this video themselves to get a buzz going for their new season. And it worked.

As usual, I didn't defend myself. I didn't feel the need to. Instead, I got together with MTV's digital team and we recorded a video. 'Everyone has been talking about my *Indian Idol* audition which has gone viral,' I said with a mischievous smile, 'but nobody's figured out who put this video out now and why. And by the way, the purpose of releasing this video has been achieved.' I hadn't lied. It *was* true, after all. But I had hinted that it could have been me who released the video for my own reasons. It was the baap of all incepticons. As a result of this, the conversation shifted from my failed *Indian Idol* audition to my new song. 'Manmaani' got an extra boost because of this unexpected publicity. Worked well for me!

◆

By the time we got done with *Roadies 9*, one thing was clear: *Roadies* had become much, much more than just a TV show. Its online and mobile presence was growing by leaps and bounds. We had close to seven million fans online, we had even won the Mashable Award for Most Social Show in the world. Unfortunately, *Roadies 9* did not draw the same audience as *Roadies 8*. It was still the highest-rated show on the channel, but it had fallen. There were reasons for this. One: the insistence that the show be launched in January. Two: auditions for ten straight Saturdays which had exhausted the viewer. Three: the tasks were close to impossible this season, and when the Roadies gave up, it wasn't their fault. For any fan of the show, giving up was unforgivable. So *Roadies 9* didn't quite work out the way we'd have liked it to.

But there was something that happened during the season which made me feel a great deal better. Remember the night when the ex-Marine and the bouncer had to beat Arsh, and who had beat me up first as I was the safety officer? Well, after they got done, both these guys walked up to me and said that they really respected me. I was taken aback. They explained that no one would have done what I'd just done: agree to get beaten up to make it easier for someone else. I was overwhelmed, because I have never been appreciated for doing this. My family is kept in the dark or they'll worry, my team thinks it's no big deal for me, MTV is only too happy to get footage of me getting hurt. And, of course, the Roadies don't know about it. So nobody has ever said, thank you, Raghu, for keeping us safe. As I smiled at them, I had a jumble of memories flashing through my mind—all the tasks I'd ever done on *Roadies*, risking myself for the sake of the contestants. The appreciation of these two strangers would be my takeaway from this season.

The end of the road

I didn't want to be part of *Roadies 10*. There were many reasons for it. I hadn't had a break since I'd signed on for *Roadies 8*—both Seasons 8 and 9 had taken a year each out of me, and they were exhausting years, to say the least. But the ratings of *Roadies 9*, like I mentioned earlier, were lower than that of *Roadies 8*. And this was one of the reasons I did finally produce *Roadies 10*—I didn't want to leave when my show wasn't at its best. That would be admitting defeat. I had to prove I still had it in me. This, despite the nagging little doubt at the back of my head that maybe it was time to end it. But no, I argued with myself. One more. One more success and then I'd leave. There was also Soin, whom I'd already asked to start working on *Roadies Battleground*. He needed this. There was a third reason, too, but we'll get to that.

Finally, I decided to make *Roadies 10*.

But there were many times when I was really tempted to walk away.

The budget was cut down to less than half, not just for the journey, but for the auditions as well. I knew why it was being done. This was the time when a lot of things were changing on the Network 18 and Viacom 18 level, which obviously had an effect on MTV and *Roadies*. The one mandate given to everyone was: tighten your belts. This had happened because, beyond a point, a channel can't keep asking for more budget from its sponsors because it has a limited inventory. So the channel needs to cut down costs. All the same, I was aghast at the number given to me.

The budget for the auditions stunned me further. Now, the *Roadies* auditions are shot unlike any other auditions of TV shows, and the reason, as I've stated earlier, is that the auditions are treated not as a TV shoot but as a ground event that just happens to be aired. So the crew and the budget are minimal to begin with as there are no frills attached. I couldn't possibly reduce the number of moderators, nor could I change the venues, because we booked venues based on the turnout, and had to accommodate them all or risk another *Roadies 6* style audition riot.

Don't even get me started on the journey. Producing a season with less than half the budget was just unthinkable—I wouldn't even be able to deliver six episodes with the budget assigned to us. This sparked off an exchange of emails between Aditya Swamy and me. I told him I wanted a bigger budget, and he wouldn't budge. *Couldn't*, rather. And then another jolt came my way. I was told that I wouldn't be paid as much as I was last time. Now, right after *Roadies 8* and before *Roadies 9*, I'd been approached by Star Plus to direct their new reality show, *Survivor*. As was my habit, I had immediately spoken to Adi about this offer, and told him I thought it was a good idea. Adi had reacted quite aggressively, however, and told me I shouldn't do it and that they wanted an exclusive contract drawn up: I wouldn't be employed by MTV but I would work only for them. Every thought, idea, concept of mine, would be theirs only. MTV even inflated my personal take-home package to make this happen. And now they were taking it away from me.

They took off the exclusivity clause from the *Roadies 10* contract but it didn't change anything. *Roadies* still needed me full-time, but I would be paid less for it. Which felt humiliating. But that wasn't the last jolt either. During one of my meetings with Adi, I was asked, most casually, to pay for a part of the budget from my own pocket. Seriously! I was being asked to produce a show that I didn't hold any rights to. It just didn't make any sense. I mailed Adi and the other heads of departments saying that I was quitting. Silence. The thing is, they didn't know how to handle the situation. They didn't know whether they could speak to me, reason with me, or order me around, because I had power. I hadn't even signed my contract yet. That's another thing you ought to know about me: I never sign contracts until I'm done with the season. No, really. It's not a conscious decision, it just happens because, like I said, I don't get things like money, contracts, etcetera. I work because I give my word to someone. I signed my *Roadies 9* contract when I had already started work on *Roadies 10*. So these guys knew that if I was serious about quitting, I could get up and walk out anytime I wanted.

And I *was* serious.

◆

Adi called me to Bandra for a meeting. There, he asked me why I was behaving like this and now I asked him point-blank (like I had in one of my emails), are *you* giving your salary to the show? Adi looked me in the eye, dead serious, and nodded. You see, Adi's bonus is dependent on revenues and ratings. Because MTV's ratings depend on *Roadies*, and *Roadies 9* made the channel dip, Adi didn't get his bonus that year. He wrote that amount off. He was asking me to give up some of my money on moral grounds. When Season 8 rocked and I asked for a certain amount, MTV gave it to me without question. When *Roadies 9* didn't, it was only fair that I give it away as well. I would earn it again. The minute these words were out of his mouth, it made perfect sense to me. I agreed with him and, within five minutes, I'd said yes, I would give up some of my money, but on one condition: if *Roadies 10* rocked the ratings again, the money would be given back...not to me, but to my team. Because I knew that to hit the target, I would have to make them work harder than ever. They would have to pull off the impossible, and a reward was only fair.

I returned from the meeting, heartened but also very concerned about how Kuhu would take my decision. It was *our* money, after all. But the minute I told her what I intended to do, she said she was proud of me. Money matters tied up, I continued work. I say continued because, even through all this drama, I hadn't stopped work on the season. Deadlines were deadlines, after all.

Somewhere, though, I felt a little resentful. Here I was, making the first ever tenth season of a reality show in the country, and I was still having to prove myself. Would it ever stop? Ah, well.

◆

MTV told me they had an idea for the season. I was taken aback again. It was the first time in ten years that this had happened. I heard them out. They had a concept: Raghu versus Rannvijay. Creator vs creation. Two things occurred to me at once: 1) It was a pretty cool idea. 2) How would we ever sell this concept to anyone? Rannvijay and I were seen and accepted as one unit. It's us against the tasks, us against the *Roadies*. Even outside of *Roadies*, we make appearances together, so people knew we were close. How would people buy into the concept, and if they didn't, how would the season work?

It was my job to make a season around this concept, and around a tag line that Zorro had come up with: 'Battle for Glory'. I wanted it to be 'Collision Course' because it had the connotations of driving and I could pitch it as Rannvijay and me colliding. But it was rejected because they felt it sounded too negative. So 'Battle for Glory' it was. I liked it too, but here is where I started feeling strange about the situation. MTV dictating the concept and the tag line to me made me uncomfortable for some reason. Regardless of that, though, I had to make it work.

While they said creator vs creation, I interpreted it as old vs new which is what everything on the season was. The first question I asked myself was, why would Rannvijay challenge Raghu? I was the guy who had begun it but was it now time for a change of guard, for a new generation to take over? It could work. There would be two teams: Rannvijay's would have new Roadies, mine would have the old ones. Every episode would have two tasks, one old, one new. This brings to life the old vs new concept and gives *Roadies* fans a highly anticipated, never-seen-before scenario. The viewers would already be emotionally invested in some of the old Roadies, which would help the ratings.

The concept also helped me practically. Since now we needed only six new Roadies, I could reduce the number of cities I went to and could work within the reduced budget. Ultimately, the budget was increased, too, although it was just a little more than half the budget for *Roadies 9*. It would have to do, however. We turned four cities into five episodes this time, not repeating last year's mistake.

I decided to shoot it in India, which again helped reduce the costs considerably. Of course, I couldn't repeat any of the states we'd been to earlier, but I also knew there was one section of India I had barely scratched the surface of. The North East. *Roadies 4* had taken us to Sikkim, but we hadn't gone beyond that. The more I researched it, the more excited I became, and soon, it didn't even feel like a step down. The sad thing is, we probably know more about America than we do about the states that make up the North East. It was sort of an opportunity to address this issue. At first, the route was Manipur, Mizoram, Nagaland, Assam and Arunachal Pradesh. But the political situation in Mizoram and Manipur was so tense that it would not be safe for the crew or for the Roadies. We were left with Nagaland, Assam and Arunachal Pradesh.

It was while I was mulling over these things that I received yet another jolt—Adi's email. Let's make a less edgy season this time, bro, it said. The focus shouldn't be on politics but on the tasks. I failed to understand what he meant. Like I've explained earlier, the tasks have always just been a tool to bring out the drama. Everything that happened during the reality shoot of the show would only fuel what happened at the tasks. And the results of the tasks, in turn, would have an effect on the interactions of the Roadies and their choices.

And it is this belief that has helped sustain a connection with viewers all these years. That's how we've been the first to reach the ten-year landmark. I explained to Adi that we always run edgy promos for every season of *Roadies*. We can't possibly promise the viewers a rip-roaring show via the promos and, finally, when they tune in on Saturday at 7 p.m., offer them a tiger that's had its claws cut off. He saw my point and backed off.

I changed one thing about my attitude for this season, though. All through Season 9, I'd been Mr Ruthless Asshole, and my way of making the Roadies perform was to insult them, discourage them, tell them they couldn't do it. But I realized that viewers picked cues from the way I treated someone. If I called someone a loser, the person was perceived as one. If I praised someone, said he'd won my respect, he automatically won everyone else's respect too. This was probably why *Roadies 9* didn't work, because I kept calling the cast 'losers' even while the tasks were equally to blame. So, this time around, I adopted a different technique: I would treat the Roadies somewhat like I treated my team. I would encourage them, nurture them, not in as personal a manner, but I would empower them instead of challenging them. Make them feel I believed in them. The unsaid brief this time was, hold back. If you're angry, don't let it out. The viewer needn't know.

But I was still wondering about the 'Battle for Glory' tag line. What battle, why glory? Trying to make sense of this is how I came up with the idea that there would first be a money task, then a vote-out in which two people would be eliminated. And these two people would then go up against each other in a battle and the winner would come back into the game, having won the glory.

On paper, the plan looked good. We even had a good chance of achieving it within the budget. But I still had to convince everybody that, this time, Rannvijay and I were working *against* each other.

◆

I had a plan for this. When we got to Pune for the auditions, Rannvijay went up on stage first and told the crowd that he was there to recruit Roadies for *his* team against mine. That way, he would already become one of them. They would be on his side, and then I'd follow and really play up my arrogance, make them feel uncomfortable. By doing this, by being opposed to them, I'd stand opposite Rannvijay, who was their team leader.

There was yet another confusion in my head: if this was Rannvijay's team vs mine, why was I involved in the selection process? I had told MTV that, ideally, I shouldn't be there while the new Roadies were being picked. It would kill two birds with one stone: give a logical answer to my question and, well, I would be able to skip the auditions which I hate anyway. But it was not to be, because MTV made it very clear that I had to be a part of the selection process, so I had to find a logical explanation for my presence.

Eventually, I worked it out with an excuse. Because my team would be full of ex-Roadies whom Rannvijay had met, interacted with, and knew, it was only fair that when it came to his team, I would also be granted the same advantage. That way, I, too, would also know the strengths and the weaknesses of my opponent.

There was also another issue with casting in my team—bringing back people like Palak and Avatar. No *Roadies* fan would want either of these two, they had pretty much been the villains of their own seasons, so what was the logic there? It was clear to me in my head. *Roadies 9* had had no villains and I wanted a couple of bad guys in *Roadies X*. Finally, we conceived the reason that Rannvijay would pick one or two people in my team, and I'd do the same for his team. That's how we explained Palak and Avatar's presence, and that's why I picked Ramandeep, who was an unlikely Roadie.

The one fun part of this whole facade was that every instance that I taunted Rannvijay during this season, or he said something about me and my team, it would have been discussed in advance between the two of us, whether it was before the auditions, during the auditions, before the journey or during the journey.

One of the most interesting casting dynamics during this season would have to be Sonal and Gaurav. Sonal, if you remember, was this twenty-one-year-old kid who had recently lost both her parents, and claimed to be emotionally numb. She seemed fragile but insisted she was strong. And then there was Gaurav, the MMA fighter, who looked so beefy but whom we nearly reduced to tears in the course of the interview. I liked the idea of casting Sonal, who was a weak-looking but emotionally strong person, along with someone like Gaurav, who was strong-looking but emotionally weak.

Anyway, the auditions were done, we had gotten ourselves an interesting cast, but I was slowly starting to lose it with MTV's constant interference. While I did understand their concern (it was their property, after all), the fact was that this was the tenth fucking season of *Roadies*—hardly the time for me to be answerable for things I've done my way all this time.

For example, I had to argue endlessly to cast Anirudh from Season 9 in my team. I won ultimately, obviously. I was so determined to have him on board that I'd gone to the extent of telling them that, look, you like Mohit and Suchit, I'm prepared to lose them. But Anirudh *stays*. The point wasn't that he hadn't done anything in Season 9, it was what I *knew* he could do if he got a second chance. I wouldn't have been so forceful but because my judgement was being questioned, I felt the need to road-roll the channel and get Anirudh on board. And I'm glad I did!

◆

The hiccups with *Roadies X* never quite stopped. This was around the time MTV got a new content head, and this guy would keep calling me, asking me to come over to the office to present the tasks and concepts. I agreed the first time. Once the auditions and the recce were done, he called again to ask whether I could share the task locations with him. Now I really got angry. What did he mean by 'sharing task locations'?! I'd been doing this for ten years, and this guy had *just* come on board. What would his feedback be? Even if he wasn't okay with the task locations, they couldn't be changed at this point—we'd never get permissions for new locations. If he cared so much, he ought to have been there for the recce. I was getting tired of this constant demand to report to MTV.

Things came to such a head just before the shoot that I quit *Roadies X* for the third and the last time. And this time I was dead serious.

I got a call from Colosceum asking me whether we were to book an economy class or a business class ticket for someone we'll call Mr Channel. I was confused. Where was Mr Channel going and why? The journey, I was informed. He'd be there all through the journey.

It was new channel policy, Adi told me breezily when I called him. He then added, 'Don't worry, bro, he won't cramp your style. He'll just be there.' I said okay, hung up, then thought, why would he need to be there in the first place? Either he was on holiday or he would interfere with my work. It was unacceptable, either way. And screw channel policy, no one from the channel had ever 'just been there' in nine years, so what was different this time? I had continuously had this feeling of interference from MTV this season and it suddenly dawned on me: they didn't trust me to do my job anymore. They wanted someone to come along to keep me in line.

It felt like a slap on the face, not just for me, but for my team, too. I'd had enough. I collected my thoughts and sent an email to Adi. After nine years of being on a show, I didn't see why MTV felt the need to send someone over to supervise me. There was an obvious lack of trust which outraged me. If they thought Mr Channel understood the brand better than me, or the show better than me, he was welcome to take my place! If not, get him out of my way. I understood channel policy but the channel needed to understand *my* policy, too. If MTV insisted on a supervisor, I wouldn't go. I hadn't signed the contract, and they could sue me if they wished to. I would pay the price but I would not be treated this way.

This has always been my philosophy. Either tell me how to do it or *don't* tell me how to do it. You can't do both! I took my team out for drinks that evening, told them what had happened and that I was quitting. My team was fuming, too, and they were glad I'd decided to leave, which was when I heard from Adi. And he stated, quite plainly, that if it meant so much to me, he wouldn't insist. No one would come on our shoot. He reassured me that he had full faith in me. I, in turn, told him I wouldn't let him down.

I packed my bags for Kohima, Nagaland.

✦

Before every journey, all of us have to undergo a full medical check-up to see whether we're fit or not. This time around, there was only one guy in the entire crew who was declared absolutely unfit. Me.

Initially I was surprised, because I had been working out. Like I'd said, during *Roadies 9*, I'd been at my most unfit and I was determined to change that. In fact, every time a *Roadies* journey is around the corner, I tell my crew to start working out because we need to be at our fittest as the *Roadies* journey is physically gruelling. I think my drinking habits from April 2011 to February 2012 may have had a little something to do with being declared unfit. Mostly, though, it was my bronchitis which had severely reduced my lung capacity. My crew was worried; if this were anyone else, the person obviously wouldn't be on the journey. I had no such option. Finally, we carried special medical equipment just in case I couldn't cope with the rigorous *Roadies X* shoot.

So, Kohima. The cast was putting up at one hotel, while the rest of the crew were staying in another hotel barely five minutes away, but with a steep uphill walk in between. I was with my trainer, Tokas, and my bodyguard, Sadiq, when we began walking to the other hotel. I was climbing up but midway, I just sat down and started coughing. I sat there for about thirty minutes, trying to get my breath back, coughing continuously. Sadiq was really scared because my eyes were bloodshot, streaming with water, and I couldn't breathe. Apparently, my bronchitis was more severe than I had allowed myself to believe. That was the rather sombre, frightening beginning to *Roadies X*. I started having doubts about whether I could do this shoot or not.

The party for the Roadies was being set up and there was to be a task here, in which the *Roadies Battleground* winner would challenge one member of Rannvijay's team. If he won the challenge, he'd replace the member, or the team would be as it was. Rannvijay and I put our heads together and decided that the task would be to perform a high kick aimed at a pot slung at a height. So a pot was hung about six feet in the air, and it was time to test the task. I stepped forward, got my knees padded up, slipped on the helmet...

...and I couldn't do it. I couldn't kick.

It was a throwback to 2006. During *Roadies 4*, one of the tasks (which couldn't be included in the season, by the way) had taken place in Pushkar and involved taking out a five-rupee note from a box with a snake in it. As always, I stepped forward to try this task. As I readied myself, I could hear the loud hissing sound within the box. It was unnerving. The box opened and this huge snake leapt out, hissing angrily.

I froze. I couldn't dip my hand in.

That night in Pushkar, I didn't sleep a wink. It had become personal; I just had to do it.

This evening in Kohima, I looked around at my crew who were staring at me with a mix of surprise and concern. I was their leader, and this was the first task of *Roadies 10*; I had to live up to their expectations. I had to do it.

That next morning in Pushkar, it was Roadies Raghu who went back to the task, dipped his hand into the box almost mechanically, oblivious to the hissing snake, and took the money out. He proceeded to do the same with two more boxes. And then, despite the snakes being defanged, he had to see what it would be like if the snake did strike. So he put his hand into another box and waited to be bitten. When he was, his doubts cleared and he stood up without flinching and left. He had done it.

So in Kohima, I took one last look at my crew, felt a change within me. I ran up to the pot and finally took off. I hit the pot this

time; it swung and I fell on my side. I had been concerned about my
spondylosis which has left my neck weak and prone to injury. I felt a
sharp pain but I was instantly back on my feet saying, 'Higher, pitch
it higher!' It was put up to six and a half feet. I went back, ran up and
kicked it so hard that it almost did an entire circle before coming back.
By now, Roadies Raghu was in full form, spitting fire as he yelled,
'Higher!' It was slung up to seven. This time, I practically flew off the
ground, hitting it so hard that it nearly cracked. I was now told that
this would be the highest point it could go. I paused to breathe as
everyone applauded. Rannvijay came up to me after the applause had
died down, beaming from ear to ear, and said, 'For a minute there, I
thought you couldn't do it. This was classic Raghu.' No one thought
I could do it and that's when I proved them wrong…and kicked *ass*
doing it. I sat back, relaxed, happy. I may have been low on stamina, I
may have been six years older than the Raghu in Pushkar that morning,
battling his fear of snakes. But one thing hadn't changed: I could still
do it. HE could still do it.

One last time

By the time we got to the third task of *Roadies 10*, I was really worried. I had been so sure, so confident of my team of old Roadies but somehow, unexpectedly and in true *Roadies* style, Rannvijay's team has risen to the challenge and beaten my guys hollow in the first two tasks. It was bad, and not because it was my team. Any match is only exciting when it's a close one; not when one team dominates the other. The season would flop this way.

So, just before the third task, Rannvijay and I gave pep talks to both teams, because that would be fair. Only, when we spoke to the new Roadies, we told them to kick ass and that they were already doing a good job. You could say that we sort of lulled them into a false sense of security. And then we went to the old Roadies and I spoke to them with so much heart that I'm pretty sure they saw the desperation in my eyes. They would have to up their game, and win. For me.

This task was like sumo wrestling: there was a mud pit where, at any given point, there would be one person from either team in it and would have to pin the other down or throw them outside the pit two out of three times. Swati came in from Rannvijay's team and, since she is a wrestler, kicked out Roopali and Roop from my team within moments. My heart sank. The rousing pep talk had apparently not worked. Then Palak walked into the ring...and totally changed the game. She pinned Swati down, once, twice. Sonal went the same way. Palak was on a rampage. And then came Ramandeep. Palak pinned her down once.

Ramandeep flipped over and pinned Palak down once. Suddenly, the air thickened, both teams shouting, cheering, the adrenaline gushed into all our veins. *Now* we were talking! Finally, when Palak threw her out of the pit, I was really proud of her. It was the boys' turn next. Mohit asked me not to worry as he walked into the pit. What followed reminded me why I absolutely *loved* my show.

It was like watching Tendulkar bat. And then bowling to him. The new Roadies had watched Mohit perform on TV, but they would realize how good he was only when they faced him. And when they did, well, Mohit buried them. He was so good that he even bulldozed the mixed martial arts fighter, Gaurav. It was awesome. I was getting pretty emotional by then and feeling really proud of the old Roadies. They had started as the underdogs and had then risen to the challenge. *That* was content.

This task set the tone for the whole season which kept see-sawing like hell. If the old Roadies beat the new ones continuously in two tasks, the new kids would rise up from the ashes. It was completely unpredictable.

Just like the Avatar-Palak equation. After *Roadies 8*, I'd mentioned that, in Avatar, we'd found another Palak. The emotion both seemed to inspire in most people was annoyance. I couldn't help but wonder what would happen if we brought them together, if they argued. Who would win? Barely days into *Roadies X*, my question was answered. In any Palak-Avatar argument, Palak beat him hollow; beyond a point, he would fall silent but not Palak, no sir. She could go on and on. She played extra smart this season, and because of that, there came the baap of all twists: she was voted out, and Avatar left.

It was entirely unprecedented, and when Avatar said he would keep his promise and leave, the cameras were rolling and we didn't know what to do. We let it happen because, well, content! I am pretty sure Avatar didn't come on *Roadies* this time to win like Sumit Suryavanshi. He just wanted his honour back—and he did get it back. This time when Avatar left, the *Roadies* were shell-shocked; Mohit and Suchit even praised him for having done what he did. And when I told him he had my respect, I meant it.

It was in Jorhat that Rannvijay and I had a fight. Up until now, we were playing the game of opposing teams but here, there was actually a moment when it came true.

Ramandeep had just won a boxing task and her prize was fifty thousand rupees and a Hero Impulse bike. She was congratulated and, in the same breath, informed that as long as she chose to keep the bike and the money, the other team would get immunity. If she gave up both, *her* team would win immunity. It was designed to put her in a very interesting spot: would she play for herself or for her team? Everyone attacked Ramandeep: the old Roadies obviously told her to hold on to her bike and the money, saying that her team didn't care for her, anyway. While, of course, her team members tried convincing her otherwise. She lost her mind completely, exploded, and stormed out. It was intense, and pure brilliance.

Just before the vote-out, Rannvijay and I had a chat. He felt she ought to return the bike, save her team and I felt otherwise. While my little brother's feelings stemmed from his 'team spirit', I was far more practical. My team had fewer people but they were better content: Suchit, Mohit, Palak, Anirudh. Rannvijay's team, in terms of content, wasn't matching up. I wouldn't be so rattled if any of them went out. So it was for practical 'content' reasons that I wanted Ramandeep to hold on to her bike.

The cameras were set up, the Roadies came by, took their positions, and now Rannvijay launched into this whole spiel of how the team came first. Survival was important, he argued. You'll get another bike if you win, anyway, he said. This happened in front of the Roadies, so I couldn't even cut in and ask him to shut up. I tried playing devil's advocate but it didn't work. It was a rousing speech, no doubt, and Ramandeep, who had written 'KEEP' on her cue card, scratched the word out and wrote 'RETURN'. My heart sank. I was mad.

The two eliminated Roadies who had to battle it out were Anirudh and Roop. And while the battle task was being set up, I took Rannvijay aside and I let him have it. If Anirudh left, I told him, we'd never see the resolution of his and Mohit's conflict. If Roop left, who among the girls would stand up to Palak? Wouldn't we rather let go of a Sonal or a Gaurav? They'd be missed less than people who were driving the content. Rannvijay heard me out and apologized. And then I said, 'This is a show we're making, not an exercise to see how good a fucking team leader you are, grow up.'

Anirudh survived the battle, Roop had to go.

Later that evening, Lalit, Tokas, Rannvijay and I were having a conversation about something and we disagreed. All of a sudden, Rannvijay just stood up and yelled, 'You know what, I'm *not* a kid!' He stormed off, leaving us standing there, stunned. Later, he came to me and hugged me, apologizing profusely. I apologized, too, and then asked him what had happened. He had been really stung by my words, he explained, especially when I had told him to 'grow up'. He said he had always strived to earn his place as a professional and wanted me to respect him as a grown-up. He apologized for his behaviour. He needn't have. Rannvijay has never been the guy who throws a tantrum and walks away but the guy who seeks to clarify things and move on. A thorough professional.

◆

New Year's Eve dawned again, bringing with it our mid-journey twist: Baba Rajiv made an appearance. I was so happy Rajiv could come on board this season because this was one journey during which I had to be the nurturing guy, and I can only conceal my nature in short bursts. This year, because of being with Rannvijay on every task and episode, the Roadies were a lot more comfortable with me. A gap had been created, which was effortlessly filled by Rajiv. With his entrance, the Roadies were again on edge, unsure of what would happen now. The teams were shuffled, the Roadies sent back to their rooms while we partied.

At the next vote-out, once the teams had been reshuffled, it was Palak, Mohit, Suchit, Harry and Swati on one side, and Sonal, Gaurav, Anirudh, Ramandeep and Roopali on the other. Palak played her cards right and voted both Mohit and Suchit out together. Best friends pitted against each other, and only one would survive. It was a nail-biting finish and, again, Suchit proved that he was indeed the unfortunate Karan from the Mahabharata, who was let down by his chariot as its wheels got stuck, leaving him helpless and vulnerable—quite literally, in this case. Suchit was quicker in the task until the end, when his bike fell and was caught in the ground. Again, as I bid farewell to him, I had tears in my eyes. The thing with Suchit is, I have never met or interacted with him outside of the show, but on the show, both times, he has made an emotional impact on me. He's a very lovable, naïve boy, with a child-like quality that speaks to me. Hold on to this quality, I told him as he left.

The strange part during this journey was that in places deep in the North East like Mokokchung, Jorhat, Bhalukpong and Bomdila, Rannvijay and I were getting mobbed. It was bizarre because, with the exception of Jorhat, these were places we hadn't even heard of, but people here not only knew our show, they knew *us*! In Tezpur, in fact, there were about a hundred people outside the hotel waiting to meet us, and just seeing them there gave me a sense of validation. I was proud that we'd created something that had touched people even in the remotest parts of the country.

◆

From Bomdila, we headed to Tawang, the final leg of the *Roadies* journey. This was when Rannvijay told me, in all seriousness, that, 'Bro, you say this is our last time together on Roadies. We *should* finish the journey on a bike.' I agreed. It was a day's worth of travel: we left Bomdila at 6.30 a.m. and it was dusk by the time we reached Tawang.

It was cold. It was excruciating. Because, despite the fact that the Impulse could handle itself on and off roads, this terrain wasn't made for bikes at all. Hardly anyone goes to Tawang except maybe tourists, and even they take a bus or an SUV. Moreover, we had to get past Sela Pass which is nearly fourteen thousand feet high and isn't exactly a motorable road. It started snowing, Rannvijay couldn't feel his fingers, my left knee had shooting pains for some reason; both of us were shivering as we rode along, and poor Rannvijay bore the brunt of the cold because he was riding the bike.

It was the time of our lives.

We rode past the Sela Lake which was half-frozen and amazingly beautiful. Here, only Rannvijay and I were on a bike as the rest of the crew were in cars. And for us, it was a moment of reckoning, unspoken but understood: of *course* we were on a bike, we had to be on one because *this* was what *Roadies* was all about. Remember how one of the first questions I'd asked myself when I was given the show was why they were on bikes? Ten years later, riding pillion with my constant companion, I had quite the demonstration. We were feeling the snow, letting the wind hit us like a million needles, but there was something beautiful about it. We were experiencing the journey, the weather, the terrain. It *was* the *Roadies* journey.

If I could take away only one memory from ten years of *Roadies*, one experience, it would be that ride to Tawang. Those ten hours were a culmination of my journey with the show. Through the wind, the snowstorm, I had one long flashback going on in my head: the first day of the *Roadies* shoot, the mad edits, the task trials, my camaraderie with my team, my bond with Rannvijay, being loved, being hated, being mobbed, quitting, coming back, fighting with the channel, being attacked by political parties, the pure shining moments in every season. Everything had culminated in this *one* bike ride. And what a ride it was.

We rode on and finally got to Tawang...where I spent one of the loveliest evenings of my life. Picture this: the second largest monastery in the world, the largest in India. No electricity inside, snowstorm outside. A few hundred monks in robes playing wind instruments and drums as they chanted mesmerizingly, and Filmy, Rannvijay, Sadiq,

Tokas and I, just sitting there, taking it all in. I was extremely thankful I made a show that showed me such places.

The journey ended and we had to come back. And if we thought it was difficult getting to Tawang, the way back nearly killed us. It's fascinating how it took us one and a half days to come back from Brazil which is halfway across the globe and *three* days to come back from the North East! And it was one scary journey. It had been snowing, the road was frozen solid, and the cliffs here had no barricade, they were just sheer drops. And you couldn't drive the vehicles; they were sliding down the mountains, even on hand brake. Though I had been able to survive the journey to Tawang despite my health, I was now feeling too sick, too nauseated to step out of the car. My crew got out and passed a bottle of rum around to steady our nerves. There was nothing else to do, you see. The road was pure ice, the Sela Lake, which had been semi-frozen when we rode up, was by now frozen solid. But somehow, inch by scary inch, we made it back.

I'm glad that the *Roadies* journey ended in India. I am glad it ended in Tawang in the North East, but most of all, I'm glad that it ended with so much difficulty. If it hadn't, it would have been an anti-climax to ten years. It should have been difficult, and it was. It was a fitting end.

Before we go any further, in the last chapter, I cited three reasons why I made Season 10. The third reason was 'Jajabor', the *Roadies* song for the season.

Let's flashback to 1996. Back when I was an intern at TV18 and completely in awe of the amazing editors, I tried hard to be with them even outside of working hours. Every night, all the editors would hang out at C-25, Pushp Vihar, Delhi. Three to four of them lived there and I'd go there as much as I could. There was a guy who would come, play the guitar, sing ghazals. He would blow us away and he had a huge influence in my relationship with the guitar. His name was Papon. He didn't teach me but I learnt from him.

I met him again, years later. He had shifted to Mumbai; this was around the time Kuhu had been a part of *MTV Coke Studio 2* and had sung a track with him. I had gone to the launch party, where I met him. He told me his wife was a huge fan of *Roadies* and he'd tell her he knew me but she never believed him. Papon added, 'But, Raghu, if you're in this position, and we're friends and all, why won't you give me a platform to sing for you?' I was stunned. I told him I was nobody to give anyone a platform, that I was going through my own struggle at the time. But I gave him my word: he would do the next *Roadies* song for me. So, one of the reasons why I made *Roadies* Season 10 and took it to the North East was because I had to keep my word to Papon.

I wrote 'Jajabor' as a reaction to a phenomenon I'd been observing all these years: parents of young kids, for most part, want them to take up safe careers. But the kids today want something out of the box; they want to be web programmers, writers, singers, photographers, etcetera. Parents aren't wrong in wanting their kids to lead a safe life, but they're coming from a place of fear. This generation doesn't. The world is open for them, and they want to chart new paths. My interactions with parents and children alike found expression when I wrote 'Jajabor'. Papon was thrilled with the lyrics and added four lines in Assamese to give it a North Eastern feel. He got it bang on. The word 'jajabor' is an Assamese/Bengali word which has its root in a Hindi word 'yayavar' which refers to a traveller, a nomad. People think he's an aimless wanderer but he's not—he knows exactly where he's going. This aptly describes this generation. And *Roadies*.

◆

Back in Mumbai, the shit began to fly. We would ready each episode and then have a fight with MTV about putting it on air the way we wanted to. I'll tell you what happened. The Information and Broadcasting Ministry was coming down heavily on MTV in general and *Roadies* in particular, and I was made the poster boy of everything that was wrong with 'youth TV'. This is why other shows, other channels, get away with murder and stinging content but not MTV. Because they're always under the scanner.

MTV was told, in no uncertain terms, that one more complaint against their content and the channel would be yanked off air. So they were definitely pushed on the back foot. Hence, *Roadies X*, when aired, was not as edgy as the journey really was. But the *Roadies* fans lapped it up anyway. *Roadies* was back with Season 10. All that was left now was the finale.

We didn't have enough money to shoot it, so I had to shoot two episodes in two days. After many hours of trying to acquire the required budget from MTV and Colosceum, I finally got desperate and said, okay, I'm going ahead with the shoot. If the money doesn't work out, I'll pay the balance from my own pocket. And that was when I was given the green light, and told that they'd figure the money situation out.

The *Roadies X* finale task was tough as hell and featured another one of my fears: going under water. It didn't help matters that the shoot was delayed. Earlier in the day, I had gone through agony because I had eaten the fiery Naga dholakia chillies, but this pain was nothing compared to the dread I was feeling about the last task. Ultimately, though, when I got into the eight-foot tank for the task trial, terrified though I was, I was also aware that this was how it had to end. I would have been disappointed if it had been easy, this final task. It had to be a push-your-limits, crazy task, and Roadies Raghu needed to come out, one last time.

Before the last episode was aired, I approached my favourite musicians, Agnee, and asked for yet another song. I wanted a clean and dignified exit from *Roadies* and wished for a song that would invoke nostalgia with a tinge of sadness, which was exactly what I felt. Agnee agreed, of course—they had never said no to me. They actually put on hold a film they had bagged to work on my song. The tune for 'Silsila', which played at the end of the finale episode, had originally been another Agnee tune, 'The End of the Road', which played every time a Roadie was eliminated in Season 9. It was kind of poetic that words were added to that very tune and it was sung for me when I was leaving. Pinky Poonawala, an upcoming lyricist, wrote it, Mohan sang it and I edited it. 'Silsila' is actually an ode from me to *Roadies*.

A word about my detractors and haters. You all know as well as I do, dear reader, that on social networking websites, or anywhere else on the Internet for that matter, the haters for anything—a concept, a person, a show—are few but loud. The fans are usually silent. And yet, the night *Roadies X* officially ended with 'Silsila', I had tears in my eyes. Because through that Saturday night right up to Sunday morning, I had been chatting with people on Twitter. And this one night, almost as a tribute to…I don't know, me, the show, my haters kept quiet. Absolutely quiet. And all I was hit with was a deluge of good wishes and people saying they would miss me, and that I had no idea what the show or I meant to them. They were right. Until that night, I didn't have the slightest idea how strongly people felt about the show. Nobody had told me.

During these ten years, whenever I've been told to quit *Roadies*, I've always argued that I had one more season in me, that I still wanted to make it. In fact, when *Roadies X* wrapped up, everyone—my parents, Rannvijay's parents, my friends—told me I should continue making it because it was a huge brand, and it paid me a lot. But I know that I can't anymore. And I won't.

In my head and my heart, it's over. Doing Season 10 was like getting to the finish line. I've reached a milestone. There was no need to run anymore. It was time to stop.

But there is a stronger reason for my leaving the show. The pressure to tone down the edginess, the rawness, the 'reality' of the content has become overwhelming. Those who have the power to pull the show off-air seem to be getting increasingly uncomfortable and impatient with my view of human behaviour. It is clear that the show needs to reinvent itself once again. And there may not be a place for me in the new and improved *Roadies* anymore. I would find it too creatively stifling. The old has to perish for the new to flourish.

The first time I officially said that I won't be a part of *Roadies* anymore was to *Society* magazine in an interview. 'But,' I said, 'my relationship with MTV can't be over just like that. Aditya Swamy, channel head of MTV, has a way of emotionally manipulating me. If they say they want to make another season, it's not like I can tell them to fuck off. Either I convince them or they convince me.' These turned out to be prophetic words. Or maybe I had a sense of impending doom.

✦

'Bro, you say you're a man of your word. You once said you have my back. How can you do this now?' Aditya Swamy was at it again. The only guy I couldn't say no to in MTV hit me where he knew it would hurt. 'You don't want to make another season, don't. You say it takes your entire year away, don't be behind camera. But you have to help us make *Roadies* transition from the Raghu show to not a Raghu show. Who can cast better than you? Do the auditions and make a few entries in the journey. Reduce your presence but be there for us.'

And so I find myself wading into yet another season of *Roadies*. I feel I cannot just desert a show that has given me so much in life. But at the same time, I feel the need to move on as well. Because I cannot simply write a song like 'Jajabor' and then settle down. There are uncharted territories, new journeys and fresh challenges to undertake. I might fail, you may never hear of me again, but it's okay. You don't fight the battles you can win. You fight the battles that need fighting. And if, by the end of my career, I'm happy with the fight I've put up, I'll be content. *Roadies* changed my life, gave me a voice and for that I'll always be grateful to the show and to each and every person who was a part of my *Roadies* journey.

As for Roadies Raghu, I don't know if I'll see him again. There will be problems, there will definitely be situations that will scare me but I hope to be able to handle them myself. I hope that one day, I'll be strong enough not to need his protection. But I will miss him.

I want to leave you with one last little anecdote, dear reader. Rajiv had that very bad fall during the shooting of 'Yahaan', if you remember. He could have died. And that same night, the sky spilled red and gold, and Manu, our director, got really excited. But I didn't tell you the full story. I'll tell you now. As Rannvijay and I were sitting on our bikes, getting ready for the shot, I saw Rajiv limping to his bike and trying to get on. I stopped him right there and said, no, Rajiv, you go back, we'll get someone else to ride your bike. You've just cheated death and this is a silhouette shot, no one will be seen, you're NOT doing this.

I turned to Manu. Tell him he's not doing it, I pleaded. Everyone agreed with me, forbade him to ride. Then Rajiv drew Rannvijay and me aside and said, 'Look guys, I've had a bad fall. I know my face won't even be visible in this shot but I'm *scared*. If I don't get on the bike right now, I'll never get over this fear. It'll take root in my head and I'll always think of myself as a guy who gives up, and I can't be that person. So don't do this to me.' I understood, as did Rannvijay. So the silhouette shot of three guys against a blood-red sky is beautiful, not just in the visuals and the composition. It's beautiful because there, in that lone shot, an entire show, an entire philosophy, can be seen. It's a true *Roadies* story. If he hadn't done it, I'd have been happy in the knowledge that he hadn't put his life at risk, but what he did reminded me again who he was. Who we all were. And when it comes to the *Roadies* spirit, the bikes don't matter. Everyone who rides a bike is *not* a Roadie. And you don't have to be on the show to be a Roadie. It doesn't matter that neither Rajiv nor I are bikers. What matters is that, even after a near-death experience, Rajiv showed us that it was possible to get back on the bike and face fear. *Roadies* is not about the road either. It's about the attitude. And by attitude, I don't mean aggression; I mean the attitude to face your problems, to face your fears. And that's what *Roadies* is.

Ride safe.

Acknowledgements

Reading books, especially autobiographies, has always been a passion, and writing my own, a dream. Finally, here it is! And for the realization of this dream, I would like to thank those who have been an integral part of my journey.

Mom, it is said there is no bigger love than a mother's, and I have seen that first-hand. Giving birth to and raising twin boys and a daughter couldn't have been easy, but you did it in style, while forging your own illustrious career. You are an inspiration, and my respect for the incredible strength of women comes from you.

Dad, the man! You've been so supportive in every role, but especially so as a father. What would I have done without you holding my hand every step of the way? You are my role model and, believe me, my biggest ambition is to make you proud.

Rajiv, I'm your biggest fan! I cannot imagine my life without you being a part of it every single day. You have been too many things to me to write here. I wish I could learn how to be half as cool as you.

Kuhu, my rockstar! Your coming into my life was its real turning point. You're always pushing your boundaries, be it in your profession or in your other interests and talents, all the while managing to make a simple boy like me shine, and I can only stand back and watch you with awe. I love you.

Rannvijay, in you I have found a kindred spirit, a younger brother, an inspiration, and so much more. I am truly lucky to have you in my life. *Roadies* wouldn't have happened if you hadn't happened to it. Or to me.

Rohit, you're not such a big part of my life anymore, but you've shaped me in so many ways! I'm grateful to you.

Saul Nasse, you are my mentor. In one short year with you, I learned more about my craft than most people do in their entire careers. Without you, this book would never have happened. Thank you!

Karthik Chintamani, you always believed in me, and gave me a chance at MTV—twice! Thank you for your support.

Ashish Patil, my work really grew with you. I'm sorry for all the grief I caused you. I really respect you as a professional.

Aditya Swamy, you are the reason I came back…and the reason I have stayed back. I owe you more than you realize. Thank you!

Akshay Rajput, you welcomed me into your home when I had nowhere to go. You understood my vision and nurtured it, taking it beyond anything I had imagined. Your hard work and talent are legendary.

My crew, for their fire and awesomeness. You have been my family on the road, and I love you all.

My friends, for supporting me, for putting up with my behaviour when I was being an idiot, and for not giving up on me.

My fans, who have understood me and stood by me all these years, no matter what was said about me. For that, I am eternally grateful.

Janaki Viswanathan, for writing this book with me, and for bossing me around, nagging me and doing whatever it took to get the job done. I'm very fortunate to have collaborated with you, jaan ki dushman!

Agnee—Mohan, Koco, thank you for everything you've done for me. You are the musical expression of *Roadies*. And though it might seem that I take you for granted, I'm actually very grateful.

Kapish and the gang at Rupa Publications, thank you for supporting and facilitating my dream—it was quite a nightmare for you, I'm sure! But if you hadn't pushed me, this would have never happened. And for that, I'm thankful to you.

Finally, those relatives, teachers and haters over the years who undermined me, told me that I wouldn't amount to anything, called me a failure. I owe whatever success I have achieved to you.

MTV Hero *Roadies XI*
Multiple Audition Form

RIDE ON

Want to be entitled for three GD rounds?

Buy the book, complete this form, and drop it in the box at the venue. By a draw of lots, ten lucky winners will be entitled to three GD rounds.

Not only that, all those who buy this book (and get it stamped at the venue) will be entitled to a Lightning GD round.

Date: _____

Name: _____
_____

Gender: ☐ Male   ☐ Female

Registration Number: _____

Message for Raghu:

_____
_____
_____
_____

Raghu

Disclaimer: Contest terms and conditions as applicable.